THE ROYAL OAK DISASTER

The First Complete Account
of the Most Controversial Tragedy in the
Royal Navy's History—
The Scapa Flow Raid of *U-47*

THE ROYAL OAK DISASTER

Gerald S. Snyder

PRESIDIO PRESS

San Rafael, California, and London, England

This book is dedicated
to the memory of those who died
in HMS *Royal Oak*

Contents

List of Illustrations

Preface

The full story of the sinking of the British battleship HMS *Royal Oak* has never really been told. Since 1940, when Germany was still at war and the first story of the celebrated German naval hero Günther Prien was published, there have been a few limited accounts—but each has been written from one side *or* the other, presenting solely the British or German point of view, as though the story could not possibly be told unless it was done so from either. There is a reason for this. Because to this day many survivors of the *Oak,* among others, continue to refute the very fact of Prien's mission, arguing that the ship was blown apart not by *U-47* but by saboteurs, all previous accounts have dwelt at length on proving a case for or against Prien.

The result is that today, thirty-seven years after the great warship heeled to starboard and sank to her death beneath the darkling waters of Scapa Flow with more than eight hundred officers and men and boy seamen, the full story remains at large. Because no one has told the story from *both* sides, using all available evidence, including much new British and German information made public only within the past few years, and because, also, no one has told the story unemotionally, objectively and without succumbing to the temptation to embroider the facts, the complete story has yet to be told. Discrepancies, inaccuracies, distortions, still cloud the facts. The first full-length study, Alexander McKee's *Black Saturday,* published while the Official Secrets Act kept a ban on the details of the disaster, nourished the erroneous sabotage thesis; another account, Alexandre Korganoff's *The Phantom of Scapa Flow,* originally published in France but published in England well after the ban had been lifted, ignored completely the startling revelations contained in the opened records and held so admiring a view of *U-47* as to appal some British survivors. Other, partial accounts have made no attempt at all to record the truth. In one fabrication, the author had *U-47* embarking from Wilhelmshaven, manoeuvring past mines and steel nets to penetrate Scapa Flow, then sinking not one but two battleships—none of which of course is true.

I have attempted to recreate the events that led up to the sinking, as well as the facts of the sinking and the aftermath on the basis of contemporary accounts, published and unpublished documents, papers, and reports, and the recollection of eye-witnesses from both sides. I have tried to avoid the temptation to extend the story to what might have happened. In this book there are no contrived conversations; all the sources I have used are listed in the Sources in the back of the book.

I first saw the scene of the sinking on a balmy fall day in 1964 when with four other American journalists on a tour of Scotland's remote Orkney Islands I was travelling by car up the narrow Orphir Road that curves southwesterly on the large island called Mainland and our guide remarked, 'There, in Scapa, the *Royal Oak* was sunk!' The Orcadians have never forgotten, and as I looked over my shoulder, at the almost landlocked natural harbour, I glanced upon the low cliffs of Gaitnip and, beneath them, a lonely buoy (marked only WRECK) which bobbed in the vast, peaceful, turquoise basin. Overhead a few clouds hurried. Some seagulls and cormorants reared tirelessly against the blue. Over the soft contours of the island wild fuchsias and lupins leaped. The wind blew through the heather, seagulls wheeled, silhouettes of cottages stood against bleak plains. It was all beautiful but sad, and I thought as I glimpsed the watery grave that on the soft silt and mud of the bottom lay the only reminder of one of the most terrible episodes of the Second World War.

Later I stood in the north aisle of ancient St Magnus Cathedral, the most precious treasure of the grey old burgh of Kirkwall, and glanced on a simple plaque placed by the Admiralty:

IN MEMORY OF 833 OFFICERS AND
MEN OF HMS 'ROYAL OAK' WHO
LOST THEIR LIVES WHEN THEIR
SHIP WAS SUNK IN SCAPA BAY BY
U-47 ON 14TH OCTOBER, 1939

Britons were horrified at the huge loss of human life, which they mourned as a needless sacrifice. But Britons too always have admired courage; so the nation did not begrudge the boldness of its enemy. Winston Churchill, the First Lord of the Admiralty, told a shocked House of Commons: 'When we consider that during the whole course of the last war this anchorage was found to be immune from such attacks on account of the obstacles imposed by the currents and the net barrages, this entry by a U-boat must be considered as a remarkable exploit of professional skill and daring.'

Prien had made submarine history. By coolly slipping his U-boat into the centre of the most important naval base in Britain, the most precious stretch of water in all the oceans, by manoeuvring there, on the surface, without detection, then sinking a ship, and escaping to tell about it, he achieved something rare in the annals of naval warfare, a feat which very well may be, as U-boat historian Jak P. Mallmann Showell recently put it, 'the most remarkable U-boat mission of the war,' perhaps 'even the most daring raid in submarine history' and, as Rear Admiral Dan Gallery of the United States Navy once called it, 'the greatest individual feat of arms performed at sea for many years'—all of which may be said even though British defences were lax and not a hand was raised against the Germans at any point or at any time between their entrance to the Flow and their exit from it. The official British view denies this last statement, the Germans minimise it, yet no real evidence is there to prove the widely held claim that the Flow 'sprang to life' after the *Oak* exploded.

Many Britons, while disputing this claim, question also the fact of *U-47*'s mission, forcefully arguing the sabotage theory. In Orkney in particular the whole episode is still a subject for debate. People talk of 'that night' as though it were yesterday. They remember it vividly, and for them there always will remain the doubt; it was too unbelievable a loss, too miraculous a feat for a submarine, too unrealistic a happening to accept.

Prien had claimed not only the *Royal Oak* but had said, as well, that he'd damaged the battlecruiser HMS *Repulse,* and the Nazi press marched this news in headlines throughout the *Reich*—when in fact the ship Prien thought was *Repulse,* one of the biggest ships of the Royal Navy, was really one of the smallest, the cargo ship-turned seaplane tender HMS *Pegasus.* How, ask Prien's detractors, could an experienced U-boat captain have made such a blunder, for *Repulse* wasn't even in Scapa Flow that night. They point to discrepancies in Prien's log, to exaggerated statements in his autobiography.

There *are* discrepancies in the log; there *are* exaggerated statements in the autobiography. But no one with any standing as a historian has suggested that Prien did not visit Scapa Flow on that fateful night. The evidence is indisputable. There can be no doubt of Prien's feat, and to all who have made it the subject of tiresome argument and controversy, the new information in this book will provide, I hope, a satisfactory, if not final, answer.

Still, perhaps the argument always will rage, perhaps anyone who attempts a restudy, no matter how deep the research, always will come upon readers whose minds will not be changed. This book is not written with the view to changing minds (although it may do that), but to put into proper perspective, for the first time, the entire story. In 1974, ten years after my first visit to Orkney, I returned to Britain, determined to learn the why and the how of the *Royal Oak* sinking. There still had been no account that examined the dramatic events from both the British and German sides, utilizing all sources, and I was encouraged by a letter from a survivor of the *Oak,* promising every assistance 'because I think that the "Royal Oak" story is worth a new book and, to my mind, those that have been written so far are a long way from satisfactory.' Being American, a foreigner, I would have no axe to grind, no particular case to argue, he felt, and that indeed is how I have approached the research and the writing of this book.

Beginning in London, I visited the Admiralty, the Imperial War Museum, the British Library Newspaper Library. I studied the *Oak*'s plans and construction history in the National Maritime Museum in Greenwich. I spent countless hours in the Public Record Office, where in 1971, hundreds of unpublished documents and papers suddenly were deposited, unceremoniously. For more than thirty years, in keeping with the Official Secrets Act, they had been held in custody by the Admiralty, away from curious eyes.

In three large boxes I found the report of the Board of Enquiry, the report of the divers who went down to the wreck, as well as the invaluable handwritten notes, also unpublished, of most of the 424 British survivors of the disaster. When combined with the recorded unpublished testimony of dozens of officers and crewmen questioned at length by the Board, and new information given me by survivors from both sides, the mass of material formed a remarkable story of high drama and extraordinary bravery and courage and afforded me the opportunity to recreate minute-by-minute, sometimes second-by-second, the agony of the *Oak* in her final moments.

For the first time, I could reveal how Corporal H. D. Jordan of the Royal Marines supported a hatch on his shoulders to allow other men to pass up; how after the first explosion three *Royal Oak* crewmen thought of the prisoners in the cell flat and ran to release them; how an unknown rating rescued by the drifter *Daisy II* jumped overboard three times with a rope's end to save other men; how Rear Admiral H. E. C. Blagrove refused the lifebuoy that was offered him and spent the last few minutes of his life helping others to save themselves.

But by far the most revealing disclosure emerged in the form of the hitherto unpublished report from divers who examined the wreck the day after the disaster. Because this single piece of evidence is so conclusive, because it should help to lay to rest once and for all the much debated sabotage theory, it bears looking at in part right here:

> Ship is lying 40 degs from bottom up. Trim 2 degs aft. Forward damage starboard side starts 80 to 100 feet from stem and extends 40 to 50 feet aft; depth extends over three plates starting one plate below the water line. Plating is blown *inboard* and the extreme edges bent *in*. Damage surveyed aft starts 10 feet aft of the after end of bilge keel and extends from water line to bilge keel. Hole about 30 by 50 feet. Plating bent *inboard*.* Bilge keel is blown away and bent outboard.

'Plating is blown inboard . . . extreme edges bent in . . . hole . . . plating bent inboard . . .' Such is what would have resulted in an external torpedo attack; only the bilge keel was bent outboard. But further, the divers' report shows, the divers brought up part of the balance chamber or after body of a torpedo and other small fragments of internal parts, and found no evidence to suggest a magnetic pistol or any explosion under the bottom. The unpublished Board of Enquiry report concluded: the evidence

> definitely suggests that all the explosions were from a source external to the ship on the starboard side, and were such as

---

* The emphasis is mine.

would be caused by torpedoes fired from a submarine in two salvoes. In addition, there is evidence from one of the survivors that he and another man, who has not been identified, saw the conning tower of a submarine in the direction and at a distance that might be expected. [The survivor, Royal Marine William Owens, was in fact emphatic that he had seen the conning tower.] The evidence available points to the attack having been made by a submarine and there is nothing to suggest that it could have been made by any other means. We are definitely of opinion therefore that HMS *Royal Oak* was sunk by torpedoes fired from a submarine.

Still, more than three and a half decades later, the loss continues to weigh heavily on the Admiralty's conscience. It is not difficult to see why, for the documents kept secret for so many years turn indirectly on the Admiralty itself—by revealing, for example, the startling fact that so slack were the defences at Scapa at the beginning of the war that a small coastal type submarine could, at high tide, easily have slipped *beneath* the anti-submarine net protecting the main entrance at Hoxa Sound—so great was the gap between the net's hem and the sea bottom. The Admiral commanding Orkneys and Shetlands admitted to the Board of Enquiry that he was unaware of the gap; he knew only what he had been told—'that the nets had been cut to fit the depth of water and I naturally assumed 'that they were right on the bottom.'

So too were there gaps all over Scapa Flow. 'Evidence given to us,' the Board lamented, 'has suggested that there was room for a small submarine to pass in at certainly five of the seven entrances if the conditions were favourable.'

Specific criteria detailing the procedures for defending the Flow had been laid down and yet, the records show, the matter was not one of priority, revealing a lack of responsibility that may never be purged from the Royal Navy's history. Not responsible for pre-war planning, Churchill was immune from reproach and ruled out a judicial enquiry which would have assigned blame to individuals, because he felt this would impose an additional burden on those engaged in the struggle against Germany. What is surprising, however, in view of the proof of negligence contained in the records, is that no one in the Navy received so much as a reprimand for one of the worst disasters in its history.

In search of the full story, I sought out as many of the survivors as I could—travelling from London to Portsmouth and north across Britain for many months; I returned to Scapa Flow in December 1974.

And what of the Germans aboard *U-47*? Had they all conspired in a hoax? Were they, as has been suggested, not at Scapa at all that night? Fifteen of the original forty-four members of Prien's crew are still alive, having transferred to other U-boats or back to U-boat school for more training before Prien's *U-47* was lost in March 1941. I located, interviewed, or corresponded with nine of *U-47*'s original crew. In the tiny village of Eastriggs Annan in Dumfriesshire, Scotland, I was welcomed at the home of Herbert Herrmann, youngest of Prien's crew, his leading torpedo mechanic, now a 54-year-old naturalised Briton and member of the Royal Navy Association who described for me—in a broad Borders' accent—details of the Scapa raid and showed me some of the mementoes of his German Navy days, including a bit of piping, a battery suction bend, souvenir from *U-47*.

With an introduction from Herrmann, I flew to Germany to meet his crewmates. At his home in the Hamburg suburb of Quickborn, *U-47*'s chief navigator, Wilhelm Spahr, 70 years old, greeted me cordially and later corresponded with me and meticulously drew the two maps that are included in this book. 'The operation had to succeed,' he told me, reflecting not so much his own thinking but the thinking of all Germans at the time. 'It was not that Germany had declared war on England. It was the other way around—England wanted to destroy Germany. With our few submarines and surface craft we found ourselves in a hard struggle of defence. We Germans were not at all prepared for a war. Peace offers by the German government to the British government were not even answered at all. Thus we had to try to damage the British Navy as much as possible.'

In the old port city of Kiel, from where *U-47* set out, I met Ernst Dziallas, the Petty Officer who was on *U-47*'s bridge in Scapa Flow. With him, and later again with him and Herrmann and Spahr, I went to the German Navy memorial at the seashore resort town of Laboe and together we ducked under and around the overwhelming array of shafts, wheels, engines, batteries, and other complex fittings of the dry-docked *U-995*—and talked about *U-47* and Scapa Flow.

I talked to British and German naval officers, both former and present, to archivists and historians. In Kiel I interviewed former German Admiral Eberhardt Godt, the U-boat Chief of Operations, and at his villa in Aumühle, some twenty kilometers from Hamburg in the presence of Dziallas and Herrmann and his Scottish-born wife, I interviewed Karl Dönitz, Hitler's *Grossadmiral,* who told me how he personally conceived and planned *U-47*'s raid into Scapa Flow.

Following every lead, I also examined the files of captured German documents which only in the past few years have been released. In April 1945 at Tambach Castle near Coburg, Allied forces captured the complete holdings of the War Historical Division of the German Naval Staff, which included the records of the Prussian Navy, the Imperial German Navy, and the Naval establishments of the Weimar Republic and the Third Reich. All of the material remained under the joint control of the US Navy and the Admiralty, which over the years returned most of the original records to the German archives, the *Militargeschichtliches Forschungsamt,* in Freiburg.

Not until 1973, however, was the captured War Diary of the German Naval Staff Operations Division made public, and here I found the unpublished first official mention of the highly-secret Scapa Flow raid, on 18 September 1939, under the heading 'Special Item'; the next citation came on 3 October, designating the plan 'Special Operation 'P'; and this was followed by a further citation, of 11 October, three days after *U-47* slipped away from Kiel and three days *before* the *Royal Oak* was sunk: '*U-47*' approaching for special operation 'P'.

By now, also, the involvement of then Commodore Dönitz, Commander of the Submarine Force, and Grand Admiral Erich Raeder, Commander-in-Chief of the Navy, was made clear—as final proof that the Prien mission was, indeed, a meticulously planned operation and not, as the disbelievers continue to label it, a result of pre-war spying or a fictionalized scheme dreamed up by Hitler's cunning Propaganda Minister Goebbels. I found no evidence to support either view.

Enough has been said and written about the horrors perpetrated in the war. The theme of this story is courage, British courage. German courage. This book, therefore, is non-partisan, neither pro-British nor pro-German, just pro-humanity. I feel, as does the Reverend A. F. Andrew, chaplain to the Thurso Royal British Legion Branch and minister at Halkirk, who said at a 1974 wreath-laying ceremony at Scapa Flow, attended by British survivors of the *Oak,* men who in an atmosphere of reconciliation today meet periodically with crewmen from *U-47*: 'We must build on the foundation made possible by the sacrifice of these men.'

For help in reconstructing the details of the story, I am grateful to many persons, particularly Norman N. T. (Taffy) Davies, the former Royal Marine who encouraged me in the project and introduced me to the survivors of HMS *Royal Oak*. I am indebted to every member of the ship's company who showed patience with me, taking the time to answer my many questions and giving me material and photographs which I otherwise would not have seen. I wish to thank former Petty Officer Richard Kerr for making available to me his personal notebook containing his story and the stories of other survivors he gathered after the tragedy.

I want to thank Herbert Herrmann for introducing me to the surviving *U-47* crewmen; I am grateful to them for allowing me to review their activities and learn their thoughts about the night of 13/14 October 1939, giving me information which has appeared in no other book, magazine, or newspaper.

Other help came unexpectedly from Monterey, California, from a villa called 'Royal Oak'—home of former Commander Philip Arthur White who retired from the Royal Navy in 1970 and told me the story of how, as an Ordinary Seaman on the *Oak,* he had been awakened suddenly about an hour before the first explosion with a premonition 'that something terrible was going to happen.'

I am grateful to Wilhelm Spahr for drawing especially for this book the *U-47* routes to and from Scapa Flow and the manoeuvres made by the submarine in the harbour itself.

For translating my German correspondence into English, I wish to thank Ingeborg Wichmann of Washington, DC.

For permission to reprint brief excerpts of copyrighted material, I am indebted to Grossadmiral Karl Dönitz and Messrs Weidenfeld & Nicolson, author and publishers of *Memoirs: Ten Years and Twenty Days,* to Frank Williams and the *Isle of Man Times,* for the right to use portions of Mr Williams' story, and to William Kimber for *Enemy Submarine* by Wolfgang Frank.

For helping in the search for photographs, I wish to acknowledge the kind assistance received from J. S. Lucas and Martin H. Brice of the Department of Photographs of the Imperial War Museum.

For moral support, and for encouraging me to write this book, I am indebted to my wife.

GERALD S. SNYDER

THE ROYAL OAK DISASTER

1

'Impregnable Scapa'

Shortly after daybreak on 6 September 1939, a lone Heinkel 111 bomber of the Luftwaffe's Air Fleet II, its twin engines droning steadily, rolled high above the northern tip of Britain, ten miles from the coast of Scotland. The pilot dropped altitude slightly, gazed out of the cockpit and spied, far below, an immense, almost landlocked expanse of water, a silvery sheet, about fifteen miles from north to south, eight miles from east to west—looking like a gigantic gash ripped through the southern half of a cluster of smooth islands. Chopping his throttle back, the pilot lowered air speed, made a wide sweeping turn, then circled slowly, while in the bubble that housed the nose machine gun a crewman held a camera and began snapping pictures.

In this way, five days after Hitler's legions tore through the soft flanks of a weakened Poland, three days after Britain and France declared war on the Third Reich, German reconnaissance first fixed on their negatives the imprint of one of the most extraordinary and strategic stretches of water on earth. With a name* to match its Nordic flavour, Scapa Flow held the key to Britain's mastery of the seas, guarding the approaches from the North Sea to the North Atlantic—from 1914 to 1918 home of the British Grand Fleet, graveyard of Kaiser Wilhelm's High Seas Fleet, and now home of the British Home Fleet, still 'doubtless the finest natural Roadstead in Britain or Ireland except Spit-Head', as the Maritime Surveyor Graeme Spence had told the Lords Commissioners of the Admiralty as far back as 1812. With depths so great, ten to twenty fathoms, with plenty of room to stow anchor,

---

* As early as 1492, the Norsemen called it *Scalpaye*, a prosaic term meaning 'something cleft in two', which has been interpreted as the isthmus cleaving the Orkney Mainland in two. To this term the Scottish added the cant term for a coastal channel, and 'Scapa Flow' the great bay became.

Scapa boasted space enough to shelter not just the entire British Fleet but the battle fleets of almost all the navies of the world.

In these Orkney Islands on this Wednesday morning, in the old and picturesque burghs of Kirkwall and Stromness, only miles from the eastern edge of Scapa, no one noticed the high-flying Heinkel or heard the thunder of its engines; no guns reached glistening barrels upward as quickly, well out of harm's way, the pilot slammed his throttle forward and turned the Heinkel home to the fatherland.

In this, the first week of the Second War, Orcadians hardly had time to adjust to its reality. During the first Great War their peaceful islands had remained free from enemy attack; as late as the last week in August, as the fateful summer days of 1939 slowly had yielded to each other, they had seemed convinced that Hitler would make his wars in Eastern Europe, not Britain. Indifferent to war, as though it would not dare disturb the tranquillity of their lives, they kept the pace of life adapted to their needs. In homely, unspoilt villages, on narrow, twisting streets, there still were smiling faces, hearty welcomes whenever people met.

The talk in August had been of farming first, Hitler second, the people choosing to discuss the cutting of oats, which had just begun, and the sudden gathering about the fields of thousands of lapwings. For the autumn migration was in full swing and the foggy weather, which had prevailed for several weeks, had tended to throw the creatures off their course. The erratic flapping of the birds was everywhere, their shrill, almost foreboding cry wrapping around the stone-built tombs, the huge barrows and cairns, other prehistoric monuments that dotted the treeless Orcadian landscape.

Yet in the hinterland, in the fields especially, it was impossible to know a war was near. To a *Kirkwall Herald* reporter sent out to explore the minds of people in the back country, a farmer summed up the judgment of many: 'I am determined not to let Hitler spoil my appetite. He did it last September and again when he marched into Czechoslovakia. I am convinced he is history's biggest bluffer. He has never fought yet, and if it is made quite plain to him, as it is being made plain, that if he tries to take Poland by force he will have Britain and France against him, he won't fight. Anyway, it's got to the stage now when we take a crisis as all in the day's work. There's been one practically every other week for the last year.'

That was Monday, 28 August, and it was as though a thousand years had passed between the time of the farmer's remark and the flight of the Heinkel 111. As the Orcadians had listened to the grim news from London, events had reeled drunkenly, uncompromisingly hard. In the space of nine days a million and a half German troops had poured across the Polish border and converged on Warsaw. In four days Poland was practically beaten, Polish air power annihilated. Incredibly, in a valiant but reckless attempt to stop the onslaught, horses were going up against tanks —while fighter planes and bombers of the Luftwaffe were screaming over the airfields, cities, and gritty roads of Britain's ally. In disbelief the Orcadians had heard the sullen voice of Neville Chamberlain over the BBC: 'Everything I have worked for, everything that I have believed in during my public life has crashed into ruins. There is only one thing left for me to do: that is, to devote what strength and powers I have to forwarding the victory of the case for which we have to sacrifice so much'.

The next day (4 September) news of the sinking of the Glasgow liner *Athenia* further shocked the cheerless islanders. It was a savage act. Steaming in the North Atlantic, some 200 miles west of the Hebrides, the *Athenia* had been torpedoed without warning. She was a passenger ship, not a troopship. Was this the way Hitler was going to conduct his war? Of the 1,400 passengers, there were neutrals, women and children aboard: 128 went down with her.

Hourly now came the news, matter of factly; and the Orcadians took it calmly. By Thursday, 7 September, they had heard of the fall of Cracow, Poland's second city, the following day they knew that the German juggernaut had reached the outskirts of Warsaw. Where next would war spread? Across the peaceful Orkneys, from Hoy and South Ronaldsay in the South to Westray and Papa Westray in the north, on Fara, Graemsay, Eynhallow, Shapinsay—places with names more Scandinavian than British—the talk now was of *Hitler* first, farming second. In pleasant little settlements, in sandy bays, in open fields, the people gathered into small groups, whispering speculations. Some grew much excited and talked on, others listened with eager ears; and rumours flew about like plovers. Might war reach Orkney? Better to halt the thought. But senses tightened. 'Learn about the respirator', warned *The Orcadian,* in a gesture of stern resolution. 'Gas Mask is your Best Friend and Safe-Guard'. Among bits of advice concerning the fitting and use of the masks, the newspaper gave the latest war news, and reminded the public to be ready 'for any emergency that may occur'.

Most needed no reminder, having to go no farther than their front door to find Orkney police officers come to tell them of lights out regulations; or to see steel-helmeted air raid wardens, armed with registers and metal instruments, come to measure them for gas masks.

Night came down eerily in Orkney at this time of year, first the murky twilight, for two or three hours, then, about six o'clock, complete darkness. But in the burghs it was business as usual, as down flagstoned streets, past gable-ended houses, the blurred forms of people pressed, gas masks tucked under arms, scurrying to fill the call for dark curtains. Among the purchasers were many country folk, farmers looking for red paper to cover stable lanterns, women seeking black cloth for tacking around windows. Many people, unable to find cloth, bought sheets of cardboard and black paint. Some settled for plain white paper and black ink.

There were moments of fear. In the absence of lights, white lines had been hurriedly painted along pavement edges, at road bends and street corners, for the guidance and safety of pedestrians; while a few blue-shaded streets lights made their appearance in Kirkwall. But cyclists were discovering their rear reflectors were useless in the glow of masked car headlamps. Several cyclists were run down.

Children too felt the emergency. Schools were closed, as were all schools in Britain this week, and many of the older boys and girls spent their unexpected holiday assisting in the work of filling sandbags. Kirkwall's only picture house, the Albert, was closed until further notice; the annual inter-county football match between Orkney and Caithness was postponed, as was the West Mainland Sheep Dog Trials. And yet life was continuing—and not unhappily. The islands' civil airways, Allied, was running a normal timetable—one of the only airlines in Britain to be so doing—and so were the local steamships still making their rounds. Well into the second week of September you could still travel from is-

land to island on any day except Sunday or cross the notorious
Pentland Firth to Scotland from Stromness or Scapa on one of the
'Saints' of the northern waters—the 'old St Ola', as Orcadians
called the mail and civilian steamer RMS *St Ola,* the ferry slated
as a troop-carrier.

In the great anchorage there was no immediate feeling of alarm,
only a routine announcement putting the Flow off-limits to all aircraft. At each of the three main entrances, the crested Sounds of
Hoxa, Hoy, and Switha, the anti-submarine booms and defence
nets were in place. At the four lesser passages, smaller ones to the
east, the Sounds of Weddel, Skerry, Water and Holm, where a
strong tidal race prohibited the use of booms, more than a dozen
sunken blockships lay, pushing rusting skeletons out to punish any
U-boat foolhardy enough to try to scrape by. Three decoy battleships and one decoy aircraft carrier sat under enfolding northern
hills, while the real ships of the Fleet, the battleships *Nelson* and
Rodney, the battle cruisers *Hood, Repulse, Renown,* other ironclads, stood out in the approaches to the Atlantic, searching for
German raiders trying to penetrate.

On the rough country roads of Orkney, three-ton lorries rum-
bled slowly, stopping occasionally to pour forth little groups of
Army and Navy men who, dragging hammocks and kitbags, could
be heard cursing those who had sent them to limbo and 'bloody
Orkney', this 'bloody God-knows where', where life was grim,
dull, monotonous, cold, where 'even the sheep wear jerkins and
gumboots!' Near the windswept slopes of Flotta, Lyness, Rinnigill,
and Longhope, wooden buildings, army tents, large corrugated
iron Nissen huts began to spring up: 'Imagine the Klondike in
the earliest days, and you have it', remembered one on whose lot
it fell to be there. Into these dwellings and into other rusty structures, real claptrap huts, some of 1914–18 vintage, the men settled down—content only in the thought that Scapa at least was a
safe place to be. Everyone knew: an attack if it came would come
from the air, not the sea; within two and a half minutes the guns
on any ship at anchor could be brought into action; within five
minutes all men not required for offensive measures could be
brought into bunkers below deck. At the naval base of Lyness, on
whale-backed Hoy, naval gunners manned a tidy eight gun
anti-aircraft battery, ready for immediate action; while at a few

other places, at Ness, Stromness, at the signal station at Stanger Head, bearded Marines in pullovers and balaclavas struggled with rough tackle to mount heavy coastal defence guns.

Yet on nature, not guns, did the defenders of Scapa Flow depend. Compressed by rocky walls of the Pentland Firth, the incoming tide of the Atlantic became a mighty torrent of rushing water: the currents and tidal streams so divergent at the various entrances that a small vessel, it was said, could point herself at a narrow passage, stop her engines, and be swept through by the tide. A U-boat trying it past blockships might graze its ballast or fuel tanks, burst them like paper sacks; one trying it through the booms might trigger rigged rockets and flares. In daylight it would be exceptionally difficult. At night it would take a small miracle; even during brief periods of slack water the tides and currents could be severe. No, Scapa was impregnable. Scapa was immune from attack by sea. The Damage Control Handbook carried by all ships of the line served to make it official:

STATE TO BE ASSUMED IN HARBOUR

III.   In a defended port, the only form of surprise attack that need be anticipated is that from the air. A gas attack becomes a practicable and likely operation, which must be considered in organising the state of the ship. Underwater damage is less likely than at sea, but possible damage by air-borne bomb or torpedo calls for the same counter-measures as are provided in the battle state.

At mid-month 'Winnie' came, twelve days after Chamberlain, the Prime Minister, had announced from 10 Downing Street the names of his War Cabinet and the famous signal 'Winston is back' had been flashed to the Fleet. Only two months from his sixty-fifth year, the new First Lord of the Admiralty rode through the waves on a fast motor pinnace to HMS *Iron Duke,* Admiral Sir John Jellicoe's flagship from Jutland. In the famous battle, on the late afternoon and night of 31 May 1916, she had proudly led the entire fleet of warships out of Scapa, the huge floating gun platforms, the smaller ships, the destroyers, the light cruisers, the sloops. Now the old grey battleship lay ignobly in Longhope Sound, minus her former glory and two of her five turrets, the dead Admiral's frock-coat sitting ghostlike in a glass case in the after lobby. Just a depot and transit ship the great *Duke* had become, yet still she had something of the dignity of a flagship, flying, as she was, the flag of Admiral Sir Wilfrid French, Admiral Commanding Orkney and Shetland.

It was a windy day and Sir Wilfrid's colours fluttered in the breeze as the First Lord was piped aboard and conducted aft with his party to the quarter-deck. Churchill removed his yachting cap, took his familiar cigar from his mouth, and waved to the assembled officers and ratings from other ships. The one time professional soldier was fit and well and happy to be close to the men of Scapa; unlike the Naval Staff, which had favoured Rosyth as the Main Fleet base, Winnie had been for the Flow all along. An officer of *Iron Duke,* Commander C. H. A. Harper, remembered how 'Mr Churchill hoisted himself on to the aftercapstan grating, and informed us that almost exactly a quarter of a century before, in the same capacity of First Lord, he had come to the same ship, in the same harbour, to stand in the same position in which he was standing on that day to address the ship's company'. For some there might be many months of waiting, the First Lord told the men: it was vital that the Fleet be prepared for any call.

For most of the next two days Churchill inspected the harbour and the entrances with their booms and nets, and the blockships: 'I was assured,' he would recall after the war, 'that they were as good as in the last war, and that important additions and improvements were being made or were on their way. I stayed with the Commander-in-Chief* in his flagship, *Nelson,* and discussed not only Scapa but the whole naval problem with him and his principal officer'.

At the very start of that war the defences had been poor, the mighty Grand Fleet, the greatest Fleet ever assembled by Britain, anchoring for months behind unobstructed entrances, vulnerable to mines and submarines. In the minds of men and commanders it seemed there were always U-boats lurking in the Flow; in the faint light of many a dim dawn even a tin can or a bottle or any other floating thing could be mistaken by a look-out for the lens of a submarine's periscope—so to alert a gun crew to battle stations, to blast the suspicious object from the water. Wrote Jellicoe as late as January 1915 to the then First Sea Lord, Admiral of the

* Admiral Sir Charles Forbes.

Fleet Lord Fisher: 'I wonder if I can ever sleep at all. Thank goodness the Germans imagine we have proper defences. At least so I imagine—otherwise there would be no Grand Fleet left now'.

Gradually the defences had improved, booms fixed across Hoxa, Hoy, and Switha, and in the four eastern Sounds more than a dozen blockships sunk. For added security, guns and search-lights were placed at all seven Sounds and, for the larger Holm Sound, an extra boom laid within the line of blockships. But Scapa gales would take their toll. In the winter of 1915–16, the seas ran high, storms raged, many of the booms were beat upon by gale-force winds and roaring seas: the boom at Holm was ripped apart and not replaced. Gradually the Fleet saw less of Scapa and in April 1918 Rosyth, not Scapa, became Admiral Sir David Beatty's main base.

Then five months later, beginning on Saturday, 23 November, the fighting ended, in Paris the terms of a peace treaty being debated; while into Scapa, into forced internment, there steamed seventy-four men-of-war of the High Seas Fleet, mooring between Lyness and the Flow's northwest corner, and waiting there—until in June 1919 when Vice-Admiral von Reuter ordered an end to the waiting and the Fleet slid under in self-destruction: the pride of the fatherland, beloved steel giants never defeated in war, the battle-cruisers *Hindenburg, Moltke, Von der Tann,* the flagship *Friedrich der Gross,* the dreadnought *König Albert,* and dozens more, some going down by the stern, some by the bow, some rolling on their sides, ensigns flying, boiler tubes exploding, masts snapping, gun turrets toppling from foundations. The High Sea Fleet was gone!

The whole German nation knew the name Scapa Flow.

The pictures taken by the Heinkel 111 travelled a circuitous route. The bomber landed at Husum off the North Frisian Islands, the film was processed in the German Air Ministry building in Berlin's Leipzigerstrasse, and on the morning of 11 September a set of photographs reached the port city of Wilhelmshaven where they were rushed to the headquarters of U-boat Command in the *Toten Weg*—a small wooden building nicknamed the 'snorkel hut' (*Schorchelbude*) because its windows were small and the air in it was often very bad—and presented to Kapitän zur See Karl Dönitz, Commanding Officer for U-boats. Dönitz, was a lean greying man of 47, an intelligent and enthusiastic submariner, commander of a U-boat in the First War, captain of a destroyer, commander of a flotilla of destroyers, and finally, until 1935, captain of the training cruiser *Emden*. In that year when the Versailles Treaty, the hated *Versaillerdiktat,* was relaxed and, under terms of the new Anglo-German Naval Treaty, Germany was allowed to resume limited submarine construction, the Commander-in-Chief of the Navy, Grand Admiral Karl Raeder, had turned to him and said, 'You, Dönitz, are to take over the job of raising our new U-boat arm'.

Dönitz was then just a junior captain (*Fregattenkapitän*) but with that order he had turned to the task of developing a new era of U-boats for Germany.* For material he had not long to wait, for on June 28, only eleven days after the signatures were put to the Anglo-German agreement, a mysterious, heavily guarded shed in Kiel harbour opened and *U-1* emerged, Dönitz in the conning tower ready to take her out to sea. *U-1* was only 250 tons, just a 'canoe' among submarines but she was nimble, easy to manoeuvre. And when by the end of September *U-2* to *U-9* materialised almost as magically, Dönitz had the nucleus for Germany's first operational U-boat fleet since the end of the First War. Over the next few months this flotilla, called the Weddigen after a 1914 submarine hero, was filled out by a further nine U-boats, *U-10* to *U-18*; and 'body and soul', Dönitz felt, 'I was once more a submariner'.

His lack of instructions or guidance was all to the good; he could develop his own methods, his own menacing wolf-pack tactics. And over the years he could, and did, influence U-boat building policy, away from the small and slow canoes toward more and faster U-boats, medium-sized, 750 tons—while the Naval High Command was opposing him, wanting even larger U-boats, huge U-cruisers, a powerful surface fleet, more warships

* When actually Germany never had ended the last. Not forgetting the potential for underwater war, nor the first German submarine campaign of 1915, when it was proved that U-boats could sink Allied merchantmen faster than they could be built, and not forgetting the second campaign of 1917, when after Jutland unrestricted U-boat warfare almost strangled British economic life, the German penchant for bigger and better submarines, and for more of them, lived on: beginning in 1922, ten years before Hitler came to power, German submarine designers and engineers worked secretly in Finland, Spain and Holland to keep up to date with submarine development and construction.

of the calibre of the pocket battleships *Admiral Graf Spee, Admiral Scheer, Deutschland,* the faster battle cruisers *Scharnhorst* and *Gneisenau,* the heavy cruiser *Admiral Hipper,* the sister battleships *Bismarck* and *Tirpitz,* each a sixth of a mile long, more than 50,000 tons fully laden.

To Raeder it was clear that to meet the demand a long-range programme was needed, so in January 1939 he presented his 'Z' plan to Hitler: six years to build six more battleships, mightier even than *Tirpitz* and *Bismarck,* eight more battle cruisers, four aircraft carriers, 233 U-boats to prowl the seas.

Britain by now had become a possible adversary; every day people were talking about war with the West. But when finally it did come, the news fell 'like a bomb shell', as Raeder would make a point of recalling. He had taken the Führer at his word: war with Britain would mean *Finis Germaniae*.

Dönitz, to whom Raeder had repeated Hitler's promise, just shook his head in disbelief. Britannia, not Germany, ruled the waves. The *Kriegsmarine* was, he would remember, like a 'torso without limbs,' too weak to maintain an effective and lasting threat against the Royal Navy. Germany had far too few surface ships—two battleships and three pocket battleships against 22 British and French battleships, two heavy cruisers compared to the Allied enemy's 22, six light cruisers against 61, 34 destroyers and torpedo boats to the combined 255 of the British and French, no aircraft carriers to counter the adversary's seven. *Gneisenau* and *Scharnhorst* were still working up, not fully serviceable; *Bismarck* and *Tirpitz* were launched but still due to commission; *Gneisenau* had not yet completed her trials; *Scheer* lay off Wilhelmshaven with engine trouble; only *Deutschland* and *Graf Spee* stood at stand-by stations, in the North and South Atlantic.

Raeder and Dönitz faced the problem: how to slip more ships through the side door from the Baltic, the Kiel Canal, and break through the British blockade line north of Orkney? To reach the open Atlantic, or to reach home ports from the Atlantic, surface raiders and U-boats had to break through the *Nord See—Mord See* in German minds: 'Murder Sea'. In the narrow sea lanes around England the Germans could not operate surface vessels, and the southern route to the Atlantic, the English Channel, was too narrow and shallow, too easily blocked with mines. U-boats would have to break through the blockade, then go full-out with all they had: concentrated, well-planned assaults against British sea commerce, troop transport and fleet units. Attack Britain's trade routes. Blockade her ports. Rapidly, unexpectedly, strike the Home Fleet where and when least expected.

The long-range plan was suspended; but where were the U-boats Dönitz needed? His submarine arm was weak—only 26 of the 57 U-boats on hand were first line operational craft, available for the Atlantic lanes. Most would be either going to a mission or returning from one; the rest were 'canoes', unsuitable for long patrols or needed for defensive positions in the North Sea and Channel. Rarely were more than eight or nine U-boats actually in position to attack British shipping.

'I have made up my mind,' Dönitz wrote in his U-boat Command War Diary on September 9.

> The obviously right thing is for me to take over control of the U-boat expansion programme as Director General, or something of the kind at Naval High Command . . . if we do not swiftly succeed in building up a numerically powerful and efficient U-boat arm, the fighting efficiency of the arm as it now stands might well deteriorate to such an extent that even the presence of its commanding officer would be of no avail.

In Berlin Hitler still hoped to avoid an all-out war with the West: his successes on land would assure him a favourable settlement. Despite the constant urging of Raeder and the Naval High Command, he refused to give priority to the construction of submarines. The Führer was fascinated by the technical details of ships, but in truth he had no special fondness for the Navy, no real maritime sense, having grown up in Austria/Bavaria with a 'warped, land-minded outlook', as Raeder would later observe.

His application rejected by Raeder, Dönitz stayed where he was, in Kiel, heading the U-boat arm, taking charge of its operations, leaving to the Grand Admiral and the Naval High Command the problem of U-boat construction. Perhaps later he could make a fresh start, press forward his wolf-pack tactics against convoys. Right now he would concentrate on strikes by U-boats operating alone.

So it was that in the very first days of the war Dönitz turned to the idea of a single dramatic blow against the British Fleet. 'From the very outset of the war,' as he wrote in his memoirs, 'I had always had in mind an operation against Scapa Flow' and now the notion was set before him like a challenge. He did not pause to inquire what manner of an idea it was. It was enough to chill his body, to quicken his blood.

To sink by submarine a British ship in a British naval harbour— Britain's *main* naval harbour!

It could be done: in the First War Dönitz had brought his own *UB-68* into and out of Sicily's Porta Augusta, past Italian defences. This was not 1914. Porta Augusta was not Scapa Flow. But this thought, the notion of penetrating the most secure of all British naval bases, stirred the deepest instincts for daring within him.

To Dönitz there appeared only one reason for making the raid— if it could be done, it should be done—yet among his small circle of confidants there was no doubt: if Dönitz could impress upon the Supreme Commander of the Armed Forces and his inner circle that the day of the U-boat was not over, that it had not been rendered obsolete by the convoy system and antisubmarine weapons, as many in Germany were beginning to feel, he might restore faith in submarines as a force against British seapower.

Dönitz lost no time in sending a 'canoe', *U-16* into waters near Scapa, nor in asking Naval High Command for a copy of its report on the anchorage. This document and the Heinkel photographs, a hydrographic map of Scapa, and a detailed report written by Korvettenkapitän (Lieutenant Commander) Wellner, the commander of *U-16,* he had before him when on 11 September he began in earnest to plan the raid.

Present in the *Toten Weg* with Dönitz was Wellner and a small circle of the top staff officers: Korvettenkapitän Eberhardt Godt, *Admiralstabsoffizier des FDU,* or Chief of Operations Division; Korvettenkapitän Victor Oehrn, staff officer of Naval Operations (*Seekriegsleitung*); and a communications expert, Korvettenkapitän von Stockhausen. There was also 'a younger officer for the preparation of written orders', Godt remembers today: 'The circle of informed persons was certainly very limited. Briefings for the mission were held for a very small group of participants only.'

The High Command report contained the best written information available, but it had been prepared before the start of the war and could do no more than note the *presumed* obstacles guarding the Flow's entrances. So Dönitz and the others concentrated on the pictures, passing a magnifying glass between them and moving from one picture to another, turning quick eyes around the harbour, thoughtfully regarding the shapes of British vessels, tiny forms in both the main fleet anchorage and destroyer anchorage: to the south near the main Hoxa entrance and just north of the desolate islands of Flotta a number of heavy and light warships, then, deeper into Scapa, in the narrow Risa Sound off the east coast of Hoy, more ships.

For several hours from the Pentland Firth, Wellner had peered through the crosshairs of his periscope, giving serious attention to details of currents, tides, patrols, and lighting at Scapa. There had been no loops or minefields that he could see. And as the best possible way in, he now told the small group, he preferred the most obvious, the broad Hoxa Sound between the islands of Flotta and South Ronaldsay. If a U-boat picked a moment when the length of floating net which formed the gate in the boom was left open, it would be possible to follow in the wake of a battle-ship; if luck was with the U-boat, if for just a few seconds longer than it took a ship to pass through, the gate remained open, a sub-marine could creep in, by stealth, under the cover of darkness.

Assuming his typical posture, arms folded, one hand touching his chin, Dönitz pondered upon the challenge. He could only won-der about the ships of the British Empire, particularly the huge aircraft carriers which naval intelligence had told him were spread apart as far as the western entrance of the Channel to East Asia. German air reconnaissance had been observing numerous steamers in the central and northern part of the North Sea up to the area of the Shetlands; but few British naval forces had been spotted. The steamers proved almost exclusively neutral.

The situation had cleared slightly on September 10 when a British plane downed five days earlier was raised and a recon-naissance table salvaged—by means of which the Radio Monitor-ing Service established that the aircraft carrier *Ark Royal,* the bat-tleship *Nelson,* and the cruiser *Sheffield* had been near Dundee. Now they were where? In Scapa perhaps. Perhaps not. On any day, Dönitz knew, the situation might change; overnight the entire

Fleet could slip from their berths, leaving nothing, not even a row-boat, with only cormorants and seagulls to greet an invader.

The meeting of 11 September broke up. No decision had been reached; yet the room seemed filled with confidence. 'The first air views of Scapa', remembered Oehrn, 'led us to suspect, even if only vaguely, that the enemy blocking was not complete.'

Godt recalled: 'The prospects for a huge success were excellent'.

For almost five years after the great scuttling of the First War, Scapa had remained cluttered with wrecks, Germany's once-proud ironclads lying underwater or with decks awash, some on beam-ends, some with bows cocked high in the air, others showing only rusting sides to British vessels that on summer cruises entered through the now open Sounds, past the now dismantled gun emplacements. In 1924 a salvage firm, Cox & Danks, began to clear the litter; in 1934 another firm, Metal Industries Ltd, took over, while over the years German trawlers passed in and out without raising alarm, sailing in at Hoy, past the still-upraised bottom of the once-magnificent battle cruiser *Derfflinger,* then out at Holm.

No one thought of Scapa as a great naval base, or of war with Germany—until in September 1938 it appeared Hitler would carry out his resolve to attack Czechoslovakia, and the Admiralty looked again to Scapa as a base for the Fleet. While at Berchtes-gaden, later at Goddesberg, Chamberlain was pleading to Hitler and the prospect of war was growing, Scapa was recommissioned and once again the Navy began thinking about blocking all existing gaps against the possibility of submarine penetration. The Hoxa boom with pendant nets was put in place, buoys were rigged to the boom moorings; other booms were fixed at Switha and Hoy. Admiral Forbes approved the local purchase of a concrete barge at Stromness, with the idea of sinking it in Kirk Sound. But by the time Admiralty approval came, in the last week of October, the Czech emergency was over, the Führer at Munich accepting Chamberlain's proposal for the occupation of the Sudetenland, for eleven months preserving the peace.

Came November, however, and with it a feeling that something had to be done to better protect Scapa. Metal Industries, which would have the job of sinking the concrete barge at Kirk, thought it would not block the Sound completely and suggested a survey.

The Admiralty, worrying about cost, disagreed; but by mid-December it had reconsidered and invited the salvage firm to tender for a shell of about 350 feet for Kirk; the concrete barge was to be used to block the narrow navigable channel in Water Sound —where in late February it was finally sunk.

Still some gaps remained, in Water one of 35 feet between the newly-sunk barge and another wreck, with a 140-yard-long passage about two fathoms deep—an extremely difficult channel for any vessel of average turning powers to navigate but a channel nevertheless. Two blockships, SS *Soriano* and SS *Thames* were sunk in Kirk Sound, others in Weddel and Skerry, near some broken-up blockships already there; but what was really needed, felt Admiral French, was a comprehensive survey to estimate the cost for more effectively blocking the eastern sounds with more hulls, more anchors, more wires, more cables—anything that would make the entrances submarine-proof.

Before any of the blocking was to be done, Metal Industries was to consult with the commanding officer of HMS *Scott,* the ship carrying out the survey approved by the Admiralty. But suddenly, on 26 May, a message was received from the Admiralty that gave dim hope to the filling in of the gaps, for *Scott*'s survey had been completed and a study of it indicated, said the Admiralty, in a report kept secret for thirty years, and not disclosed until 1971, that:

No risk at present exists of submerged entry of submarines by Holm or Water Sound and that entry on the surface would be extremely hazardous. Their lordships doubt if further blocking measures proposed would be final or could be relied upon to provide 100 per cent security against a determined attempt at entry of enemy craft on the surface, though such an attempt is considered extremely unlikely. It has therefore been decided further expenditure on blockships cannot be justified. The Rear Admiral and Commanding Officer, Coast of Scotland is requested to inform Metal Industries of this decision expressing Their Lordship's appreciation of their valuable assistance in investigating the question. The Commander-in-Chief, Home Fleet, is requested to report in view of this decision, whether he considers it will be necessary to provide security by provision of any patrol vessels.

On this single report did the Admiralty depend for analysis of the defence and security of their principal base. The Assistant Chief of the Naval Staff, Admiral H. M. Burrough, approved the report, routinely, and since the matter was not considered a major one of policy and strategy, it did not go beyond Burrough to the First Sea Lord, Sir Roger Backhouse. At the time Backhouse was ill, it is true, but the report did not go to any member of the operational side of Naval Staff; the Acting Chief of the Naval Staff, Admiral J. H. D. Cunningham, was not consulted; neither was the Deputy Chief. To Metal Industries went simply 'Their Lordships' appreciation of their valuable assistance in investigating the question'.

The chief salvage officer for Metal Industries, Thomas McKenzie, was *not* appreciative; his duty he felt lay in pointing out the danger signs. He wrote to the Admiralty:

It is fully recognised that the navigation of the Sounds, even now, presents difficulties, owing to the strong tidal streams and the existing obstructions, but it is safe to assume that an intrepid submarine officer, in war time, would take risks which no discreet mariner would think of taking in peace time.

If the entrances were left as present, he wrote, a hostile submarine could enter Scapa Flow.

and the fact that any such craft successful in passing through one of the Sounds could be within torpedo range of Capital ships in 15 to 30 minutes, makes it of vital importance that the Sounds should be efficiently blocked.

Admiral French agreed. In mid-June he visited Scapa, went down to Kirk and Skerry Sounds, going in and out of both on a young west-going tide in a picket boat. Couldn't a submarine do the same, provided it had slack water and light enough to see? It's 'complete rot talking about swirls and eddies putting you on the beach or sunken ships,' French told Forbes. 'The sunken ships provide you with an excellent beacon'.

Immediately Forbes responded, suggesting improvements: he wanted the existing chart, which showed all manner of non-existent obstructions, to remain as the official chart, with a 'Notice to

Mariners' stating that new obstructions had closed all passages, and he wanted more blockships in Kirk and Skerry. In other channels, fast, shallow draught surface craft, such as motor torpedo boats, could patrol for submarines. The Admiralty agreed, but only casually. Lulled by the *Scott* survey, Whitehall assigned no urgency to the task.

In time three more ships would be sunk to block the channels between *Soriano* and *Thames,* south of *Thames* in Kirk, and the main channel in Skerry. But the days, then weeks, wore on, war broke, and no more blockships were sunk. At the end of the second week in September, as Churchill was preparing to leave Scapa on Forbes's flagship *Nelson,* to visit the rest of the Fleet at Loch Ewe, on the north of the Scottish west coast, only a taut 12-inch hemp had been slung between *Thames* and *Soriano*; backing that up were slung two 7-inch and one 6-inch loose wires, and from the stern of *Thames* toward *Soriano* a 7-inch wire leading down to a 7½-ton anchor; similarly, from the stern of *Soriano* to abreast the quarter of *Thames* a 6-inch wire led to a 7½-ton anchor.

The moral effect was very good.

Alternately in Wilhelmshaven and Kiel Karl Dönitz continued to think upon Wellner's suggestion; it did seem plausible, but it would work only if patrol boats in Hoxa or on the seaward side of the gate did not notice the submerged submarine and if no Hydrophone or Asdic watch was maintained at or inside the entrance. The Hoxa boom was long and difficult to watch from shore and at night the watch in the gate vessels would have a hard time seeing the far end of the boom, where a gap was kept to keep from having to open the gate for small craft passing to and fro. Wellner had made no mention of this in his report to Dönitz, fearing perhaps the guns that covered the gap, perhaps the Asdic, suggesting only the possibility of entering in the wake of a ship—yet like most others not unmindful that in the First War, in the same Hoxa Sound, two U-boat commanders had tried to force entrance and failed: in November 1914, Kapitänleutnant (Lieutenant-Senior) Heinrich von Hennig had guided his *U-18* through Hoxa in the wake of a steamer taking supplies, was detected by a patrol boat, rammed, drifted down to the Skerries, sank with all but one crewman taken prisoner.

Then in October 1918, the war nearing its end and German

naval officers wanting a final blow at the Grand Fleet, *UB-116* under Oberleutnant zur See (Lieutenant-Junior) Hans Joachim Emsmann, the son of an admiral*, crossed the North Sea in safety but at Scapa triggered the defenders' listening equipment, detonated a net of mines, fell to pieces—and produced one of the grimmest stories of the war: when the next day British divers found three bodies in the smashed conning tower, through the fore hatch they cleared the way aft to the control room bulkhead, past more bodies and kitbags packed with new, clean clothing, and after some days' work they reached the control room bulkhead. Finding the door partly off its hinges and jammed, they dug away bedding and debris from around the door and found the forearms and hands of a man thrust out through the crack at the lower part of the door seating. Was this Emsmann? It could not be known as no more of the man than the arms and the elbows could be reached; his body was on the other side of the jammed door in the collapsed and inaccessible control room.

In the Second War the memory of Hennig's and Emsmann's fates at Scapa were not forgotten and the Germans would think twice before they would try again to push through the front door—when actually, unknown to the Germans, unknown even to British naval authorities, the front door was more vulnerable than it had ever been. For the foot of the Hoxa net, far from being at the minimum safe distance, two or three feet from bottom—to keep from fouling and bringing the whole defence down—rested a full twenty-five feet from bottom at low water. Like a strange and mysterious curtain, slowly swaying, playing to the coming and going of the current, the net wondrously rose and fell, at spring tide lifting ten to eleven feet, at high water to thirty-five, enough for a small 'canoe' to slip beneath it, creep close to the bottom, scrape or bump along it. A U-boat could navigate for miles this way; and if it succeeded, it could get out in like manner, slipping beneath the net while the tide remained high.

Without even thinking of going in under the net and without accepting the likelihood of any single plan working, Dönitz looked to prospects for success. An operation against Scapa was too overwhelming an idea to dismiss; yet over the days as he gazed intently at the first set of Heinkel photographs he felt compelled to

* Konteradmiral (Rear Admiral) A. D. Hugo Emsmann.

conclude that it would be, on the face of it, the 'boldest of bold' enterprises. The principal difficulties arose out of the exceptional currents prevalent in the Scapa area. East of Hoxa, in the Pentland Firth, where North Sea and Atlantic meet in a narrow channel, there flowed one of the worst stretches of water in the world, where a current of ten knots per hour was regularly to be met with.

Dönitz reasoned: 'As the maximum underwater speed of a U-boat was only 7 knots, this meant that the current could carry the U-boat wherever it liked, without the latter being able to do anything about it'.

He also was well aware of Scapa's status as a Main Fleet base, knowing it had to be heavily defended: the Admiralty 'with all its great experience in these matters, and the Commander-in-Chief of the Home Fleet must have complete confidence in the effectiveness of the measures taken and felt quite sure that the British warships were perfectly secure in their anchorage'.

More than this, Dönitz was reluctant to send a U-boat to Scapa because of 'the very great difficulties involved, from the point of view of both seamanship and navigation'. Still he did continue to grapple with the idea, compelling his mind to think of it. In his memoirs he tells how one day he was sitting in front of a map of the Flow, thinking of the possibility for success, when of a sudden his glance fell upon Oehrn.

Oehrn turned to Dönitz.

'You know, sir', he said. 'I'm pretty sure we *could* find a way to get in'.

And Dönitz felt with those words just 'the final impetus I required to tackle the problem in earnest and in detail'. For more than any other officer on his staff Dönitz trusted the opinion of Oehrn, whom he regarded as a man with an exceptionally clear and determined mind.

Yet Dönitz remained not entirely convinced. He knew full well that he needed more information about the defences. He asked for more photographs.

In the great port cities of Wilhelmshaven and Kiel life went on as usual, the people convinced the Reich was going to win. How could this not be? The war was going well. Not a bomb had yet been dropped on Berlin. Although the British had raided ships in the Schillig Roads anchorage off Wilhelmshaven, others lying off Brumsbütel in the Elbe, bringing the war home to the German people, reminding them that they would have to defend the fatherland, morale remained high. There was not yet any rationing. Cinemas still were featuring foreign imports; at Kiel's popular Schauburg theatre the public was flocking to see *Cafe Metropol* starring Loretta Young, Tyrone Power, Adolphe Menjou. The bookstores were doing a banner business, still selling works of foreign authors, including *Gone With the Wind* (*Vom Winde Verweht*), A. J. Cronin's *Citadel*; also selling well was a propaganda book about England, *Look Up the Subject of England,* and *Fifty Years of Germany* by Sven Hedin, a Swedish friend of Hitler (the Führer's own *Mein Kampf* had sold more than five million copies nationwide).

As for Dönitz, he was too apprehensive to remain anything but grave. On the afternoon of the 4th, while Bristol Blenheims ('Tommies') of the RAF had delivered their low-flying attack on ships off Wilhelmshaven, he had been standing on the deck of a submarine depot ship, and saw two 500-pounders hit the deck of *Scheer* but bounce harmlessly into the sea—while U-boat officers around him let out a cheer and anti-aircraft defences poured fire on the retreating Tommies, sending several down in flames; only one Tommy inflicted any real damage, crashing against the bows of *Emden,* ripping a gash that killed the pilot and more than a dozen German sailors. When it was over, Dönitz called his officers together and told them, in a warning that he and they would remember long after the war: 'This war must be taken very seriously. Make no mistake about it—it may well last for seven years, and we shall probably be only too happy to see it end then in a peace by negotiation'.

On 14 September, as he waited for his new pictures of Scapa, Dönitz's U-boats lay in a widespread pattern to intercept any ships they could, yet without a precise pattern to spring a trap for particular ships. Three U-boats lay off the Firth of Forth, one east and one southwest of the Firth of Moray, one somewhere between the Shetlands and Norway, three approaching the western outlet of the Skagerrak, nine on a return passage between the Shetlands and the Kattegat—while the Navy's Operations Division was cautioning from Berlin: 'It is a strategic task of prior importance for the Radio Monitoring Service to obtain exact data on the whereabouts and operations of the enemy aircraft carriers'.

Were they in Scapa? When on the 14th Dönitz received a report from Aelesun that fishermen in the area had reported sighting four destroyers and two submarines on a southwesterly course sixty miles west of Trondheim Fjord, he thought the carriers might be out with them. But the Germans could not be sure what kind of vessels the destroyers and submarines were—British perhaps but also possibly Swedish or Danish.

The same day there occurred the first U-boat loss of the war when west of the Hebrides two torpedoes fired by *U-39* at Britain's newest and finest carrier, *Ark Royal*, exploded prematurely and the destroyers counterattacked with depth charges, forcing *U-39* to blow her tanks and surface, the entire crew stumbling out of the conning tower hatch; *U-39* scuttled, *Ark* picked forty-three men from the choppy sea. Meanwhile three Skuas which had flown from *Ark* before the action found *U-30* surfaced two hundred miles to the southwest, trying to finish with her guns a steamer just torpedoed. One Skua popped a bomb on the U-boat's bow, climbed away, leaving two torpedo tubes out of action; the other two hit the sea after flying so low that exploding bombs shattered their afterparts, killing the air gunners, forcing the pilots to take to rubber dinghies—to become the first men of the Fleet Air to be captured by Germans.

A fortnight after the start of the war, the Führer himself visited the submarine base at Wilhelmshaven and reviewed the crews of several returning U-boats. In his open Mercedes-Benz, wearing his military cap, his double-breasted field-grey uniform, Hitler offered a gloved hand in salute as the crew of *U-29* stood at attention on the afterdeck, a triumphant Kapitänleutnant Otto Schuhardt watching on the bridge, fresh from administering the first major British loss of the war. On 17 September in Bristol Channel Schuhardt had found the old British carrier *Courageous,* 22,500 tons, torpedoed her as she was turning into the winds to receive planes for landing, made her to suffer the fate that narrowly had missed *Ark Royal*; *Courageous* went down with more than 500 men and Schuhardt received one of the first Iron Crosses of the war.*

---

* An honour that was later denied to the man who sank the *Athenia*, Korvettenkapitän Fritz-Julius Lemp of *U-30* who the next week nervously reported to Dönitz

On the lock gates in September bands were playing, flowers passed among crews, the first phase of the submarine war in the Atlantic and Channel nearing its end, U-boats accounting for almost 120,000 tons of British merchant shipping; and they might have sunk more if all torpedoes had functioned as they should.

Dönitz next flew to Berlin to put before Raeder his proposal for the raid on Scapa Flow. On Berlin's *Tirpitzüfer*, at the Supreme Naval Staff (*Seekriegsleitung*) headquarters, he discussed the mission with the Grand Admiral. A Special Item, previously unpublished from the War Diary of September 18, records the details of the meeting:

> Commander, Submarines plans to send out a submarine with torpedoes to Scapa Flow, since the evaluation of photographic reconnaissance by the Operational Air Force indicates that such an operation would be very promising. Chief Naval Staff agrees with this but orders an investigation as to whether it would not be more advisable and effective to have the operation carried out by a minelaying submarine, and reserves definite decision on its execution for himself.

German reconnaissance was ordered to watch Scapa constantly. By 25 September it was established the British Home Fleet was at sea in the strength of five battleships, three cruisers, numerous destroyers: 'Speed: 20 knots . . . west of Norway . . . enemy destroyers southwest of the Dogger Bank and about 90 miles west of Lindesnes', according to Radio Monitoring.

Over the Flow itself on the afternoon of the day following, photographic reconnaissance spotted the grey silhouette of a battle cruiser of the *Repulse* class, thought by Naval Intelligence to have been the *Hood,* 42,000 tons, the biggest warship in the world, the pride of Britain's Navy. Where was *Hood* going? Might not a U-boat catch her at Scapa? Perhaps, thought Dönitz, but not with

---

that it was he who had torpedoed the liner, in error, mistaking her for an auxiliary cruiser. Lemp had violated the Prize Ordinance Regulations governing surprise attacks on ships, which Hitler had wanted to remain in effect for fear of drawing more countries into the war. Ordered to keep the matter secret, Dönitz had all mention of the incident stricken from *U-30*'s logbook and the Nazi Propaganda Ministry charged Churchill with deliberately sabotaging *Athenia* to give the British an excuse for attacking German ships without warning.

mines—although already many dozens had been sown, in sensitive inshore areas of the North Sea, in approaches to such ports as Weymouth and Dover, in the middle of shipping lanes, in harbour mouths themselves. Unloaded by 'canoes,' these lethal eggs—the efficient and new TMB, which carried between 800 and 1,000 pounds of explosives, detonated at 12 to 15 fathoms by magnetic fields of ships moving overhead, the acoustic mine, detonated by sound made by ships' propellers, the pressure mine, set off by change in pressure created by passing vessels—were damaging and sinking ships with astonishing success. But Dönitz reasoned that mines were for targets which *might* appear in a certain area, while in Scapa there already *were* targets. He would urge upon Raeder only torpedoes.

Loosed at short range, they would be deadly.

At midday on 26 September Dönitz was handed his second set of Scapa photos, taken also by Air Fleet II. With Oehrn, Godt, and von Stockhausen he pored over them hungrily, his eyes fastening upon the plain black and white prints and discerning immediately that they showed more detail than the first prints. 'They were clear and disinct and even the direction of the current at the time the pictures were taken could be discerned on them', recalled Oehrn.

The Germans set upon the pictures. First they studied the obstacles blocking Hoy, Switha, and Hoxa Sounds, noting that each was closed with booms but that each boom had a permanent unnetted gap at its shore end, and that each gap varied in size. In addition, from their hydrographic map they could calculate the width of the gaps up to the 7 metre line—the limit of manoeuvrability for submarines.

Lifting magnifying glasses over the photographs, they saw that in the narrow gaps a few possibly navigable channels existed; if patrol boats could wind through the gaps, why not a small U-boat? Dönitz moved his glass slowly, spanning the harbour. In Hoy Sound, western gate between Mainland and northern end of Hoy, second largest island in Orkney, he spied at the isle's south end a passage about 500 feet wide. A passable gap.

Then turning his gaze downward, to the area of Switha Sound, he could see that to the north of the island of Flotta there lay at anchor heavy and light warships. At one end of the boom, near the tiny island of Switha, another gap loomed but one which only could have looked exceedingly narrow and difficult to navigate; then to the east, across main Hoxa Sound and close to the Flotta shore, another, more considerable gap lay, one large enough for a U-boat drawing 12 to 15 feet of water to pass through: but immediately after navigating the gap it would have to make a sharp turn to starboard, increasing the danger of touching the boom, of becoming entangled in netting. The booms themselves, the officers knew, were not infallible, not designed to stop a determined U-boat on the surface: one heavily armed with explosive cutters could without difficulty force its way across or cut through a single line of anti-submarine nets. To enter or exit, it could fire a torpedo at a boom and penetrate through the hole—although at great risk, of fouling propellers, of carrying some part of net and boom with her, thus alerting patrol drifters which likely were fitted with depth charges.

The men turned to the smaller narrows, the four eastern entrances, where the velocity of tidal streams had swept away all thought of using booms, where much as they had in 1918 blockships poked rusting skeletons above the sounds—the newer blockships sitting astride the channels but many still askew them, moved by two decades of Scapa storms. In Water Sound, they could see, a blockship lay on the south side, then northward of another portion of a different blockship lay still another blockship, forming a gap about 200 feet wide but one that must have seemed foolhardy to try to navigate. Skerry Sound appeared completely barred with, at most, only a small passage south of two blockships. Weddel also gave the appearance of being submarine-proof.

But now Dönitz noticed something unusual. Looking at a small leg of the larger Holm Sound, which curved into the Flow from the North Sea, his eye was caught by the narrow channel of Kirk Sound, where there was not one but two gaps, one about 200 feet wide, west of the westernmost blockship, another about twice that width, south of the blockship close to the western shore. To the U-boatmen leaning over the pictures, the gaps had to look inviting. They knew the depths would vary at high and low water, but it was clear there was a weakness in the enemy's defences. Could Scapa be vulnerable here?

'The pictures', Oehrn would remember, 'showed that apart from the scuttled ships the passage was not otherwise blocked or secured by stationary observation posts. Without a doubt, the navigational difficulties for passage of a ship were very great, but we felt they could be overcome'.

Might not a daring U-boat commander, cruising on the surface and following a prearranged timetable, on a dark, clear night, creep through one of the narrow openings around the anchored blockships, and, like a torpedo boat, attack, then by the same stealth, still fully-surfaced, slip out the same way? If the U-boat made minimum noise, if the tides were right, if no patrols were encountered—the 'ifs' played with Dönitz's mind—his First War career in a U-boat had ended off Sicily when *UB-68*, under less strain, had suddenly turned on its bow and plummeted out of control, only to shoot upward, like a stick suddenly released from a plunge into water, after Dönitz had ordered air tanks blown, engines thrown full astern, hard rudder over.* But whatever doubt Dönitz had was fast fleeing; for on the surface the U-boat was the perfect instrument, the best boat imaginable, really a *Tauchboot*, a Submersible, and not an *Unterseeboot*—as always Dönitz had known.

Despite the misconceptions of laymen, the U-boat primarily was a surface vessel which only occasionally moved under water. With a small silhouette, with for the most part only the conning tower showing above surface, it was highly manoeuvrable, quick to dive, capable of constantly altering its course; if it let go its torpedoes within the short range of 600 yards, it could hardly miss.

As for the chances of getting out of the Flow after the attack, they were, in the words of Godt, 'as acceptable as they could possibly be in any war. Neither the entrance nor the escape were safe risks. They were calculated risks. Safe risks probably do not exist'.

In the days that followed, Dönitz kept his idea from his U-boat commanders. Sure only that he wanted to proceed, and with a night surface attack, he announced that he wanted reconnaissance of Scapa stepped up. On 27 September *U-10* was sent into the operational area of the Orkneys, the next day two more U-boats—*U-19* and *U-22*—were ordered into Orkney waters. And the War Diary of the 28th was encouraging:

* *UB-68* crashed to the surface, was hit by a barrage from a British cruiser, the crew abandoned ship, Dönitz was rescued by a destroyer and taken to Malta and a British prisoner of war camp.

According to Radio Monitoring, the main body of the Home Fleet is probably lying again in Scapa Flow. One cruiser (the *Glasgow*?) near Rosyth in the evening of 27 Sept.

On the same day Hitler returned to Wilhelmshaven. Dönitz met with him, trying to impress upon the Führer anew the importance of the submarine as a weapon of war: with three hundred U-boats he could force the British to beg for mercy. Hitler listened to his U-boat leader but seemed unimpressed, and Dönitz did not push the point; as with all who came in contact with the Führer he felt awed by his power and personality, too uncomfortable to try to insist on anything. Dönitz said nothing to Hitler about his planned raid on Scapa—and if Raeder told the Führer about it, Dönitz was not informed.

Later, after lunch in the officers' mess, Hitler surprised a group of officers who pressed eagerly around by saying nothing about the U-boat arm, only that, 'Field Marshal Göring and his Luftwaffe are going to chase the British Fleet right around Britain!' The words stunned the young submariners, who knew Göring had little respect for the Navy. The corpulent *Reichsmarschall,* the Number Two man in Germany, rumoured for becoming sea-sick whenever he set foot aboard ship, for years had refused to cooperate with the *Kriegsmarine,* turning down both Dönitz's and Raeder's constant requests that the U-boat arm be given its own planes—a Naval Air Force—for reconnaissance missions. The war would be won in the air, the boastful Göring wanted everyone to believe: his planes would be needed elsewhere, 'Everything that flies belongs to me', one of his favourite comments.

The days wore on, and Dönitz decided to wait no longer, penning in his U-boat Command War Diary a summation of the situation on Scapa:

1. To penetrate the obstacles in Hoxa Sound seems hardly possible. Penetration through those on Switha Sound and Clesstrom Sound quite out of the question.
2. Holm Sound is completely blocked by two merchant ships, apparently sunk, which lie diagonally across the channel of Kirk Sound, and a third vessel to the north of the other two. To the south thereof and running as far as Lamb Holm is a

HMS *Royal Oak*

The Third Reich's first hero

(*Below*) Kiel, October 23, 1939. Sailors of the cruiser *Emden* cheer the *U-47*

Kiel in the summer of 1939 and five Type VIIA U-boats

U-47 was a Type VIIB in the U-boat design arsenal, predecessor of the most widely used combat sub in the war, the VIIC

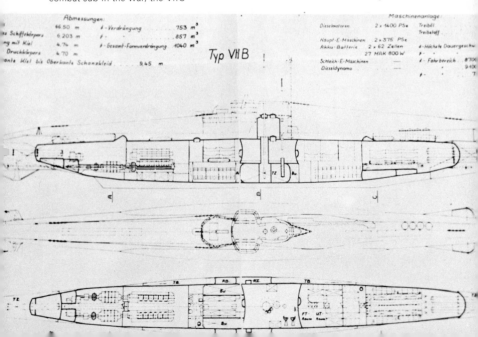

General view of Scapa Flow

Tot time in HMS *Royal Oak*. Every crewman over 18 years old was entitled to draw his share of rum

narrow channel about 50 feet wide, in which the depth is about 3½ fathoms and on either side of which are shallows. To the north of the merchant ships is a further small channel. The shore on both sides is practically uninhabited. Here, I think, it would certainly be possible to penetrate—by night, on the surface at slack water. The main difficulties will be navigational.

Dönitz now had only to seek and obtain the approval of Raeder, then cast about for the right U-boat commander to lead the raid: someone with an iron nerve, a cool head, a superb sense of navigation.

2

Special Operation 'P'

At 1655 hours—4.55 p.m.—on that first Monday of the war, the fourth of September, the sound of feet suddenly clattered on the conning tower ladder of U-boat number *47* and the face, then the head and shoulders, of Oberfunkmaat (Petty Officer Telegraphist) Hans Blank appeared through the hatchway. '*Kapitän*, Sir,' said the young wireless operator, 'an urgent signal from U-boat Command.'

On the bridge, side by side with his *Eins WO*, his Number One, first officer of the watch Englebert Endrass, Oberleutnant Günther Prien contemplated the wireless teletype signal. In his first command, Prien was, at thirty-one, the 'Old Man' to the crew, four years older than Endrass, fair-haired, square-jawed, broad-shouldered, of medium height, and as *47* rode easily over the sea, its diesels driving her steadily into the jagged waves, he braced his stocky frame against the spray deflector and read the terse one-line directive. From Dönitz in Wilhelmshaven it had been decoded in the coding machine, reported and logged in plain language: EXISTING ORDERS FOR MERCANTILE WARFARE REMAIN IN FORCE.

Three times already Prien had grappled fundamentally with this fact, first when from the south that morning he found a freighter, a Greek, about 5,000 tons, lumbering casually upon the sea. *U-47* gave chase, diving first, then surfacing, then closed on the Greek, sending a warning shot across her bows, making the neutral merchantman to heave-to, break out her flag, swing out two boats; but suddenly the men in the little boats tried to flee.

In an outburst of effort they began rowing feverishly, which struck Prien as amusing, for *U-47* just followed calmly, came level with the boats, stopping when Prien ordered the captain to give up his papers. This whole impetuous business was unnecessary, for Prien allowed the freighter to sail free; she was a non-belligerent, bound for Germany with a non-suspect cargo of minerals, a few hundreds tons at most: no reason to doubt the truthfulness of her papers, to examine her on the high seas. And when next two west-ward-steering vessels, weak ships, the first Swedish, the other Nor-wegian, crossed Prien's path, they too were allowed to sail on: even if their cargoes had been in doubt, it would have been im-practical to bring them in as prizes, to claim them by condem-nation.

So what might have been a formidable undersea weapon was turned in effect into a surface warship, for 'mercantile warfare' meant attention to the Prize Ordinance Regulations which out-lawed unrestricted submarine war; if surfaced, *U-47* could stop its quarry, but then it must search for 'contraband,' munitions of war, foodstuffs destined for armed forces. It could sink a ship, a merchantman even, but only if this vessel was directly helping the war effort—and then only after its papers and crew had been taken on board.

Lifeboats, said the Rules*, were 'unsuitable' for the high seas.

In the small curtained area amidsection that passed for his 'cabin,' a cramped nook to port, just off the *Zentrale*, the control room directly opposite the radio room to starboard, Prien re-viewed his instructions, paying special attention to the Regula-tions. *U-47*, he knew, would take no foreigners into her already overcrowded quarters, no *Englisch* to get in the way of his diesels and motors, his delicate instruments, men jumping to action sta-tions; every available cubic metre of space was taken; there was barely enough storage space for torpedoes. But he would other-wise comply with the tenets of this senseless code of conduct; and so *U-47* idled about, west of the Bay of Biscay, scornful of the wrath of the waves and veering, it seemed, neither one way nor the other but rather cautiously waiting to cut the life-lines of Brit-ish commerce, to intercept any ship making for the British Isles, to seek out the dark shadows of fighting vessels: the battleships *Nelson* and *Rodney* perhaps, *Ark Royal*, the battle cruisers *Re-pulse, Renown, Hood,* or any of a dozen or so other destroyers and cruisers, the main body of the Home Fleet (which unknown

* The articles of the London Naval Treaty of 1930.

to Prien was standing out far west of the Hebrides on this second day of the war).

On the morning of the day before, from the *Grossdeutsche Rundfunk*, the German wireless network, martial music had poured through the narrow corridors of the U-boat, creating the mood for some startling news:

'The British government in a note to the government of the Reich has demanded that the German troops which have advanced into Poland shall be withdrawn. If a satisfactory reply is not received in London by eleven o'clock, Great Britain will consider herself in a state of war with Germany.'

The tension had been unimaginable, the crew seized at once with a sense of anticipation, and now, on the fourth, after the Reich had refused to yield to the British ultimatum, and after, at 2353 hours, Prien had been handed a further W/T: BY ORDER OF THE FUHRER, PASSENGER SHIPS UNTIL FURTHER NOTICE WILL NOT BE ATTACKED, EVEN IF IN CONVOY, the crew believed to a man, from the captain down to the most junior rating, that England, not Germany, had started this dreaded war. They felt caught in a struggle to defend the fatherland: the orders from Wilhelmshaven, the strict adherence to prize warfare regulations, bore 'proof' of the Führer's desire for peace.

No sham gestures were the orders from the High Command— they were a direct consequence of the *Athenia* incident. But they were not altruistic either, for Hitler, back in the Chancellery, was reasoning that after his steel juggernaut had crushed Poland, might not Britain and France make peace? Britain, though determined, seemed 'hesitant.' The French, far superior to the Germans in the west, were showing no eagerness to help their Polish allies.

U-47 looked a vision of power, built at the *Germania Werft* in Kiel, the leading Krupp yard, commissioned as a unit of the 7th U-boat Flotilla, the *Flotilla Wegener,* on 16 December 1938, a time of steadily rising international tension, two months since Chamberlain, carrying in his pocket an Anglo-German declaration of the 'desire of our two peoples never to go to war with one another again,' announced to the world: 'I believe it is peace for our time.' In three months Czechoslovakia would cease to exist.

In Kiel at year's end, there was music at *47*'s commissioning, flags everywhere, beaming sailors in pressed uniforms bedecked with shiny buttons, the loud raucous blare of a band.

'It was my birthday, the date when we put the boat into service,' remembered Machinist First Class Werner Lüddecke. 'The commander made a good impression on me and, I may say, on the whole crew.'

There was jubilance everywhere. The family of U-boats was growing and Prien, from Leipzig, a child of the depression, the product of a broken home, a sailor since his teens, stood proudly on the bridge of the new submarine, four million marks worth of steel ('such an expensive coffin' was the running joke at the constructional briefing) and while she glided lazily, gracefully, from her fertile pen, the band played, the Nazi ensign of the *Kriegsmarine*, a smart white, red, and black, black swastika, black cross, fluttered at the bows, a prayerful hush fell over those who saw her slip by.

Though capable of bearing the main brunt of any war at sea, she was at the time Germany's best design: 218 feet from stem to stern, listed as a 500-tonner—to comply with the Anglo-German Naval Treaty—but in fact 750 tons, looking like a dark fat sausage to some, to others a lean grey wolf, a stiletto upon the water, hiding beneath her smooth pressure hull a complex array of vital organs. Type VIIB in the U-boat design arsenal, actually the 6th production type (after Types IA, IIA, IIB, IIC and VIIA), she was the first modification of the Type VII, longer, heavier, faster, more powerful than her predecessors, her range boosted from a radius of 6200 to 9100 miles, her saddle tanks modified to improve her seaworthiness, her armament increased to up her fighting power. Surfaced, her twin 375 horsepower electric motors, battery-driven, gave her a top speed of slightly more than 17 knots. Submerged, her twin diesels, rated at 1400 horses each, could reach a maximum 7.6 knots. There never had been a class of U-boat like her.

For the next eleven months, in peace, *U-47* continued fitting out, fought the seas, sailed on shake-down voyages, once to Spanish Morocco with six other boats, *U-45, U-46, U-48, U-51, U-52, U-53*—the entire *Flotilla Wegener*. The crew practised target shooting, diving, five seconds to close the hatchway, one and one-fifth seconds for each man, thirty seconds to submerge; they tested her fittings, her 21-inch torpedo tubes, four in *der*

Pairskammer, the 'House of Lords' at the stem, one in the bow, fired her 3.5-inch and 88 mm automatic AA guns, and gradually officers and crew worked up to full efficiency: to fix in light and darkness breakdowns in engines, to steer and hold the boat at the right depth by matching engine speed with proper tilt of the broad hydroplane vanes. The boat's complement, boys mostly, average age twenty, volunteers in the most dangerous trade in the world, handpicked for physique and temperament, Meyer, Dittmer, Scholz, Winzer, Hölzer, Sollig, some thirty-five more—cooks, mechanics, electricians, wireless operators, torpedomen, stokers, the corps-elite of the German Navy, sworn by a holy oath to obey Hitler himself—went about their business mechanically, moving with a quiet cheerfulness, without any visible expression upon their faces save a general one of devotion to the fatherland.

Prien and Endrass, and the other officers, Oberleutnant Hans Wessels, and Oberleutnant zur See Amelung von Varendorff, and the chief navigator, Obersteuermann Wilhelm Spahr, who later, like Endrass, would command his own U-boat, meshed well together. Prien was pleasant, witty, popular with officers and men, the skipper obviously of a 'happy ship.' Because he hailed from the Merchant Marine and held an A-6 commission as *Kapitän auf grosser Fahrt* (literally 'Captain on Big Voyage'), the crew felt great confidence in him, admired him personally.

'He was always cheerful,' said Spahr, 'and since most of the crew consisted of young people, his cheerfulness carried over. During training in the Baltic, North Sea, Atlantic, and Mediterranean, and during wartime operations, morale always was high. Prien demanded a lot of himself and expected the same spirit of readiness from every member of the crew, which was forged into a unit in the Dönitz–Prien spirit.'

Der Löwe, the Lion, as Dönitz was nicknamed, thought highly of his new commander. At war games, while practising group tactics—attacking heavily-escorted convoys—the Commodore,* from his own submarine, saw in Prien a first-class submariner, discerned with pride that he displayed special aptitude for torpedo work. He was inexperienced as a U-boat commander, yet he was plucky, cool and clever; he possessed just the right touch of boldness. Dönitz watched him closely.

---

* Dönitz was given this temporary rank while performing the duties of a *Konteradmiral* (Rear Admiral).

In the early light of 5 September, a second Greek freighter, the *Bosnia*, 2,407 tons, zigzagging without lights, sent *U-47*'s alarm klaxon blaring, forced overawed sailors to action stations, made them tumble from bunks, scramble fore and aft.

'Alarm, *tauchen*—dive, dive!'

Throttles closed the main air inductions. Main vents opened. Ballast tanks filled. Down like a rock slumped the U-boat, hydroplanes set to level her off, to an even keel, to periscope depth; then she waited, then surfaced, poured on full speed, rapidly overhauling the freighter. It was easy, just like manoeuvres.

'*Artillerie Gefechtsstation!*'

The gun crew rushed up the conning tower, dropped the gun-covering, swung the 3.5-inch deck gun into position, boomed a shell, a warning to stop, afore the starboard quarter of the startled Greek—who *refused* to stop, instead put on full speed, tried to slip away, the wireless operator flashing a new call, a frantic 'SSS'—Submarine, Submarine, Submarine—thus breaching the legal conduct of international law. When in return Prien ordered the gun crew to fire on target, three of five rounds struck hard amidships, smoke curled over the freighter's bows. She stopped, lowered lifeboats, and in the desperate push to get free, one capsized.

On *47*'s narrow deck casing two ratings stretched out on their stomachs to pull a frail Greek boy aboard, handing him moments later to the second lifeboat. Then suddenly from the southwest a Norwegian freighter sailed onto the scene, heaved to, lowered a boat, hauled the dripping, half frozen survivor in, while *U-47*, using shells to save torpedoes, finished the crippled coaster.

So the Germans were behaving with humanity—no treacherous monsters of the deep were they, as some British accounts already had them. Indeed about this time, only miles away in *U-48*, Herbert ('Vaddi') Schultze, to become the first commander to sink 100,000 tons of enemy shipping and win the Knight's Cross for it, was signalling the Admiralty in London the very position of a British merchantman he'd just sent down. The victim (SS *Firby* from Hartlepool) 'did not have time to send an SSS call,' Schultze explained, 'and would Winston Churchill please come to pick up the survivors?' Schultze signed his message 'German Submarine,' but the First Sea Lord, as later Churchill would tell the story in Parliament, was 'in some doubt at the time to what address I should direct a reply.'

Prien hadn't Schultze's flair for grim humour: and when on the 6th, while surfaced west of southern Ireland, there hove in sight another steamer, the *Rio Claro* from London, 4,806 tons, he thought only of the interception, turned, made a run for her; and so again the warning shot, the frantic SSS, more shots, a bridge ablaze, seamen leaping to tossing boats, torpedo loosed, water pouring into a broken steamer. Success again, so easy.

On the morrow another ship, the *Gartavon*, heavily-laden, low in the water, bearing 2,900 tons of ore for Glasgow, found *U-47* in her way. *Gartavon* lowered a boat, showed sign of submission, but suddenly she swung hard round, made straight ahead, sharp prow ready to ram to death the German submarine. With guns firing, *U-47* passed by yards under the bows of the fast-ploughing freighter, then turned and closed on the arrogant foreigner. Prien sent out a torpedo, which ran off target. But with his 88 mm, he tore holes in *Gartavon*'s side, until she rolled over.

On the evening of the fourteenth, the submarine sailed through the narrow Bay of Kiel, came to rest at the Wig, the naval base at the northern end of the city, and at the *Tirpitzmöle,* a large wooden jetty named after Alfred von Tirpitz, founder of the modern German Navy, she moored, fastened on the pier's wooden poles. Prien changed into double-breasted blues, was awarded the Iron Cross, Second Class, his crew given a fortnight's home leave: plenty of time to toast their successes, initial blows as staggering as those garnered in the opening of World War I. In the first two weeks of War Two, the British, just setting in motion their convoy system, had lost 111,000 tons by U-boats.

At the jetty Prien took his share of compliments, basked in the smiles of his comrades, then walked alone to his place of residence, a picturesque brick dwelling about half a mile from the *Tirpitzmöle*, and as the faint sun gilded the slanted rooftops of Kiel, he cast his eyes upon the winding streets, saw flags flitting from a multitude of balconies, perceived scattered groups of sailors and soldiers, like dauntless heralds bustling, in neat blue, brown, white, and grey uniforms; and in whatever manner he must have fathomed the sights, he could only have been filled with a good measure of satisfaction, for he had crossed the gulf from poverty to naval hero.

Born in the Baltic seaport city of Lübeck, eldest of three children, son of a judge, student at the Katerineum preparatory school, he had seen his parents separate before he was ten, had gone with his mother to Leipzig; in the struggling, inflation-plagued *Reich* saw her face stained with tears, watched her scrape an income by doggedly selling to shops and private customers lace made by peasants, occasionally earn some marks by disposing of her own cheap pastoral scenes.

Günther tried to earn some money of his own, at fifteen made some Swedish crowns by escorting foreign visitors to the Leipzig Industries Fair. But his thoughts lay always on distant places: he'd read tales of the sea, there was glory upon the sea, great voyages and battles, and like his boyhood hero, Vasco da Gama, whose picture looked down from above his bed, Günther was adventurous, determined, given to shaping visions of himself as a sea captain. He thought of becoming a cabin boy, shipping out to sea, and at the Advice Bureau of the local Labour Exchange he was given a prospectus for the 'Seaman's Factory,' moniker for the Hamburg–Finkenwärden Seaman's School where for a small fee a lad of his age could find his sea-legs.

Young Prien attended, learned to hoist a sail, read a compass, take bearings, climb a halyard, to knot, splice, signal; and three months later he tried to ship out, went from ship to ship, signing finally as a deck-boy on the square rigger SS *Hamburg*. It was a short cruise. The old windjammer sailed to Pensacola, Florida, on the return made Falmouth but foundered in a gale off the Irish coast, leaving Prien lodged for a month and a half in a Salvation Army hostel in Dublin. It was 1925, and in a sketchy autobiography* he'd write fifteen years later he'd recall how the Irish would clap in the cinemas whenever there appeared on the screen any show of German soldiers, while appearance of British babies got catcalls and whistles. The *Lützow* brought the stranded crew back to Bremerhaven; and next on the freighter *Pfalzburg* Prien served as a seaman, learning navigation; then from the German Merchant Service he earned a gold ring for his sleeve, status as Fourth Officer on the steamer *San Francisco*.

For the next few years on a variety of ships he sailored, then at age twenty-four, he passed an examination for his Master's ticket. It was 1932, however, the depression, bad times standing in the

---

* *Meig weg nach Scapa Flow*, translated as *I Sank the Royal Oak*, Gray's Inn Press, 1954.

way of his shipping out. Without ever commanding a ship, he had become an unemployed ship's officer, so he returned to his mother in Hamburg. To keep from idleness and receive free board and lodging, in exchange for ordinary road building work, he joined the Voluntary Labour Service, where through hard work he made it to foreman. Yet he wasn't happy; he was out of his element; all the while he kept looking for a way out to sea.

The Nazi movement was deepening, scoring successes in local elections, the revolutionary party rebuilt by Hitler in 1925 spinning a web of intrigues: in January 1933 the 'Austrian corporal,' the former vagabond from Vienna, was given the chancellorship and in their desperation millions of unemployed, Prien among them, turned from the inept democratic Republic—democratic 'nonsense' they called it—and gravitated towards Adolf Hitler and the authoritarian Nationalists. Prien was not interested in politics; his passion was the sea, not the world of Nazism—there is no evidence to suggest that he embraced its criminal character. He joined the Party, for its social, not military, appeal; at a time of near despair it was giving him confidence, a security he never had. He regarded with admiration the new stature of Hitler, falling victim to him along with almost the entire upper crust of German society.

Generally the Navy kept aloof from politics, the officers absorbed in professional duties, not exempting them perhaps from a certain moral complacency but the party's statements on national and social questions, words 'honour and dignity' like magnets to men like Prien, who had felt badgered by frustrating earlier attempts at democracy. When he heard, in January 1933, that the naval reserve of the resurgent German Navy was looking for officer material from the Merchant Service, he joined as an ordinary sailor, was sent at once to the training school at Stralsund on Dänholm Island, over three intensive months was licked into shape, trading finally his hateful grey uniform for a blue one and going off to the U-boats' training school in Kiel.

As his first post after graduation Prien was made watch-keeping officer aboard *U-26*, a Type I boat commanded by Leutnant zur See Werner Hartmann, who years later would remember his first meeting with the jaunty officer.

'In the canteen of the Torpedo School a youngster was standing on one of the tables. He was lecturing the sailors in the craziest

pidgin-German on the customs, morality and immorality of Asi-
atics, Africans and Americans. And in the small hours he led us in
singing the rousing choruses of the grandest sea shanties in the
world, the old sailors' songs known everywhere from Hamburg to
Hong Kong, from Santiago to Genoa. This astounding young man
with the twinkling eye knew verses to them by the hundred. "Who
is he?" I asked. "His name is Prien," I was told. We sat down together behind a wall of tobacco smoke and grog fumes, chewing
the rag and spinning endless sailors yarns. The outcome was that
Prien just had to be my Number One. And we managed to wangle
it.'*

U-26 had the unsettling habit of wobbling sideways. One of the
boats constructed at Cadiz by the German U-boat development
bureau, she proved so unstable that she operated only briefly, in
Spanish waters during the Spanish Civil War. In the summer of
1938, while Franco's Nationalists were forcing the Loyalists to internment in southern France, Prien left her and returned to
school, then passed the commanding officers' examination, mar-
ried, became the father of a daughter, and took control of U-47.
He could hardly wait to get back to sea, one day astonishing his
crewmates by remarking, typical of him: 'I get more fun out of a
really good convoy exercise than out of any leave.' It was statements like this that would endear him to men like Dönitz.

On a balmy day in August 1939, a critical moment in world
history, Germany on the precipice of war, threatening to attack
Poland, U-47 started up engines, cast from her moorings, made
for the Kiel Canal and the open sea.

September tumbled forward; and soon the Germans could forget
their fears of provoking the British and French, for on the 26th
Raeder convinced Hitler of the need to take off the wraps, relax
restrictions limiting U-boat operations. The Führer agreed, and
adopted a more realistic general policy about naval warfare as well,
directing that, with very few limitations, 'trade war' could be
waged at sea. Merchant ships and troop-ships definitely established as hostile could be attacked without warning, and this
also applied to ships sailing without lights in waters around England. Still forbidden were attacks on passenger ships or large ships

* Wolfgang Frank, *Enemy Submarine*, William Kimber, 1954.

obviously carrying considerable numbers of passengers in addition to cargo, but it was almost unrestricted warfare; *Graf Spee* and *Deutschland*, at loose in the Atlantic, could seek out mercantile foes, hunt at will.

On the 26th, while Hitler was formulating his 'Führer Orders', Churchill was announcing from Parliament the arming of British merchantmen against U-boat attack. It was his first major speech since returning to the government and the First Lord spoke out with pride: 'In the first week our losses by U-boat sinkings amount to 65,000 tons; in the second week they were 46,000 tons; and in the third week they were 21,000 tons. In the last six days we have lost only 9,000 tons.'

Yet hard experience had taught him to avoid all optimistic forecasts. 'One must not dwell upon these reassuring figures too much,' he warned, 'for war is full of unpleasant surprises.'

In Orkney a few days before September's end a tug brought into Kirkwall harbour a reminder of the war's first U-boat victim. It was a heart-rending sight, an empty lifeboat, a scarred and leaky vessel that emitted visions of a nightmare at sea: of shaken and weeping people clinging to slippery sides, struggling in oil-clogged water, sitting or kneeling inside, bailing out with boots and shoes the inrushing black oil scum. Large numbers of Kirkwallians had come to stare at the salved relic, to gaze at the name, *Athenia*, in gold letters on her bow, to study her floor boards, slightly damaged, wonder how the fragile craft had remained in such good condition despite its fortnight and more adrift.

As yet no gun defences covered Kirkwall harbour; there was no boom at all to protect the large number of neutral ships brought in for examination—only about 400 yards of indicating nets and a line of buoys; yet everywhere seen and felt were the signs of war. Although the rush for black-out material, blankets, and first aid equipment had slowed, and although the distribution of gas masks was finished and the obscuring of lights completed, the heaviest income tax in British history now was promised, the use of water to hose cars, lorries, buses, and windows was strictly prohibited, and the newspapers stopped publishing weather statistics. Every day from the Orkney Medical Officer there came appeals for beds, blankets, sheets and pillows for an emergency hospital. Rationing schemes were just beginning, motorists queueing for petrol to keep tanks filled—only farmers, now in the limelight, were excluded from fuel plans.

All over the islands complaints were heard of the sudden marked increase in prices: black-out material made and sold before the war for 1s 6d per yard jumped to 3s or 3s 6d, rainproof gas-mask cases (for 1/6d) were going briskly, and the prices of the five principal items in the housewife's daily budget—potatoes, butcher meat, milk, butter and eggs—were fixed (good hen eggs selling for 1s 6d per dozen, pullet eggs making 1s per dozen, home produced fresh eggs controlled at 2s to 2s 6d per dozen).

So tension was mounting; but so also was the people's confidence, for the general life of the community was maintained, the war news in particular exerting an uplifting force. 'The British Navy,' assured the *Orkney Herald* on the 30th,

is driving the enemy slowly but surely from the seas. Day by day our ships are remorselessly tracking down U-boats. The magnitude of this task can be gauged when it is realised that the hunt goes on over a radius of from 7000 to 8000 square miles. The Royal Navy's anti-submarine campaign has been so effective that for over a week no British ship was sunk or molested by enemy U-boats.

And from the First Sea Lord, already a leader essential, carrying the weight of the world on his shoulders, moving toward the peak of his achievement, more words of encouragement, majestic, inspiring phrases. Warsaw had fallen on the 27th and 'Poland,' said Churchill, in a broadcast from London on 1 October, 'has again been overrun by two of the Great Powers which held her in bondage for a hundred and fifty years, but were unable to quench the spirit of the Polish nation. The heroic defence of Warsaw shows that the soul of Poland is indestructible, and that she will rise again like a rock, which may for a time be submerged by a tidal wave, but which remains a rock.'

At Scapa Flow on the same day a routine Orkneys and Shetlands General Memorandum was issued, which in the wake of Winston's eloquence must have sounded weary; but for the men of Scapa, for every seaman, stoker to Admiral, the words served to augment the feeling of security given off by the hills that locked the anchorage in. Referring to Commander-in-Chief, Home Fleet's

plan of February 1939, the new document, entitled 'Scapa Flow—
Provisional Defence Scheme,' stated matter-of-factly that patrols
were to be established at Hoxa, Switha, and Hoy booms 'to prevent enemy submarines entering Scapa Flow either through the
booms or through the gates when open'.

The drifters, each armed with a three-pounder mounted forward, a .303 Vickers machine gun, six rifles, two depth charges
and two chutes, were to move outside the booms in Hoxa and
Switha and to the westward of the boom in Hoy, patrolling the
length of the booms, keeping a watch on the whole of the nets and
side gates. The orders were clear:

> A submarine trying to pass through the booms will carry
> some part of the net and boom with her and a portion of her
> hull will be in front of the buoys which are displaced on the
> surface; any submerged submarine entangled in the net is to be
> attacked with depth charges bearing the above in mind. A spe-
> cial watch it to be kept on the waters each side of the gate
> when it is open. A submarine sighted on the surface is to be at-
> tacked by gunfire and subsequently with depth charges if she
> submerges.

The memo covered much more ground, went on to order the
responsible officer 'to get into touch with the Chief Constable,
Kirkwall, and other local authorities and co-operate in their
schemes for:

a) Blacking-out all lights as an air raid precaution.
b) Obtaining intelligence of air-raids from air raid wardens.
c) Obtaining intelligence of movements of ships in the vicinity
   of the Orkneys from coast watchers.
d) Keeping a watch on any suspicious characters in the neigh-
   bourhood, in which connection, if the police cannot give the
   necessary assurances, arrangements are to be made for the
   protection of Lyness Naval establishment and oil fuel depot.
e) Issuing permits to fishermen and persons proceeding to and
   from the mainland.

Admiral Forbes, in keeping with the spirit of the memo, whose
provisions applied to the main entrances only, thought of doubling

the Hoxa boom, placing anti-torpedo baffles inside the Switha boom. He did not consider necessary the laying down of baffles for the Flow generally but instead preferred a system of 'indicator loops'—cables laid on the sea bed to induce and record the electric current of ships; on detection of a ship, rows of mines laid down the loops' centres could be fired from shore.

Yet for all of this there seemed no urgency; and neither baffles, loops, nor controlled minefields were laid. As for Kirk, Water, Weddel, and Skerry, the defence scheme routinely concluded they could be effectively blocked 'by the use of wire hawsers, nets, or some other method.'

The men of Scapa waited. It was wartime, true, but no one really knew what 'war' was all about; they had left behind their homes, their wives, their sweethearts, and now, in steel, in uncomfortable ships, at isolated and lonely billets or batteries ashore, they hung about, idled away the hours, staring across the sullen water of the Pentland or at the grey, grim world of vessels of all shapes and sizes sitting sombre and ghostlike on the eighty square miles of Scapa expanse: the end of the world it was for some, who loathed it, cursed it, as endless purgatory; yet for others, in awe of it, it was a strangely beautiful place, grand and severe, gripping, frightening in its eeriness, idyllic, yet sad.

Most took it in their stride, made the best of it, manned the guns, watched the nets, saw sunrise and sunset, hosed the decks, ate, read, spun yarns, and sometimes jumped to action stations, to check the reports of coast watchers in close vicinity of Scapa entrances—in almost every case the 'sightings' turned out to be basking sharks, submarines never.

Some sailors, off-duty, reaching out for release from boredom, fell into trouble. On the 2nd, two ratings from HMS *Royal Oak*, a 29,000-ton battleship anchored in the distant northeastern corner of the Flow, were brought before Provost Slater on the bench of Kirkwall Police Court, charged with fighting on Harbour Street, behaving in a disorderly manner, breaching the peace. An officer appearing for the sailors told the provost that whatever the judgment, the two accused, Able Seamen William Carter and Charles Testor, would be dealt with by the Navy. Both pleaded guilty, paid fines of 10s each, were hustled onto a bus bound for Scapa, stared glumly from the windows as the vehicle rolled from the royal burgh.

The long spell of dry weather was over, most farmers had completed their harvest work for the season, and whether Carter or Testor noted or not, it must have been obvious that things had gone well through the cutting and leading stages; very little rain had been falling and the stocks and stacks alike had received a thorough airing, the drying winds earning the farmers' gratitude, the crops comparing favourably with the bulk of the previous year, the grain of better quality, the potatoes particularly good.

As Carter and Testor stepped from the bus and boarded a tender for the *Oak,* to be locked in her cell flat, the summery weather was beginning to break, turning colder and more seasonable. In the distance, farmers could be seen making preparations for housing their cattle, which up to now had grazed contentedly and slept in the fields.

Carter and Testor could hardly have cared, just scrambled up the side; but in less than two weeks both would be dead.

Sunday, 1 October passed like any other Sunday before the war in Kiel. Though the Schauburg had switched to more Germanic fare —Maria Andergast, Fritz Eugens and Albrecht Schoenhals (playing in *Roman Eines Arztes*) replacing the *Cafe Metropole* lot— church bells still tolled the hour, the streets and plazas filled with the spirit of fellowship; and in the harbour, one of the finest in Europe, lying at the end of a striking Baltic fjord, there swung gently at anchor on the deep blue water an old cruiser stripped to serve 'crews in waiting,' the depot ship *Hamburg,* now offering hot food, the fresh smell of white linen, the subtle brotherhood of U-boatmen off-duty.

Günther Prien was in the mess, feeling the comfort of the ship, letting it warm him, draw him close together with his comrades, *U-16*'s Wellner, and Kapitänleutnant Sobe, chief of the 7th U-boat flotilla, when in strode Kapitän zur See (Captain) Hans-Georg von Friedeburg, a tall, well-groomed officer, Chief of the U-boat Arms' Organisation Department, later to succeed Dönitz as Commander-in-Chief of the U-boat Arm, just before the end of the war to become Commander-in-Chief of the *Kriegsmarine* and the man who in May 1945 would sign the surrender document before Field Marshal Montgomery.

There was a stern expression upon von Friedeburg's face, something severe in his voice, for he had an unusual petition for a

Sunday: Korvettenkapitän Sobe and Kapitänleutnants Wellner and Prien were to report to the CO U-boats.

Von Friedeburg had not been involved in the planning of the attempt on Scapa. But he had been let in on it, personally by Dönitz, because of the preparations, the readying of equipment, the technical inspection of *U-47*, the need for a special communications code; it was with respect that von Friedeburg fixed his eyes upon Prien. He saluted as he departed but left the three completely in the dark, alone to throw questioning glances at each other, twist their heads a little uneasily, wonder what was up. After a few tense minutes they boarded a small motor launch, then were speeding across the broad harbour, on past the *Tirpitzmöle* where Dönitz was inspecting the crew of a U-boat, then on to the submarine depot ship *Weichsel*, tied by heavy manilla hawsers to metal bollards on the dock, four U-boats tied to her starboard side.

In the *Weichsel* the three waited, suspecting something big up, some special mission, but they had received no explanation, had not even a hunch to go by. Then came a runner who asked Wellner and Sobe to go on to see Dönitz in the Admiral's Mess, leaving the puzzled Prien to wait by himself. He slipped up to a porthole and gazed out at the harbour, watched the gulls fly over, sit upon the sea, while his mind sought to reason the mystery of why he'd been summoned. Finally, the runner returned and asked Prien to the Admiral's Mess, preceded him up a few stairs, then waited while the U-boat commander knocked and entered—finding Wellner and Sobe with the 'Lion' himself, in quiet discussion, in the centre of the cabin round a large table covered with charts, and while Wellner and Sobe stood by and watched, Prien shook hands with Dönitz, cast his eyes upon the uppermost chart, saw immediately in large letters the words *Bay of Scapa Flow*, a name well known to him, known to every Navy man in fact, for the story of the scuttling of the High Seas Fleet played a vital role in German history: the humiliation still rankled.

Dönitz opened the discussion by telling Prien to listen to Wellner, who at once bent over the table and began to describe the seven entrances to Scapa and the boom and net barriers to submarine penetration. It was as he had written in his report, said Wellner, and he placed his forefinger on Hoxa, held it there for an instant, moved it to Hoy, then Switha, and then to Water, Kirk,

East Weddel and Skerry Sounds. Prien followed, and while his thoughts still roamed round the name Scapa Flow, Dönitz took up the discussion and pointed to the defence booms he knew existed in the First World War. The U-boat leader hunched forward, with the point of a compass indicated where from 1914 to 1918 the timber floats and lines of wire mesh nets were rigged from surface jackstays, the lines patrolled by no fewer than ninety-six trawlers and drifters—at least one for every 200 yards of each line of net between the booms.

The booms were removed in 1919, knew Dönitz, but in all likelihood the British would lay them at the same places: he pushed the compass point to Hoxa Sound, 'Here Emsmann was stopped,' he said. 'And here von Hennig.'

More strokes with the compass, toward the usual anchorages of the Fleet: *Iron Duke* off Lyness, *Royal Oak* in the northeast corner, elsewhere berths for famous ship names. There the *Hood*. There the *Repulse*. There the *Birmingham,* other places for other monoliths, like lambs waiting, spreading funnels and craggy towers, barbettes, turrets, and gun barrels across the broad sweep of water, a spectacle to open the eyes, Dönitz knew: when the fleet was in, it was said, you could not see the water for ships.

Every entrance would have some kind of protection, said Dönitz, 'but nevertheless I believe that a determined commander could take his boat through right here.' And the point of his compass, which until now had been wandering all over the chart, rested upon the wrinkled gooseneck at the extreme eastern approach to Scapa, the channel called Kirk.

Dönitz was looking at Prien, and no one, he felt, was better suited for such a mission: Prien was aggressive, circumspect, possessed good nerves, was an excellent sailor—a 'clear thinker, not given to complex pondering,' as Oehrn had told him when Dönitz asked for his opinion the week before, and Dönitz had agreed, seeing in Prien 'all the personal qualities and the professional ability required.'

Now he raised his head, under lowered brows gazed at Prien searchingly.

'It will be a difficult task because the current runs strong. But I think it is possible and if it is possible, it must be tried. What do you think, Prien? Do you believe a determined commander could get his boat inside Scapa Flow and attack the enemy naval forces lying there?'

In his wartime autobiography*, Prien told how he stared at the chart, but before he could give his answer, Dönitz said he did not want it now. He told Prien to gather all of the information he needed and work out the possibilities, taking at least forty-eight hours to decide. On Tuesday he'd see Prien again. If Prien didn't think the mission was possible, he was to report this opinion; but it was to be the product of his own mind; and Dönitz was emphatic: 'However you decide, it will not be a black mark against you, Prien. It will not affect the high opinion we have of you.'

There was nothing more to say: Prien clasped Dönitz's hand, gathered up the charts and notes, the entire file, including all of the Air Fleet photographs, saluted, and left. He reboarded the motor launch, ordered it back to the *Hamburg*, placed everything in his desk, which he carefully locked, and then again he shuttled across the bay, but this time to Kiel-Wik and the shipyards where at the iron gate in the high brick wall surrounding the naval complex he showed his papers, returned the sentry's salute, and began the short walk to his home in the suburbs.

His mind turned the chances, but already he was determined to carry out the mission.

Prien stepped briskly, within fifteen minutes was home, finding supper already on the table; but he seemed not to notice the food, only absent-mindedly acknowledged his wife Ingeborg; with supper over, he told her he had work to do, was soon alone with his thoughts about Scapa Flow.

He left the house, retraced the familiar path back to the pier, shuttled again to the *Hamburg,* unlocked his desk, removed the Scapa file, and for the second time that Sunday went home. At a writing table he spread out the charts and notes, all the photographs, and worked through the whole thing like a mathematical problem.

* The book is obscure in many details, heavily censored in the Germany of 1940. Yet Prien declared the account truthful, and although he was helped in its preparation, and here and there the writer may have tried to add a touch of drama to the story, still-living German witnesses, including Dönitz, Oehrn, and Spahr, bear out that this is what actually did happen. Almost every previous account has drawn on Prien's book, some authors have attacked it for its inaccuracies, which do exist, but as a general chronicle of the major—and minor—events as they relate to Prien and his Scapa Flow mission, it can be relied upon.

Kirk Sound, he could see, was narrow, just over 15 metres wide, about 3½ fathoms at its deepest point, and any attempt at entrance would probably have to be made with an east-moving stream, at *Stauwasser,* stagnant or calm sea, between the tides when there could be little or no current. This would increase the minimum depth of the water and, most important, significantly increase the breadth of the navigable channels, making it easier for a U-boat feeling its way fully-surfaced to manoeuvre round the blockships. A medium-sized submarine such as *U-47* could draw 12 to 15 feet on the surface, at high water pass straight over any obstructions.

The trouble was, however, as Prien must have realized, that the period of slack water did not last long: at Kirk Sound the tide ran up to ten knots to within half an hour each side of high and low water, slack water lasting only for about fifteen minutes. He might have somewhat longer than this to operate within the Flow since the velocity of the tides decreased slowly from about half an hour before high water and low water reached its maximum velocity about half an hour later; yet timing was vital: if he spent too much time inside, he might get caught by the outwardrushing tide, never get out.

Could he come in against the tide? Perhaps, but he would be creeping in, probably making no more than two or three knots, weaving through the blockships on the mainland side. If he went against the tide, he would be further slowed; and besides, the tide was unpredictable, could run between two and three knots, vary considerably in direction. At the netted entrances sometimes one section would be bowed to the flood, while the adjacent section sagged to the ebb; at times there might even be a lateral tide, one that turned the nets around sideways.

For all that Prien had to worry about, it must have been the unpredictable that troubled him the most, for the Germans had no way of knowing whether the same blockade conditions which were observed at day also prevailed at night; nor did they know whether there would be enough light to allow recognition of details within the narrow passage. There might be Asdics* or other echo-sounding apparatus to cover the entrance—the Germans suspected the Royal Navy to possess some secret submarine detection

---

* An English term, derived from the group which developed it, the 'Anti-Submarine Detector Indicator Committee'.

devices. And what if he was seen or heard? Any noise might suggest a submarine passing through.

On the northern shore of Kirk Sound, Prien knew, he would have to pass the tiny village of St Mary's, and could only hope no one noticed him. And if he did get in, if conditions proved favourable and he did force the entrance, what would he find? Enemy ships at close range, a whole armada, perhaps the entire British Fleet. But if observed inside the Flow, if spotted by just one fast surface ship, one equipped with guns, there'd be no time to bring his own guns to bear. Then if the weather was not clear, the sea not calm, accurate firing would be difficult, the boat hazardous to manoeuvre. And how would he get out? The same way he came in; but time was the invader's worst enemy. Assuming he entered at slack water, remained half an hour, by then the tide would be running against him, by as much as eight or ten knots. He might make it out, Prien must have felt confident of this, but he must have felt too that he might not, not if the Flow was running at full strength.

From the beginning, there had been no doubt in Prien's mind that he'd take to the challenge; he seemed determined to tempt Providence, so he studied the charts, indoctrinated himself well in their details, preparing to commit all to memory: not for a second in the breakthrough would he have time to refer to things written or drawn.

On Tuesday the 2nd, Prien called for an interview with Dönitz, and von Friedeburg was waiting. Immediately he asked if Prien was going, and when Prien replied yes, von Friedeburg relaxed, sank into his chair, reached for the phone, called Dönitz directly, got a two o'clock appointment for the Commander. Prien reported promptly, 'Yes, or no?' the ferretlike Dönitz wanted to know, not bothering to return the salute.

'Yes, Sir.'

Dönitz smiled for an instant but suddenly became very serious. 'Have you considered every angle? Did you consider Emsmann and von Hennig who never came back?'

'Yes, Sir.'

'Well,' said Dönitz, 'make the necessary arrangements.' Then he got up, said no more, just shook Prien's hand firmly, and years later would state simply of this meeting: 'After a thorough examination of all the available information Prien accepted.'

By 2 October almost all Atlantic U-boats had returned to home waters, the exceptions being *U-35*, still operating in the western outlet of the Channel, and two overdue submarines, *U-27* and *U-39*, which had failed to respond to repeated requests for positions. The Germans, presuming both *verlohren*, lost, had yet to know that *Ark Royal*'s escorting destroyers had sunk *U-39* on 14 September, that six days later *U-27*, after stopping and sinking fishing trawlers off the Butt of Lewis, had been hunted down, sunk by Asdic-fitted destroyers and naval aircraft, her entire crew captured.

Still the Germans had more than enough U-boats to watch Orkney constantly: *U-10* was roaming in position west of the islands, *U-20* and *U-23* approaching the operational area, *U-18* just leaving Kiel for it, seven more submarines ready to put out for the North Sea. On the 2nd too, German Radio Monitoring established *Ark Royal* north of Scotland, with the 6th and 8th Destroyer Flotillas, while near Rosyth moved *Furious*, the 2nd Cruiser Squadron, the 7th Destroyer Flotilla, and, farther north, the light cruiser *Diomede*.

'Within the Home Fleet,' added the efficient Radio Monitoring, 'the new unit "Scotland Forces" made its appearance; to this apparently belong the vessels reported in the Rosyth area and the heavy cruiser *Norfolk*.'

Up to now, no German battleships or cruisers had seen action. For psychological reasons alone, therefore, Admiral Alfred Saalwaechter, Commanding Admiral, Group West, a U-boat commander in the first war, later to perish in a Russian prisoner of war camp, favoured a major sweep with *Gneisenau,* two cruisers, and all destroyers as far as the latitude of the Utsire Light. The appearance of German battleships in the North Sea would tie down the Home Fleet, help the pocket battleships in the Atlantic, give U-boats off Scapa a chance to attack if British heavy forces put out to intercept *Gneisenau*, most of all, give the Luftwaffe an opportunity to score. Raeder agreed in principle, approved the operation for five days before the new moon; and then the next day, the 3rd, he turned his attention to Dönitz, who had flown from Wilhelmshaven to present in person his plan for *U-47*.

Dönitz trod lightly around the subject, began by telling the *Grossadmiral* that the Prize Regulations, only partially lifted by Hitler on 30 September, still were impeding him in the war against merchant shipping. To stop neutrals, his U-boats still had to surface, needlessly exposing themselves to attack from the air. It was wrong, he told Raeder, to waste his few available boats in the Atlantic: better to use them collectively against convoys, make war on merchant shipping in accordance to the Regulations only on the approach against convoys, and only outside the coastal waters of England. If the commanders exercised caution, if the operational areas were favourably situated, the practice promised success.

But time was important, he warned, for the supply of new U-boats was lagging behind demand. In 1939 there had been only a slight increase in the number of submarines, and now, he pointed out, according to the conference minutes: '1940 must be regarded as a year of weakness as regards submarines. At present there are 29 Atlantic boats available; there will be 9 more by 1 April 1940, making 37 boats theoretically available at that time. On the basis of previous experiences, however, a loss of at least two boats monthly in the Atlantic must be expected. In other words, there is no relation between the replacements and the possible losses. Accordingly, it may be presumed that fewer boats will be available in 1940 than at present.'

Finally, they came to item three, the planned raid on Scapa Flow. Exactly what was said we do not know; but three short sentences in the minutes of Dönitz's conference with Raeder record what transpired:

Commanding Admiral, Submarines reports on Special Operation 'P'. Prospects of success appear favourable: Chief, Naval Staff gives his approval.

So the scheme to penetrate the British naval stronghold was on. Dönitz felt relief, Prien could go: but for the moment at least he thought no more upon it, his discussion with Raeder moving quickly to other areas, the purchasing of submarines from neutral countries, the idea of Russian support of the German war effort; they talked of the possibility of German vessels refuelling, taking on supplies in Murmansk and Vladivostok.

The same day Dönitz returned to the *Toten Weg*, heard in the evening, routinely, that *U-10* and *U-20* still were standing off

Orkney. Only to Oehrn and Godt did he mention that Raeder had approved the attempt by Prien.

'For the operation to be successful,' as later he'd put in his memoirs, 'it was essential that absolute secrecy should be maintained.'

Prien too kept the secret—in his mind was locked the details of Kirk Sound; but he had to select the time, was forced to take into his confidence key men around him: there must be no moon to shine upon the operation, expose it to someone who by chance might spot *47* threading its way.

On the 6th, the day after air reconnaissance had determined that the bulk of the Home Fleet still lay in Scapa, Prien ordered Spahr to bring the charts and books of the Scapa Flow sector and with Endrass report to his cabin on the *Hamburg*. Spahr remembers vividly the scene:

'Since I had the charts and books of the Scapa Flow sector under my control, I had to come, with the *Eins WO*, Oberleutnant Endrass, to the Captain's cabin. In the cabin we took a written oath and signed our names to secrecy. Only then did Prien tell us of the plan to penetrate Scapa Flow to attack the British Navy there. I now fetched the sea chart, ocean handbook, the hydrographic atlas, and the Nautical Yearbook. We got the assignment to establish, independently of each other, the most favourable point in time. We were to hand in, each for himself, our answers in envelopes. In taking account of the moon (it was new moon) and hydrographic conditions (backwater), we decided it was to be the night from 13 to 14 October 1939. We said nothing about our defence. For secrecy reasons the crew was not informed. My reaction was clear and unequivocal: the mission had to succeed.'

Dönitz agreed to the timing. In this period the northern lights would be dark: no dazzling columns of light—'Merry Dancers' they called them in Orkney—to stream across the heavens, throw luminous arcs across the bows of the invader. In his memoirs Dönitz would write: 'Both periods of slack water would occur during the hours of darkness and there would be a new moon.'

Apparently he did not know of or attached no significance to the fact that almost to the day a quarter of a century before, on the night of 17 October 1914, the Grand Fleet, of about a hundred large vessels, was driven to sea by an alarm, premature, that a German submarine was inside the harbour—a misadventure that

The tidal race before the Churchill Barrier was built and (*below*) Churchill Barrier, built to block the sound forced by *U-47*

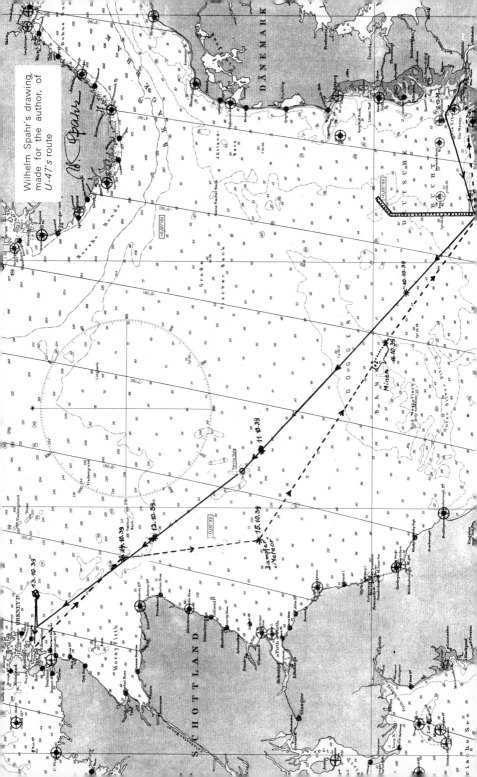

Wilhelm Spahr's drawing, made for the author, of U-47's route

Prien with the man who sent him into Scapa Flow : Admiral (later Grand Admiral) Karl Dönitz

Prien and the 'snorting bull' of Scapa Flow

On *47's* conning tower

The name 'Bull of Scapa Flow' painted on *U-47's* conning tower also was applied to Prien himself

Churchill, however, never forgot: 'Guns were fired, destroyers thrashed the waters, and the whole gigantic armada put to sea in haste and dudgeon.'

In Kiel on the 8th, a beautiful clear Saturday, *U-47*'s crew assembled at the *Tirpitzmöle* for what appeared to be a normal operation in the Atlantic, the usual long patrol, of four to eight weeks, requiring plenty of provisions, fresh water, ammunition, torpedoes. In the busy harbour von Friedeburg stood on the pier with the adjutant of the Chief of the Flotilla, both trying hard to convey no expression of special concern; but already the crew had sensed something up, for several times over the course of a week the departure date had been postponed. Now further reason to suspect something odd: not enough stores were going down the hatchways. The stores taken on—potatoes, vegetables, bread, other items—all in watertight sacks, the men were careful to evenly distribute about the long narrow boat, to make sure they didn't shift during dives, didn't block gangways or touch the controls; yet it was clear there was not enough supplies for a normal patrol.

'And then,' said Spahr, 'there was this: I happened to be standing on the bridge with Prien when *U-40* was returning from a trial run under the command of Leutnant Barten, and he hollered over to us, "Pruentje (Prien's nickname), the old man is not going to be so insane as to send you into the lion's den?"'

Prien was stunned for an instant. His face flushed at the inappropriate remark: how could Barten have known that Dönitz was planning a mission on Scapa? Spahr said nothing, threw a glance at Prien, heard him shout back to Barten: 'No, only you could get such a crazy idea.'

But now, said Spahr, the crew 'started a big guessing game.' As the equipment being loaded was different from what normally would be taken, it was fairly easy to suspect some special mission. All secret documents were removed; on the 6th a special sea-mapping folder on Orkney had been received, known only to Spahr and his assistant, boatswain Ernst Dziallas, who also happened to notice that Prien placed in his locker an English warflag—'meant to serve as deception in an emergency, but incurring of course a risk to the men that, if captured, they would be treated as spies.' The flag would have to be scuttled, the *Bootsmaat* knew, and before *47* moved into Scapa Flow.

The mutterings of 'something big up' had not surprised Seaman

First Class Gerhard Hänsel; for suddenly he remembered how two weeks earlier on that Sunday he had been called to Prien's cabin on the *Hamburg*:

'There the new Second Watch Officer, von Varendorff, was introduced to me and I was informed that I had to go with him in Submarine Commander Dönitz's boat to the wharf to get the maps of Scapa Flow.'

Hänsel had wondered whether he should fetch the navigational handbooks too, and told no, only the maps, he'd made the trip with von Varendorff, retrieved the maps, placed them in a small briefcase, then together the two had gone to Prien's cabin and, while von Varendorff watched, Hänsel had locked the case in Prien's desk.

The crew moved around normally, eager to return to sea, anxious to claim their share of good hunting. Quickly, efficiently, through the hatchways forward and aft were loaded the demolition charges, the torpedoes, each a ton and a half, the shells and bullets for the deck artillery, the single 3.5-inch and one 88 mm. automatic AA gun, and the machine-gun kept in the conning tower. The sub's air-purifier was renewed, the oxygen cylinders filled. The torpedoes—the usual G7e's, powered by an electric motor, showing no wake, propeller driven, charged with 500 kilos of explosives, the G7e's, powered by compressed air, charged with 380 kilos—winched up one by one by chains into the fo'c'sle's four tubes, four more stowed under the deck plating, two in the stern loading rails ready for immediate reloading; all would be readied for firing, the batteries brought up to strength on the voyage itself, to give them the needed range capacity.

The mechanics began fitting the detonators, placing pistons into the tubes. But curiously, the usual procedure of storing the two reserve torpedoes into the upperdeck stands, was ignored; and then, in the middle of the loading operation, Endrass, the *Eins WO*, also the torpedo officer, who was supervising the loading, announced new orders from Prien: 'A' torpedoes were to be turned in, some of the fuel and provisions unloaded as well. And when the outside fuel containers were not filled, it became obvious to everyone that the radius of the mission had to be smaller than normal—clearly a short, special operation.

'We were glad,' remembered Leading Seaman Willi Loh, 'that we would be back home soon.'

On the 7th *U-46*, after having had repair work done to her engines, slipped from the *Tirpitzmöle*. *U-47* was still loading; and in the War Diary of Flag Officer, U-Boat West, it was recorded:

U-47, which should have sailed for the Atlantic on 4.10, has been given a special operation and will not take part in this Atlantic patrol.

The next morning the youthful crew mustered on the pier, in best uniforms, closed ranks, near *47*, which was made fast to the pillars and was rocking gently in the sun-flecked water. Under the bill of his white cap, the emblem of a U-boat commander, Prien wore a look of composure upon his face. For a short while he stood with von Friedeburg and the adjutant, then the three walked up and down the pier, saying hardly a word.

Von Friedeburg broke the silence, as the commander readied to board. 'Well, Prien,' he said, 'whatever happens you are sure of many thousands of tons and now the best of luck, my boy.'

Prien saluted smartly, shook hands in silence, walked across the narrow gangplank to the U-boat. He was piped aboard.

'*Leiner los*—cast off.'

Endrass gave the order, and the men bent to their tasks, as *47*, powered by her electrics, droning slightly at slow speed, separated from the pier, manoeuvred in reverse into navigable waters, careful to clear her submerged hydroplanes; when she swung around, her diesels took over, began their steady hammering.

From the Atlantic, *U-15* was returning, bringing back observations on the buoys and lights along the eastern English Channel coasts and in the Strait of Dover.

Unobtrusively, without pomp and circumstance, *47* steered through the locks of the Kiel Canal, seven hours to pass from the Baltic to the North Sea. The wind whipped the swastika on the mast, and Spahr set the course, nor' nor' west. The objective: Scapa Flow.

3

'We are In!'

Not only *47*, and a few other U-boats, but a major portion of the *Kriegsmarine* was standing out on the 8th; for the previous evening Admiral Saalwaechter had begun his sweep of the North Sea. In the feint to lure British ships within range of the Luftwaffe, the flagship *Gneisenau*, the Fleet Commander, Admiral Hermann Böhm aboard, the cruiser *Köln* and nine destroyers, set course in a north northwest direction towards the Skagerrak and Kattegat to Utsire Light.

At Scapa, upon hearing of the sortie, Admiral Forbes immediately brought to short notice his battle cruisers and light forces; then shortly after one o'clock on the afternoon of the 8th a Hudson reconnaissance aircraft of British Coastal Command spied the *Gneisenau* force off Lister Sound on the Norwegian coast, flashed word to Forbes, who suspecting the Germans of trying to break out into the open Atlantic, ordered the main body of the fleet to full alert, ready to intercept. He bunched his ironclads into 'Hunting Groups,' each capable of scouring a wide area, covering most courses the Germans might take.

Repulse and *Hood* with the cruisers *Sheffield* and *Aurora* and four destroyers sped toward the Norwegian headland of Stadlandet. From the Firth of Forth an hour later steered another group, the Humber Force, steaming for the mouth of the Skagerrak; then from Scapa early in the evening of the 8th, a huge phalanx of naval vessels, the main body of the fleet, *Nelson,* with Forbes aboard, two other battleships, *Rodney* and *Newcastle,* the carrier *Furious* and eight destroyers, raised anchor to scan the water northeast of the Shetlands; His Majesty's venerable *Royal Oak,* labouring forward, too slow to take her place on the line, left Scapa with an escort of two destroyers for a position west of the Fair Isle Channel between Shetland and Orkney.

It was a new form of sea warfare, designed to overwhelm any raider caught in the field of search; but German air reconnaissance lost no time in noting the strategy: 'Radio Monitoring,' declared the Operations Division War Diary for the 8th, 'report that the 2nd Cruiser Squadron, destroyers, and Commanding Admiral, Battle-Cruiser Squadron are at sea. Further data established Commanding Admiral, Battle-Cruiser Squadron in the immediate area of Scapa, the 2nd Cruiser Squadron and the 7th Destroyer Flotilla in the Rosyth area . . . Radio Monitoring reports in the course of the evening that Commanding Admiral, Home Fleet and Commanding Admiral, Battle-Cruiser Squadron are *not* in Scapa.'

The *Gneisenau* armada stood out on a mission distinct from that of *U-47*—neither Prien nor Saalwaechter knew of the other's intentions—yet the North Sea sweep was to foreshadow an operation which would, in a way, prophesy the outcome of the attempt on Scapa.

Immediately upon entering the North Sea, lest she be seen by enemy aircraft or by British, Dutch, or Danish vessels, and be reported, even by the neutrals, *U-47* submerged, operated under a schedule in which day was turned into night, night into day, which meant the midday meal at midnight, breakfast at night, supper in the morning, sleep during the day; only in darkness did the submarine dare to come up and breathe and recharge her batteries, dump her garbage (in weighted burlap sacks).

At 9 a.m. on the 9th, before reaching the sanctuary of Heligoland, *47* test-dived, three hours later she entered the harbour, made her usual trim trial, settled down nicely, waited for sunset, then stood off again; then early the next morning she ran to starboard of the German mine barrier—the so-called Western Wall—and at dawn, while south of the extensive shoal of Dogger Bank, Prien saw through the crosshairs of his scope the disquieting shadows of fishing vessels: who could know whether one or another of those little boats were not deployed to spy? Prien ordered *47* down, to settle on bottom, wait it out. The watch officer hit the diving alarm, throttles were shut to halt the diesels, close the main air inductions. In the *Zentrale,* the valves to flood the diving tanks were opened; the undersea propelling machinery and the electric motors were turned on.

The *Unterseeboot* angled heavily down.

At dusk on the 10th, *47* rose from the bottom, continued on, surfaced, following a general northeastern course. The sky was the colour of slate, and the sea, unvarying, rolled and broke over her bows. As she passed the Dogger Bank, the watches took their places, mechanically scanning the horizon, the crew settled about their tasks, off-duty a little horseplay, still guessing the purpose of the mission.

Spahr, navigating by dead reckoning, would remember: 'I had to keep all the sea charts and nautical books up-to-date, entering the changes and corrections on them. During surface trips I was the watch officer of the third watch, and my battle station was at the map table in the control room.'

In Scapa, if *U-47* got into Scapa, he'd stay below, to draw the battle sketch, enter the enemy's positions, *47*'s own attack route with its torpedo tracks and the enemy's course and speed moving off. After, he would enter the new position in the sea chart, and maintain the logbook, check the position as often as possible astronomically, during the day by the sun altitude lines, at dusk or dawn by a constellation made up of three stars. 'Off-duty I would normally be in my berth at mess reading a book or old magazines. The war diary was written by the captain.'

Uninspirationally at first, Spahr might have added, for during the first three days Prien used the log only to echo the routine of the mission. *Left port (Kiel) on special operations, Operational Order North Sea No 16, through Kiel Canal, Heligoland Bight, and Channel 1*, he wrote on the first day, noting in the margin *Exact positions cannot be given as under special orders all secret documents were destroyed before carrying out of order.*

On the 9th, while south of Dogger Bank, he penned: *Lying submerged. After dark, surfaced and proceeded on our way. Met rather a lot of fishing vessels.* On the 10th: *During day lay submerged; at night continued on course.* And the next day only: *As on previous day.*

Oddly perhaps but the same monotony was to be found among the men of the *Gneisenau* sortie and the British hunters. For neither group found the other, the operation a failure on both sides. All through the day and night of the 9th the British had hunted for the Germans. While Wellington bombers sent in to attack could not find the sortie, Heinkels and Junkers had snapped at the

Humber Force, turning the hunters into the prey, claiming hits but actually not doing damage to a single ship. Forbes's force meanwhile had steamed between the rocky, lonely Faeröes and Iceland, still seeking out the *Gneisenau* unit—when unknown to Forbes, the Germans, having wished to be seen but failing to entice the Home Fleet toward the Skagerrak, had withdrawn after dark on the 8th, turning about off Utsire for passage through the Skagerrak and Kattegat into the Baltic Sea and Swinemunde.

On the 10th, while German Naval Operations was reporting *U-47* APPROACHING THE SCAPA OPERATIONAL AREA, the British turned back, having made no contact with the German thrust; Saalwaechter with his ships unscathed was safely back in Kiel.

But Forbes didn't head for Scapa. On his own initiative he opted to take the main body of the fleet to the subsidiary base of Loch Ewe, leading the Germans to presume, as a 'Special Item' in the Naval Staff War Diary would note the next day, 'The forces subsequently returned to Scapa'—when in fact the great harbour was left bereft of its principal occupants.* Only HMS *Royal Oak*, which in a biting force-nine velocity gale had lost contact with her escorts, turned to home water, to the serenity of her protective ring of islands around her anchorage in the northeast corner of the Flow.

Already war-weary, the elderly lady ached in her joints, clumsily lumbered into her appointed place, barely making it, for the rough seas had put her port battery completely out of action, damaged ventilators and exhausts on bulkheads, caused many of her rivets to loosen, side plates to leak, letting salt water into her starboard aft fresh water tank and into the Royal Marines' mess deck, as well as into the implement store immediately below, which stood awash in two feet of salt water.

This wasn't *Royal Oak*'s style, for usually she was a smart and efficient fighting unit, spotless from truck to waterline, gun muzzles burnished, gangways washed and polished, enamelled paintwork gleaming, bright work glittering, mess decks and flats the same—and yet a long history of mishaps she had. Laid down in

---

* Why did Forbes take the Home Fleet to Loch Ewe instead of Scapa? 'Unquestionably,' according to the official British naval historian Captain S. W. Roskill (in a letter to the author) 'because of the known insecurity of Scapa. Thus it could justifiably be said that his use of Loch Ewe contributed to the comparatively few ships there when *U-47* infiltrated into Scapa Flow.'

January 1914 by HM Dockyard in Devonport, just before the outbreak of World War I, going down the slipway in November 1914, commissioned in May 1916—as one of the five Royal Sovereign class battleships*—she'd been plagued in her firing trials by faulty gear—difficulty with her cordite dropping mechanisms, her air blast apparatus, her electric locks, pinions jumping out of racks: once the deck beneath one of her twelve 6-inch guns gave way on firing, badly twisting the deck's supporting beams. Years later a hatch dropped on a Marine's chest, suffocating him; a Leading Seaman fell off a pier and drowned while waiting to come off liberty; her stern anchor, seven tons of iron, once parted, dug its flukes into a launch, near killing three men.

Yet when war came, the 'Mighty Oak', as they called her, and as she was, the proud bearer of an honoured name,† stood ready. Serving with distinction in the Grand Fleet's First Battle Squadron during the famous battle the Allies would call 'Jutland' (the largest naval encounter in history and the most decisive), she steamed next in the line to the fleet flagship HMS *Iron Duke*, on 31 May, fired seven salvoes at 14,000 yards and claimed two hits.

Two years later, in 1918, she steamed down the Pentland to meet the surrendering German naval might, leading one line while other ships steamed parallel on the opposite side. Despite her earlier misadventures, superstitious sailors from then on would call her lucky, for she 'carried Drake's Drum,' they said. A former lieutenant commander who was in the *Oak* that day has explained: 'As we sighted the Germans the order was given to shut off the engines. A similar order went throughout the fleet, and we glided on in an uncanny silence. I was then on the bridge awaiting instructions from the captain when suddenly we heard it—the muffled sound of a drum beating to quarters. I was ordered, "Find out what damn fool is beating a drum." The ship was searched. We thought we had been imagining the drum, but the cruiser immediately behind us sent up a flag-signal: "Who is beating a drum in your ship?" There may have been—must have been—some perfectly conventional explanation for the noise, but it was never

---

* Her sister 'R' class capital ships: *Royal Sovereign, Revenge, Resolution, Ramilles.*
† She was the eleventh and greatest ship to hold it, the first built in 1663 to commemorate the tree near Boscobel in Shropshire in which Charles II, King of England, Scotland, and Ireland, hid after the Battle of Worcester in 1651.

given. And in the decks, manned by Devonians, it was freely said
that Drake's drum was acclaiming victory.'

At Jutland she had sounded no drum, but she had worn a
badge of honour, a silken ensign presented by the women of
Devon—and more steel sheathing than most of the battlewagons
around her: the full thickness of her 13-inch armoured belt carried all the way up to the main deck. Instead of being reduced to
tapering off above the Low Water Line, the belt extended to a
depth of five feet below, compared to four in most other battlewagons, enabling the *Oak* to roll to a greater angle without exposing the unarmoured portions to shell fire below the belt. Then, to
shield her from bombs, which by 1922 already had become a
highly developed method of attack, she displayed a layer of 3-inch
steel on each of her three main decks, each a thousand feet long;
and her ventilator openings were protected by tiers of armour
grating—although, it must be said, none of this was expected to
make her invulnerable to armour-piercing bombs that might burst
between decks (seven in all), destroy her oil-fired boilers, her engine room ventilators, cause fumes from the explosions to be
drawn into her machinery compartments.

Even below her armoured belt, however the *Oak* was well
protected, for in '22, out of fear of submarine attack and the loss
of battle cruisers at Jutland, her two funnels were merged into
one, her deck protection increased, and she was 'bulged'—fitted
with a new feature of battleship design: tubeless, watertight cham-
bers, or monstrous 'bulges' to boost her buoyancy, lessen her
tendency to excessive roll, minimise damage to her hull, by prematurely exploding any torpedo fired at her. The rounded humps,
thought 'proof' against torpedo warheads of 450–500 pounds, decreased the *Oak*'s draft, looked, as one observer would put it, 'as
if someone had sliced a huge sausage down the centre and stuck
one half to her starboard side, the other to her port side.'

If *Royal Oak* made no pretensions to looks, neither did she to
speed. She could do no more than 21 knots; but she was a big
ship, more than an eighth of a mile long, 102 feet wide, her distribution of armour good, her 6-inch guns better laid out than the
faster and more glamorous *Queen Elizabeths*: she carried eight
massive fifteen-inch guns, in four revolving turrets, each with shell
rooms containing 208 fifteen-inch shells, next to magazines holding the solid propellent cordite. So between the wars she formed,

along with others of her class, the backbone of the Home Fleet, becoming from 1926 to 1934 a unit of the First Battle Squadron of the Mediterranean Fleet, then right into the second war, a flagship, flying the St George's cross with two red discs of Rear Admiral, Second Battle Squadron of the Home Fleet. On 3 September, she struck her topmast—lowered it in order to give the enemy less on which to use his rangefinders—and in the wardroom at noon that day officers gathered to drink a peculiar mixture of champagne and stout—'black velvet,' navy men called it—to toast 'the downfall of Hitler.'

The *Oak* was old, it was true, almost twenty-five years at the start of the war, but as long as she remained in harbour she could serve as a floating AA battery. It made no difference that in this second month of the war she was a mess, littered with large pieces of Carley rafts that had broken up in the heavy seas, tearing loose from stowage positions below the boat deck and on the forecastle and quarter-deck amidships. She was, after all, secure in the shallow water of her anchorage, very safe in Scapa Flow.

At about 10 p.m. on Wednesday, 11 October, civilian deckhand Montgomery Bryden on the Hoxa boom watcher vessel *Dragonet* was lying in his bunk wide awake when suddenly from up forward around the starboard side he heard two or three turns of a propeller, as though, he thought, a ship were trying to give herself a 'kick ahead.'

Bryden turned to a deckhand sitting nearby, Andrew Davidson, and remarked, 'I wonder what the steam pinnace is doing alongside this time of the night.'

Bryden knew the gate was open; there was nothing unusual about this, for as the main entrance into Scapa, it had been opening and closing with frequency, to allow several ships to enter, namely a destroyer, the *Furious*, a battleship, a cruiser, and now, at exactly four minutes past ten another destroyer; but ships usually entered from the *opposite*, Flotta side, on *Dragonet*'s port —never before from his bunk on the starboard side had Bryden heard ships on the side away from the open gate.

Deckhand Frank Glasgow, who'd been reading in his bunk amidships directly above *Dragonet*'s keel, also noted the grinding of the propeller, also had never heard this noise before, so quickly rose, lay down his paper, and not bothering to put on his shoes he walked barefoot to the next messdeck where he mentioned the sound to Bryden, who guessed a boat coming along the starboard side.

Glasgow felt differently. He suspected it might be something else, possibly a sound produced by a submarine's propeller scraping against the boom wires: if attacked by a submarine, he knew, the boom would have yielded to the vessel's forward motion, lifting eight ton weights on the chains, allowing the submarine to press forward but then the weights would have brought the chains up taut, holding back the invader—as might the various steel cross sectors, or the net itself, which could only be penetrated by a submarine with very efficient cutters. To make sure no one was trying anything like this, Glasgow went on deck, looked around, saw nothing, found a fireman named Allerdyce on watch up front, at the winch which controlled the opening and closing of the gate.

Then he saw that the gate was still open, heard from Allerdyce that another ship was due to come in. There was no requirement that ships arrive at the gates at the time they were ordered opened and no Asdic search made in or outside any of the booms; and since a few minutes later another ship did pass through, and Glasgow felt no unusual movement of the gate boat and saw nothing odd about the wires of the boom—none of the rockets or flares fixed to it had gone off inadvertently—he turned in again, thought nothing more upon it. Neither apparently did anyone else worry about propeller sounds, for on this night the stream was running strongly to the westward along the boom and ships passing through the gate were swept down towards *Dragonet*; in a few cases ships even switched on their searchlights.

Davidson, who also had gone up on deck, had peered over the starboard side and found nothing.

'On coming back to go to the port side,' as later he'd tell the Board of Enquiry, 'I met the fireman of the watch who told me that a big ship had just passed our stem going through the gates. On hearing this I went down below and just took it for granted that the noise was that ship's propeller that I had heard and thought no more about it.'

At exactly 2227 hours Allerdyce winched the Hoxa gate closed.

The next morning, the 12th, the gate swung open again, at 8.55 o'clock to allow a ship to pass through. The gate remained open; but not until fifty minutes later, at 9.45, did any ship enter. And

then the gate was kept open, for a second ship, which did not arrive. A third ship, unannounced, arrived at 10.10, was allowed in,
and finally, at 10.34, the gate was closed, which meant, as Captain Robinson, the 'XDO', Extended Defence Officer stationed on
Flotta at Stanger Head, overlooking Hoxa, was later to testify before the Board of Enquiry, 'The total time the gate was open was
one hour and 39 minutes.'*

Shortly after midday on the 12th a German air reconnaissance
plane suddenly circled overhead, 1,800 metres, covering Scapa
thoroughly, well out of reach of the only anti-aircraft guns, the
eight near the naval base of Lyness at the southwest corner. Because of the possibility of air attack, *Furious* raised steam and
Repulse moved to dock, German Naval Operations noting later in
the day, in a 'Special Report on the Enemy': '*Furious* and *Repulse* in Scapa; the *Hood* probably also in the Scapa area. The
Renown in the Channel, war readiness and position unknown.'

U-47 was closing quietly on Orkney, electric engines humming,
words of command given softly, rumours whispered, producing
questions from the crew, general ones about the purpose of the
whole thing, and the answers, from officers and PO's, merely, as
Spahr would remember: 'We've got to conduct ourselves absolutely in such a way that we won't be seen or located, so we can
attack a worthwhile target.'

Every hour the turning of the screws was taken in account, the
depth of the water taken by an electrical depth sounder, which
Spahr was careful to turn on for only brief periods, lest the sound
be picked up by the British. Radio silence was maintained—*U-47*
knew nothing of the latest Operations reports (moving the Germans themselves to later question the tactic of air reconnaissance
while *47* set course).

On the 12th the *Unterseeboot* approached the islands from the
southwest, dived at dusk, lay submerged, and while the crew was
downing supper, Herbert Herrmann, a *Mechaniker Gefreiter,* a
Leading Torpedo Mechanic, at 19 the youngest aboard, also the
PO *Backschafter*, was serving up meals to the Chiefs, the PO's

* The laxness in security was repeated. 'On Friday, 13 October,' as Robinson would
go on to tell the Board, 'the gate was ordered by the Flagship for 0130 and the
ship passed out at 0212. The gate closed at 0228. Time—one hour and two
minutes.'

and officers. He was supposed to wash the dishes afterwards. But
he didn't do too much of this as he was off and on very seasick,
fortunately had help and understanding in this from the PO's, especially Ernst Dziallas and his own PO's, Kurt Bleeck and Willy
Meyer.

'They washed more dishes than I did,' Herrmann would remember. 'I was mostly OK when we were lying at the bottom of
the sea. On the whole it was routine, as we were not to intercept
or attack anyone until our main aim was accomplished. The spirit
of the crew was excellent; there was a very close relationship between superiors and ratings; we all had the same food made by
one cook and in the same galley, and we all had to live together.
When the worst came to the worst we all had to die together. Everybody laughed and made jokes about gathering potatoes in Scotland as POW's. But nobody really believed this would happen.'

At times the boat pitched and rolled or bumped over the heavily wrinkled sea. Herrmann remembered: 'In rough weather one
would stick the table cloth in a bucket of water and ring it out and
slap it on the table, put up all the slinger latts and put all the
dishes on the side against the latts where the boat rolled over to.
By the time one made his way to the control room, shouted
"Bridge" with the answer "Eye" then "To Skipper such and such
a meal is served," the boat heeled over to the other side and everything went onto the deck or the chief engineer (Hans Wessels)
had the contents of a can of cocoa in his lap. Prien would arrive,
look at the mess, look at everyone and say, "Never mind Herrmann, just make me a sandwich" and nobody else would ask for
anymore.'

Thursday, the 12th, and Prien's log indicated an end to the waiting. *Surfaced in the evening and came in to the coast in order to
fix exact position of ship. From 2200 to 2230 the English are kind
enough to switch on all the coastal lights so that I can obtain the
most exact fix. The ship's position is correct to within 1.8 nautical
miles, despite the fact that since leaving Channel 1 there was no
possibility of obtaining an accurate fix so that I had to steer by
dead reckonings and soundings.*

The kind English, burning their lights for units of the Home
Fleet; they were helping to imprint coastal contours on minds of
the watch in the bridge on *U-47*.

Leading Seaman Gerhard Hänsel, two hours on watch, saw the lights come on, cast a glance at the coast, the low-lying islands, the first time he had seen the Orkneys and 'my impression was "It will be hard to get into them".'

Dziallas, also on the bridge, taking bearings, marking bearing points for the site location and course determination, spotted the lighthouse beams, found his job much easier; he was chatting loosely with Prien and Spahr, who had climbed up, were breathing deeply of the cool night air, Spahr feeling especially good about his dead reckoning, for he had brought the boat to within less than two nautical miles from the islands; and now the lights, the *Englisch* were letting him steer terrestially; he needn't bother with astronomical position finding.

Thankful, Spahr raked the coast with his glasses, saw the shape of the land—its silhouette 'sombre,' he'd remember—and then the lighthouse. Rose Ness. Very clearly he could see its beams, about eight nautical miles distant. Haze blocked the Anskerry lighthouse but beams from the Copinsay lighthouse flashed very strong.

'I felt serene,' Spahr would recall, 'even though the outcome of our operation remained a big question mark.'

For Prien this was enough, they were there, the boat risked discovery; he altered course slightly, then ordered the U-boat down. Endrass banged the diving alarm. The diesels stopped clattering. The electrics began whining, the ballast tanks filled.

U-47 settled on the seabed, to pass the early hours of Friday the 13th.

At 0437 lying submerged in 90 metres of water, according to the log. *Rest period for crew.*

But not everyone slept, for soon after the dive Otto Strunk, the *Stabsobermaschinist,* Chief Engine Room Artificer, passed word to Wessels of a problem, an unusually high degree of sea water had got into the port engine's lubrication oil. The engines didn't use diesel direct from a bunker; it was always transferred to a daily usage tank first, and the tank had a glass peep-hole for spotting water. But perhaps the water had got in while it was being pumped out with sea water for transfer to the overhead reservoir between the engines; from there it flowed naturally into the fuel pumps.

Wessels, the 'LI,' *Leitender Ingenieur*, Chief Engineering Officer, informed Prien at once, and Prien recognised it as an un-

pleasant situation. But nothing more. Couldn't this be fixed after
the mission? No, said the LI. The problem could become serious.
If in Scapa, if they made it into Scapa, and if they had to pick up
speed, put pressure on the engines, it might be impossible to lubri-
cate the gears; the seawater might turn into steam. Once the salt
crystals lodged in the gears, a *Branderburger*—stalling of an engine—might occur. They might succeed in entering Scapa Flow,
might even succeed in manoeuvring around it, but if chased, if
called on to get out at top speed, they might fail completely, find
the boat unable to move against the current.

It was an easy decision now. The problem had to be found,
Prien knew.

The lubricating oil was found to have 7–8% water in it.

Wessels and his machinists located the leakage. In the cylinder
liner separating the combustion chamber from the water cooling
chamber the water was flowing freely into the crank chamber,
blending with the lubricating oil.

Could they change the cylinder? No, that would take too much
time, Wessels told Prien. But he could improvise; so he went to
work on a temporary remedy, had his *maschinists* fashion a make-
shift thing, a kind of gutter, like a rain gutter, built of sheet metal
and this was fastened around the defective cylinder liner—and it
worked; it drained the salt water into the bilge before the water
could mix with the lubricating oil.

*All hands worked feverishly to change the oil, i.e. to get rid of
the water and to isolate the leaking point.*

Through it all, the crew had slept, all save the machinists, a few
others who oversaw the air supply, added oxygen as it became
necessary, maintained the trim of the boat.

Wessels and his men could rest, as could Prien; but a few hours
later Prien was at the map table in the *Zentrale*, comparing with
Spahr the sea chart against the enlargements of four reconnaissance photographs of Scapa taken by Air Fleet II. Then Prien
ordered a general stand-to in the front torpedo and ratings quarters. Herrmann has never forgotten how it was.

'Everyone somehow found a place to sit or crouch down. The
last one to come was the Old Man with some papers under his
arm. The Chief Engineer called attention, but the Old Man declined with a "Thank You, as you were." He looked around,
looked in everybody's eyes and suddenly said, "We're going into

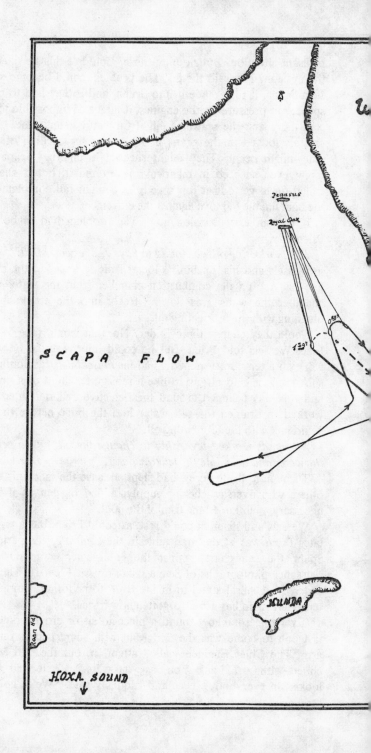

SCAPA FLOW

HOXA SOUND

MUNDA

Roan Hd.

Pegasus

Royal Oak

069°

139°

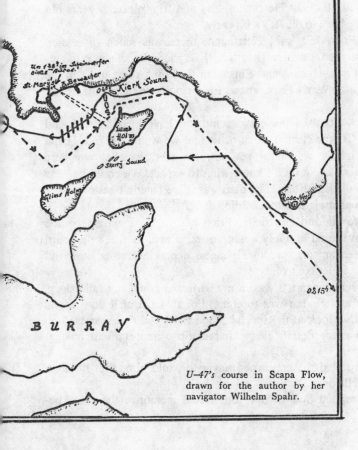

Karte „U-47" - 13.10.1939 zum 14.10.1939

W. Spahr

Um 139° im Scheinwerfer
eines Autos.

St. Mary's 2 Bewacher   Kierk Sound
                      040°

                      Lamb
                      Holm

              Skerry Sound

Glims Holm

                                Rose Ne...

                                        02.15ʰ

B U R R A Y

U-47's course in Scapa Flow,
drawn for the author by her
navigator Wilhelm Spahr.

Scapa Flow! First we're going to sink aircraft carriers, then battle-ships and cruisers, and all we can get." The room seemed to get a lot lighter, as nearly everyone went pale. Nobody spoke and the silence was eerie.

'Prien again looked at everyone and continued, "I am deter-mined to get in, do what we have to do and I am more determined to get you all out again and back home." He told us then that we had aerial photographs to get through the minefield and get through the barrier. He knew the entrance was barred by block-ships which were connected with chains and he could get in there at a certain height of water.

'He also told us that the High Command was sure we could get in—but not so sure we could get out again. But he was convinced we could do both and have some success.'

'My God,' thought Herrmann, 'my first trip, nineteen years old and maybe have to die. It's a bit early.'

After Prien left, said Herrmann, there was much discussion among the men, much anxiety felt. 'Everybody knew about the at-tempts by von Hennig and Emsmann to do the same thing in the First World War. They knew Emsmann was never heard of again.'

But the mood of the crew 'could not have been better,' said Dziallas. 'It was clear to each of us that we would get into Scapa Flow. Whether we could get out, however, is what we were worried about. We didn't know what to expect. We could become prisoners of the British. The plan was if we couldn't get out, we'd run the boat straight onto a landing dock.'

To save air and electricity, Prien had ordered extreme quiet. Most men turned in. Only a handful remained, to check outboard breech mechanisms, pressure gauges, depth indicators, keep all other gear under control.

Spahr remembers: 'I was in my berth but could not fall asleep, too tense about what was to come. For that reason I got up and took another look at the special Scapa Flow chart. I impressed on my mind every detail, every characteristic important to naviga-tion.'

Prien spotted the concerned navigator, told him, 'But it's time for you to lie down.'

'Yes,' replied Spahr, 'but you should memorise the chart because after we surface, you won't have a chance to as much as glance at it.'

Prien, who already knew the chart well, made for his 'cabin,' lay down, drawing the curtain behind him.

When in a moment someone came by, a bit noisily, the radio operator snapped 'Quiet, the Old Man's sleeping,' and from behind the little green partition came a voice in characteristic reply.

'The Old Man never sleeps. He just rests his eyes.'

U-boats did well for food and in the evening all the delicacies the cook, Friedrich Walz, could produce were brought forward, the meal a warm one, coming at just the right time for a change, for there would be no time to dine at midnight. Herrmann remembered:

'It was like the last supper with all the trimmings. Soup, *Kassler* (salted pork), potatoes, green kale and gravy, a sweet and strong coffee. We called it the hangman's meal. Nevertheless we enjoyed it and cracked jokes which helped to ease the tension. After the dishes were washed and stowed away, everybody became very busy. All the bunks were lashed to the side. The gratings on top of the torpedoes were dismantled, the loading beams were lowered and the (spare) torpedoes lifted and put into quickloading position in front of tubes 1 and 2 and made fast. The detonators were taken out of the hold and laid down handy. Ammunition for handfire weapons was taken out. Explosive charges were placed between the tubes and placed all over in readiness to destroy the boat when it became necessary. Radio code key machines were dismantled and secret papers, log book, signal book, were heaped together and an explosive charge placed on top. Escape apparatus was checked and placed to be handy.'

Preparations for attack on Scapa Flow. Two torpedoes are placed in rapid loading position before tubes 1 and 2. Explosives brought out in case of necessity of scuttling. Crew's morale splendid.

Between bow and stern tubes more charges were laid, von Varendorff, the second watch officer, overseeing their placement. For hours in training the men had practised the procedure: on order 'Abandon ship!' time fuses activated, the explosives, pressure-resistant, triggered by delay-action ignition, from ignition to detonation five minutes to get out. Von Varendorff and his mechanics, the last to leave, would hit the plunger on the first fuse, wait a second or two to ensure the fuse was all right, then on to the next fuse they'd go, then to the next, then in the control room meet, get out, pour over the side, swim away from the boat as fast as they could.

More jokes went among the crew, relieving the tightened senses, the line about 'gathering potatoes in Scotland as POW's' repeated often; but very real was the possibility of falling into the hands of the British. Among the crew many still wore proper round caps with ribbons, reading *Unterseebootsflotille Wegener,* only a few having new caps without the name *Wegener*; so all who had the old ribbons tore out the name of the flotilla, leaving them with ribbons that said only *Unterseebootsflotille.* This left the tails, which usually were at the back, trailing down the side. Signaller Gerd Hänsel got the idea to cut the tails and tie them into a bow as the British sailors did. Everyone laughed but they did it, then cigarettes and bars of chocolate were passed around, tucked into their escape apparatus, a kind of life jacket with oxygen bottle, potash cases, air funnel with mouth-piece, a pouch for emergency food supply.

'Prien asked some to let him see the chocolate,' remembered Herrmann. 'But they owned up that they had eaten it, as they thought it was better having it now than never getting the chance to have it at all.'

At 1915 hours the U-boat surfaced and set course for Holm Sound.

Everything goes according to plan until 2307, when it is necessary to submerge on sighting a merchant ship just before Rose Ness.

Prien ordered Battle Stations, was soon using both periscopes, the sky scope and the surface attack sight, trying to get the hazy contour of the ship in the crosswires, using the hand controls to train left and right, adjust the angling mirrors, change the magnification: but in spite of the very clear night, bright lights from the heavens, he could not make out the ship, which soon vanished completely from sight.

At 2331, surfaced again.

U-47 was now feeling her way to Holm Sound, following the tide, and close to midnight Prien sighted the Rose Ness lighthouse on his starboard side, parallel to *47*'s bow, a distance of only 600 metres.

'Course three-two-oh,' called Prien; and *U-47* ploughed on, past the cliffs and caves of the eastern South Isles, but keeping away from the coast of South Ronaldsay, steering round the Bay of Lime, then closing on towards Burray, heading north past one of the most vulnerable of all Scapa's entrances, unguarded Water Sound where below the dark coasts, extremely hard to see, lay two openings, one 400 feet wide, the other 200, both with a depth of 15 feet or more at high water. British coasters—five-six hundred tonners—recently had entered this Sound at high water; the Metal Industries tug *Imperious*, draught 12-feet, 6-inches, had done it at low water, passing in and out round the bow of the rusty red wreck *Naja* lying just off the Burray shore. Between the stern of *Naja* and the broken stern portion of another blockship lay another, narrower gap, probably not navigable; but the Sound was far from blocked against submarine attack.*

'Course two-seven-oh.'

Prien had measured the current and was changing course, making for the mile-wide entrance of Holm Sound, on a bearing which would take him, he believed, directly into Kirk Sound.

The wind came up in the north and in the sky there were glimmering lights, 'It was a bright moonlight night,' said Dziallas, one of five on the bridge. 'The moon was reflected in beautiful colours in the water. The sea was quiet.'

To Prien it seemed eerie, uncomfortably light.

On land everything is dark, high in the sky are the flickering Northern Lights, so that the bay, surrounded by highish mountains, is directly lit up from above.

Then of a sudden a blockship, clearly visible, hove in sight.

Kirk Sound already?

I believe myself to be already in Kirk Sound, and prepare for work.

Prien was looking at the *Cape Ortegal*, successfully sunk on 12 September, but in Skerry Sound, not Kirk. He had brought his craft into the wrong Sound, could only have found the channels odd, not at all what the Kirk Sound chart had shown, for here lay

---

* 'Between South Ronaldsay shore and existing blockship there is a wide shallow channel which could be navigated by shallow draught surface craft,' Thomas McKenzie of Metal Industries had warned in his report of 12 May.

only one opening, about 350 feet across, stretching from the north side of the Sound between the blockship and Lamb Holm, with a depth of 25 or 30 feet, and extending from the bows of the block-ship to the four fathom line off Lamb Holm. There was no second channel, however, only a number of small, extremely narrow ones, navigable, but by fast shallow draught surface craft, not by a sub-marine, not a 750-ton U-boat.

While the light in the north kept flickering mysteriously, from Spahr belowdeck there came a quick warning: this wasn't Kirk Sound. The turn had been made too soon.

The navigator, by means of dead-reckoning, states that the preparations are premature, while I at the same time realize the mistake, for there is only one sunken ship in the straits.

Spahr, after noting Prien's course change, had switched on the sonic depth finder, keeping track of the depth, at the 1-metre line had brought the error to Prien's attention and given him a new course—30°. At the same time Dziallas from his position on the bridge also had discerned the false course, like Spahr had brought the error to Prien's attention, told the skipper the boat absolutely would have to change course.

'Hard a starboard!'

Prien immediately altered course with hard rudder, avoiding in time the danger of being forced by the strong inrushing current into the sunken hulk.

'Damn shame,' muttered Prien after the crisis had passed. 'That's all we need.'

Then down the voice pipe: 'It's all right, situation acknowl-edged.'

The imminent danger is averted. A few minutes later, Kirk Sound is clearly visible.

Dziallas and Spahr began taking new bearings, from both sides of the Kirk Sound passage; and with this data Prien determined the accurate course.

The sky poured down light, making shimmering reflections upon the water.

Maschinist Obergefreiter, Friedrich Schmidt, who happened to be passing through the control room, remembers looking up.

'Saw the Aurora Borealis through the turret hatch. Fantastic!'

'It was,' said Hänsel, on the bridge, 'almost as light as the morning sun.'

Endrass, who as the torpedo officer would aim on target, fire the torpedoes, while Prien would do the navigating, turned to the skipper, who never liked bright nights, not even in the open Atlantic.

'What about it, lovely night for shooting!' said Endrass.

Prien was too busy to answer. Kirk Sound loomed on the port side.

The blockships lie in the sound, ghostly as the wings of a theatre.

During this Friday the 13th, there were no nets, no mines, no shore lights, no lookouts of any kind, and no Asdic-bearing vessels; there was only the dark background of silent headlands.

Feeling 'repaid for having learned the chart beforehand,' Prien guided his boat towards Kirk, somewhat behind schedule, past high-water (which had come this night at 2338 hours), *with* the current instead of in slack water, but in calm and navigable water. He reduced speed, slowing engines, which made the boat harder to handle, but now he was on the right course, soon faced with a choice. But easy to make, for of the two channels ahead, the narrowest stretched 200 feet wide, the other twice that at least, just as Dönitz had pointed out in the Air Fleet photos: a technically primitive blockade. Both channels were navigable, the southern passage the deepest, about 15 feet or more down, but the wider, northern passage would offer the best course. Prien ordered the boat hard a-port, the diesels turned off, the electrics on, the tanks slightly pre-flooded to give a little more draught.

Suddenly the twisted wreck of a two-masted bark, an ineffective hulk, loomed up ahead, *U-47* passed it easily. Fifteen metres to spare. A wonder it was there at all. Then there was a foaming of water. The current was growling, the boat having trouble using its rudder effectively. Prien ordered her steered to starboard, to hug the shore, and she now rode easily upon the water.

On a course of 270 I pass the two-masted schooner, which is lying on a bearing of 315 in front of the real boom.

Keeping to the lee shore, avoiding entirely the channel closest to the Lamb Holm shore, the five hands on the bridge, Prien, Dziallas, Hänsel, von Varendorff and Endrass, now gazed over the rim of the tower and saw ahead, about a hundred and fifty metres, on the northern side in a line abreast, the blockships, the 'real boom' Prien wrote of. The men were looking at the blockships *Thames* and *Soriano* (paying no attention to the broken up portions of the blockship *Minich* near the opposite Lamb Holm shore), ships the Admiralty had accepted as constituting 'an effective barrier to passage through the main Kirk Sound channel.' *Thames*, Prien saw, he could pass easily, going to the south around her. The biggest obstacle lay in crossing the chains and wires connecting her with the other blockship: he did not fear the cement-filled hulks themselves.

An aggressive navigator, Prien decided in a moment that he'd manoeuvre between the sterns of both ships, putting on just enough speed to counteract the current, which played free and fast but was navigable. He ordered a course of 270; and all eyes fastened on the two scuttled ships, which lay where the channel narrowed with masts cut away, showing only the trunks and bridgework, each ship fixed to the shore by anchor chains.

Prien wanted more draught. He feared running onto the blockships; so ordered the medium dip cell flooded, giving slightly more draught, about 50 centimetres more. And without referring to the chart, he manoeuvred the *Unterseeboot* into the gap between ships, a passage 136 feet wide. As the boat felt its way on, he called down the rudder angles—he did not give the steerers the course—but to each rudder angle the boat reacted well, the steerers pressing brass buttons, to turn starboard or port.

In the flickering lights of the Aurora, the eyes of the men must have glinted strangely, the excitement something wonderful, for *U-47* was facing no armed resistance whatsoever, nothing other than the wires and cables quietly strung.

The penetration proceeds with unbelievable speed.

But of a sudden, straight ahead, there hove in view the anchor chains of the second bulk, *Soriano*, extending obliquely downwards, and more cables dipping under water.

I recognize the cable of the northern blockship at an angle of 45 degrees ahead.

Prien would have to pick out the point where the cables dipped at an angle under the water, then slide over them. The current was helping, doing its best to show the way, for round the cables there turned up white foam which swirled and marked the danger spots. Prien had to be careful, guess the right place, hope the water was deep enough to let him clear the obstruction. He kept his eye on the echo sounder; but the current kept pushing, the tide rushing

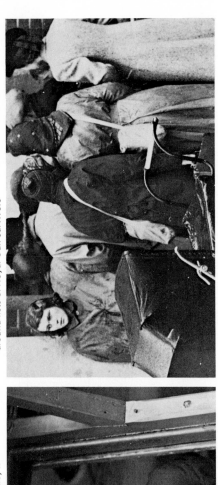

around lists of *Royal Oak* survivors

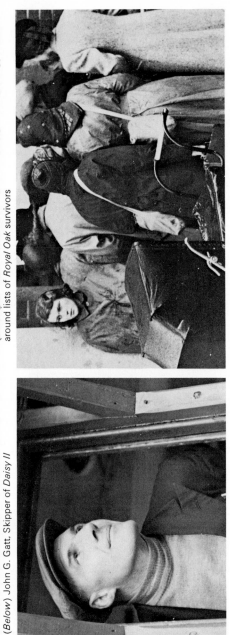

(*Below*) John G. Gatt, Skipper of *Daisy II*

In Thurso survivors of *Royal Oak* wait before the long train ride back to Portsmouth

One survived : of the five Royal Marines who posed for this photograph in the *Royal Oak* in September 1939, only one, Henry Pattison (extreme right with eyes closed) lived

On leave from the *Oak* at the time of the sinking, Ordnance Artificer John G. Faulkner was presumed dead, his wife was sent the Admiralty's sympathy on his 'sad death'. Faulkner keeps the items below as a souvenir today

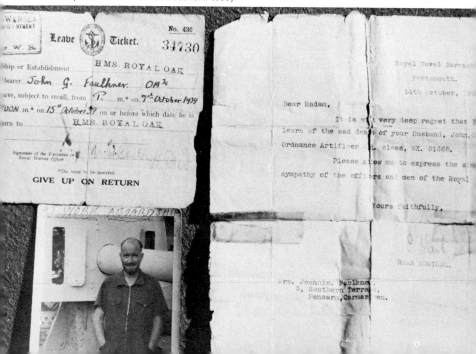

SUNDAY GRAPHIC

No. 1,280.   SUNDAY, OCTOBER 15, 1939   TWOPENCE.

1,200 In Torpedoed British Battleship

370 SAVED FROM ROYAL OAK

Gale Hinders Rescue

ABOUT 370 OFFICERS AND MEN ARE KNOWN TO HAVE BEEN SAVED WHEN THE BATTLESHIP ROYAL OAK WAS SENT TO THE BOTTOM.

The Royal Oak, which is believed to have fallen victim to a U-boat, had a complement of 1,200 officers and men.

The "Sunday Graphic" learns that the Royal Oak was sunk on Friday night. Rescue ships rushed to the scene, but were hampered by a strong north-easterly gale.

Among the rescued are Capt. W. G. Benn and Commander R. F. Nichols. Names of survivors on middle and back pages.

HOW GERMANY HEARD THE NEWS

Germany first received news of the sinking of the battleship from a B.B.C. announcement. Several hours later it was officially stated that the Nazi Government was still without confirmation from any German source.

"We must wait for a report from whatever German units may have been involved," it was stated, but the hours passed and still Berlin had received no news from those "German units."

Berlin began to wonder how significant that silence was. Screaming headlines in the Nazi newspapers boasted of the sinking of the Royal Oak.

SYMPATHY IN ITALY

"Great new success . . . Another bitter lesson for England." . . . shouted.

. . . . received with great regret and there were widespread expressions of sympathy.

Vessels of the Royal Oak class have very good internal protection, and with protective bulges their defence against under-water attack is considered to be very strong.

News of the loss of the Royal Oak follows the Admiralty announcement of the sinking of three U-boats on Friday.

Seventeen or eighteen U-boats have been sunk by the British and French fleets, according to a report in Paris.

Several others are believed to have been sunk, but their loss cannot be definitely established.

CONTINUED ON BACK PAGE

RUSSIA IS FORTIFYING HER FRONTIER WITH GERMANY—See Page 3.

When the final count was made, it would show 424 survivors

Sonntag
15. Oktober
1939

Reichsausgabe   Tageszeitung der Deutschen Arbeitsfront

der Angriff

Sie wollen neutral bleiben

Das siegreiche U-Boot in die Heimat zurückgekeh[rt]

„Royal Oak" und „Repulse" wurden in der Bucht von Scapa Flow torpedie[rt]

Kreuzer „Southampton" und „Edinburgh" getroffen
Auslandspresse bestätigt die Treffer der deutschen Bombe[r]

Trotz Minen- und Netzsperre!
Deutsches U-Boot in der Bucht von Scapa Flow

Berlin, 17. Oktober.

Die getroffenen Kreuzer
„Southampton" und „Edinburgh"

Berlin, 17. Oktober.

Einer der Gründe für Englands Mißgunst
IV.
Das gewaltige Ausmaß der Sozialarbeit der Deutschen Arbeit[sfront]

Von Dr. Robert Ley

Das OKW. berichtet
Handelsschiffe mit 54 000 t im Atlantik versenkt

Berlin, 17. Oktober.

Half-true, half-false headline in the Goebbels-founded Nazi party organ *Der Angriff* (The Attack) misled the German populace. The battle cruiser *Repulse* was not at Scapa Flow when *Royal Oak* was torpedoed inshore, moving the U-boat slightly to starboard, and finally her rudder would not respond; the boat was pushed astern, close to an anchor chain—then right up against it.

Suddenly the U-boat's keel ran afoul of the chain, scraping it, making a horrible sound. Leading Electrician's Mate Friedrich Schmidt, in the battery room below, thought it like a 'shuffling noise.' Then followed, he'd remember, 'shock and excitement.' More than a few must have thought they'd struck a mine cable.

To Leading Seaman Willie Loh, one of the four torpedo mechanics, who was tending his two torpedoes in the stern, one in the tube, one in reserve, the brushing of the chain sounded like 'a heavy rattle against the hull,' and to Herbert Herrmann, standing near him, 'a scraping sound, like when metal strikes metal.'

At this moment someone shouted 'contact,' and the reply came back, calmly, 'acknowledged.'

The chain pushed the U-boat toward the land and made it touch bottom; so the invader had grounded and was being held fast.

Prien acted quickly: he ordered the port engine stopped, the starboard engine slow ahead, the rudder hard to port; and when the stern still pushed on the chain, held fast to the blockship, the fear of discovery must have pressed hard on the minds of every man. 'Backwater was gone, low tide still flowed, everything was moving very fast,' remembered Spahr, tensely keeping the track of the course below.

The stern still touches the cable.

Prien had to work her free, and quickly, confidently, he ordered the air pressure valves opened, the flooded diving tanks blown.

The boat was in such good form that I was able to switch on to charge in the harbour and pump up air.

At once the boat shook and trembled, in seconds, had extricated itself, coming under control again.

The boat becomes free.

Prien ordered *U-47* around to port, brought onto course with difficult, rapid manoeuvring. The boat veered a little, threatening to ground again; but then it steadied, headed on. *U-47* had penetrated the fleet anchorage and Scapa Flow was set before it like a vast and solemn panorama, the brilliantly tinted lights of the Aurora casting streaks upon the dark mass of the surface. There were no more obstructions.

'We are in!' Prien said down the voice tube.

We are in Scapa Flow.

The time was twenty-seven minutes past midnight, Saturday the 14th.

U-47 fairly drifted into the bay. There was no cheering, all hands were rigid with the tension of the moment, the crew's mood 'excellent and confident,' remembered Spahr, who'd been busy watching the courses the boat was taking, checking engine revolutions, water depth; he had the precise location at all times.

Prien was loose, almost jubilant. 'We're in for a big thing tonight,' he told Hänsel as the U-boat entered the harbour, began a western course, heading for the very heart of the British base. Her electrics stopped humming, the diesels turned on—the sudden noise, said Dziallas 'had a truly nerve-whipping effect.' Then as they crept past the little settlement of St Mary's the boat was suddenly caught in the high beams of a car: light from a British motor car pouring over the whole starboard side of Germany's finest underwater weapon!

Probably from a car on the road running eastward from the village along the north shore of Kirk Sound.*

The men stared out in horror. Dziallas would remember, 'we could clearly make out vehicles parked on land and a guard walking up and down.'

But no one noticed the submarine.

While the Merry Dancers still flickered, playing upon the water, *U-47,* undetected, anxiously began its search for ships.

It is disgustingly light. The whole bay is lit up, Prien would write.

To the south of Cava, he knew, strong English forces usually concentrated. *U-47,* her guns unmanned, closed on the area for torpedo shots. But not a single ship could be seen.

To the south of Cava there is nothing.

Prien ordered the still-surfaced boat on.

I go farther in.

Into the voice-pipe, for the benefit of the men below, the captain carried on a running commentary: 'We are cruising on a quiet

---

* Prien would tell this story later, and although no motorist made a report, the Admiralty would state in an item in its Board of Enquiry report, 'He (Prien) is hardly likely to have invented this.'

sea and in the Northern Lights like a sitting duck. But nothing can be seen of a fleet.'

The crew stood at battle stations, waiting for orders: they heard only course changes.

Prien ordered the boat turned to port, in the direction of the small isle of Flotta: those on the bridge recognized the coast, saw in the distance Hoxa and Hoy Sounds, and two small skiffs patrolling, one at each boom.

They were the only vessels patrolling that night. Of three other drifters available, one was boiler cleaning, and two standing off. The boom at Switha was not being watched at all.

Prien had before him a sort of infuriating experience.

I recognize the Hoxa Sound coastguard, to which in the next few minutes the boat must present itself as a target. In that event all would be lost; at present south of Cava no ships are to be seen, although visibility is extremely good. Hence decisions: South of Cava there is no shipping; so before staking everything on success, all possible precautions must be taken. Therefore, turn to port is made. We proceed north by the coast.

Prien had got through; he was in an enemy harbour, running surfaced about it, but where was the prize? Where were the heavy ships—the carriers, the 15-inch battleships. Where were the 'small' ships, the destroyers and cruisers? The submarine had rounded Cape Howequoy, sighted not a warship of any kind, for about three and a half nautical miles, had steered slowly in the direction of Flotta, turning finally in a wide circle.

Prien dared not take the submarine down, for if discovered, he'd have to surface, lose precious time, perhaps never make it out. So he took her in deeper, north for about 1.2 nautical miles, steering a course due 50°; but aimlessly, for what seemed an eternity, he went. Every inlet was deserted.

It was about 55 minutes past midnight, at least twenty-eight minutes since *U-47* had snaked a course through Kirk Sound; and not a single fighting ship had been seen. More than one crewman must have wondered why he was there, for *U-47*, it appeared, had the vast anchorage all to herself.

'God,' said Stoker Werner Sollig in the engine room, 'Let them open their eyes on the bridge and they'll find something for sure.'

Every ship out on manoeuvres?

'The entire fleet can't be gone,' Willie Loh was thinking.

Prien muttered into the tube linking him with the crew below: 'Still nothing in sight.'

Herrmann, who for a minute had been on the bridge, to mount for surface attack the aim optic on the telescope stand, was waiting forward with other torpedomen, waiting for the signal 'Tubes Ready!'—after the bow tubes had fired, he'd head aft to join Loh at tube five. But now all he was thinking, as he kept glancing at the lights above the tubes, was that something had to be found— 'not to have made all this effort in vain.'

Almost an hour had passed before there emerged at last the first faint shape of a ship, a shadowy bulk lying dark and motionless in the northeast corner of the Flow, wearing an air of sleeping, burning shaded anchor lights at both extremes: obviously by the solid appearance of her superstructure and tripod mainmast, her eight-barrelled pom-poms and 15-inchers, an 'R' class battleship. Then to the west behind the first ship there appeared the fore part of another ship, but bows only, the rest hidden by gun turrets, bridges, masts, and deck structures of the first.

Two battleships are lying there at anchor, and further inshore, destroyers. Cruisers not visible, therefore attack on the big fellows.

Prien was wrong: only the nearer vessel was a battleship, HMS *Royal Oak*; the other a cargo ship turned seaplane transport, HMS *Pegasus*, 6,900 tons, lying a mile from the *Oak*. At the time, Prien knew the identity of neither—there is no mention anywhere in his log of any ship by name.

As *U-47* drew closer and reduced speed, the ships grew larger, then the U-boat's motors stopped, Prien trimmed the boat into firing position, then Endrass took the enemy's measure: he called off the range; distance apart, 3,000 metres; estimated depth 75 metres. There'd be impact firing, a fan of three, the first torpedo of the salvo aimed at the protruding bows of the farther, northern ship—a difficult target—the next two torpedoes on the closer, southern vessel—a 'sitting duck.'

The tubes already had been loaded in Kiel, the torpedoes, the 'eels,' as the Germans called them, pulled out in rotation and adjusted on the trip, batteries brought up to strength before entrance to Scapa, the tails well-greased, inscribed with fingers, 'With Love,' 'With Luck,' 'To Chamberlain,' embellished with hearts and arrows, one inscribed with the name of a crewman's sweetheart for luck.

Endrass hunched over the torpedo aiming device, bringing the thin cross hairs to bear on the bows of the farther vessel, the hull of the closest. He determined the firing sequence, the velocity and degree of the torpedoes, then shouted down the pistol-settings—details for the detonators.

'Flood tubes one to four and tanks two and three,' shot the order from the voice tube.

Herrmann remembered: 'Peter Thewes and I did the work and PO Kurt Bleeck called out the orders he received and repeated them back as a check that they had been understood.'

Valves to tubes one to four opened, the tanks put under air pressure, and Endrass was informed, 'Tubes one to four are being flooded,' then 'Tubes one to four are flooded,' and a quick flurry of other orders and replies, one shouted statement chasing another.

'Open outer doors.'

'Outer doors opening.'

'Outer doors open.'

'Tubes one to four ready.'

Endrass's order for a fan of three meant the electric torpedoes in the two portside tubes, one and three, and the electric in starboard number two. The air torpedo in tube four was not called on at all.

Los!

Endrass pressed the electric button on the bridge, a mechanic punched a manual firing switch—as a precaution in case of electric failure—and the first torpedo leaped out, making the boat lurch slightly, rocking gently.

Two seconds elapsed, then automatically the second 'eel' hissed out, then the third—'Torpedo started,' someone shouted, it was running normal under its own power.

'One felt,' remembered Herrmann, 'elation and relief to get rid of the torpedoes.'

Spahr held the stopwatch: 'I took a breath and watched the dial in order to compute the precise range from the seconds it took up to detonation. The distance was about 3,000 metres. Visibility considerations kept us that much apart, and we wanted to keep from being discovered as long as possible. My hope of course was that the ship would be destroyed.'

In the radio room starboard, the wireless operator followed the shots with his earphones, he could easily hear them running, while Spahr took up the count, his eyes fastened on the dial of the stop-watch and the seconds ticked by, the wait agonizing, as the running time lengthened. There was no shock wave to indicate a hit. The 'eels' should have hit. Wrong horizontal or vertical steering? An error in the distance given? Perhaps faulty detonators? The targets were stationary, easy hits, but the detonators might not have gone off, might have underrun the target, sunk to the sandy bottom.

But then a hit, from the bridge a geyser of water seen, a light tremor felt in the boat.

After a good 3½ minutes, a torpedo detonates on the northern ship; of the other two nothing is to be seen.

A few anxious minutes passed but the Flow's defences did not spring into action and not a searchlight swept the water.

Prien was thinking. 'He thought for a long time,' said Dziallas. 'Should he reload or break it off. In this situation Endrass made the suggestion to put off from shore and then reload, so that a second attack could at once be started.

Prien ordered the boat swung around, the stern tube put in firing position.

About!

4

Like a Sleeping Giant

At 1.04 a.m. on Saturday the 14th Ordinary Seaman Leonard E. Soal, on watch on the compass platform of *Royal Oak*'s upper bridge, heard suddenly a near thunder, an explosion, saw linked cable shackles jump into the air, white and yellow smoke rise from the deck forward, then pieces of wood floating in the water, ten feet off the starboard bow.

Soal remained disbelieving: the forecastle deck stood drenched by a large spout of water, an odd acrid odour hung about, rust dust filled the air; and round about the compass platform and in the vicinity of the bridge, others on watch, including a commissioned officer, a midshipman, a chief petty officer, a boatswain's mate, a bugler, all raised their heads, turned eyes skyward: nobody worried about an attack from anywhere but the air. But no airplane could be seen, the drone of none heard. A murmur of voices broke upon the ship, for the water thrown up in the bows seemed much bigger than could have been caused by the anchor cable running out.

Below the fo'c'sle, on the starboard side forward, Petty Officer Higgins, Gunner's Mate of the Watch, expected to hear a pipe ordering gun crews to close up; he waited a moment and when he heard no pipe, nor bugle, he walked with several members of the gun crew around the 15-inch guns, stopped on the starboard side of the fo'c'sle abreast 'B' turret, leaned over the side, spied two beams floating in the calm water, being carried by the tide; he took them for baulks of timber, like the piles used in pier construction—about nine to twelve feet long, they were, fifteen inches to two feet in width. Could the beams have had something to do with the explosion? Higgins had no idea, nor could anyone with him figure it out, as now a strange quiet spread across the *Oak*'s bows. The men at Air Defence Positions grew much puzzled.

Below decks the explosion aroused equal astonishment. In the alcove in the Engine Room Artificer's mess next to the cable locker flat far forward, Chief E.R.A. Charles Cartwright had first thought 'the cable has gone mad—under no control.' When the cable was worked normally, it was frightening enough; but this sound, this roar, it was nothing like he had heard before: 'It shook the dust free and the lights dimmed, my messmates sprang from their hammocks in a flurry of blankets and ran from the mess.'

Cartwright acted much the same as dozens of others at this very moment: 'I stood upright for seconds, must have thought, angrily, nothing to do with me—let somebody else do something—and turned in again and went to sleep.'

All over *Royal Oak* men were doing the same, rubbing their eyes, cursing the noise, sitting up in a daze, going back to sleep, too drowsy to leave their hammocks.

Many, however, had no choice. Engine Room Chief Petty Officer F. J. C. Hobbs, sleeping directly aft of the cable locker flat, felt a thud, found himself on the deck, pitched there by an explosion he'd remember as 'lifting the bows of the ship and causing the bulkhead of the mess to bulge.' Fearing the bulkhead would give way at any moment, suspecting an explosion in the cable locker flat, or the next compartment, forty or so feet from forward, well below the waterline in the Inflammable Store containing petrol, paraffin and other combustibles, Hobbs moved quickly, in pyjamas and shoes, his nostrils flared by an odour 'like that of gunpowder.'

'An aerial bomb or torpedo,' he thought, as he bounded aft.

'A bomb or a 6-inch gun going off,' thought Lieutenant A. M. Seymour, officer of the watch of the first watch who, also sleeping forward, had been pulled from his slumber by the force of the explosion, had tugged on some clothes, hurried onto the fo'c'sle, smelled fumes, sniffed, but couldn't recognize the odour—not like anything he knew, certainly not like cordite—he saw no fire but noted the rust dust, spotted the bonnet of the port navel pipe (the standby anchor) lying upside down. The lights were on and Seymour looked down the pipe, observed the atmosphere between decks misty with puffs of greyish smoke.

'Slips on the cable have parted—cable's run out!' Seymour heard it said, then he, like others, made for the slips, well back from the bow, to have a look. A small knot of men had gathered, present among them Captain William Gordon Benn, the *Oak*'s skipper, who'd been asleep in his cabin, upon waking had suspected immediately an internal explosion in the Inflammable Store. Benn sent aft for his Engineer Commander, J. W. Renshaw; then on the now crowded fo'c'sle, alive with senior officers, he bent to examine the cable slips: all of them on both cables, port and starboard, had parted: the cast iron had fractured under the stress, allowing the port cable to run out, letting go the single starboard anchor by which the *Oak* had been riding. Benn turned to First Lieutenant Commander Ward, ordered him below to inspect the forward compartments, for a few minutes more stayed on the fo'c'sle chatting with the ship's navigator, Lieutenant Commander Richard A. V. Gregory, who like Benn suspected nothing more than a small internal explosion, agreed with the captain's observation that 'the ship was not listing or going down by the bows.'

'I realised that the latter was difficult to be certain about but I did not think she was going down by the bows,' Benn later would remember, 'I was quite certain the ship had not listed.'

In mess after mess, stem to stern—upper deck, main deck, middle deck, lower deck—the story was repeated: men awoke, bothered by the sound of men stirring, sat up, blinked for a moment, lay down again, quiet or snoring, as if lacking strength to leave their hammocks. They were the picture of exhausted sailors after a day of tedium. Arms and legs protruded from blankets, heads dropped over sides. Some sailors, hearing the disturbance, gave no thought to making inquiry, just shifted their bodies to new positions, fell back to slumber, grunting annoyance. The reason was simple: no one had told them what to do. They arose upon direct order. They had received no orders at all.

In the Chief Petty Officer's mess forward, CPO Writer Stanley W. H. Thompson, who'd been asleep for about forty-five minutes —exhausted from a long walk in Kirkwall that afternoon—had been yanked from his sleep by the sensation of a jolt. Some of his messmates awoke at the same time, remarked 'What was that?' then turned back to sleep.

But Thompson felt edgy. 'I'm going up and see what it is,' he said. When he reached the Torpedo Flat (long removed were the two pairs of 18-inch torpedo tubes at upper deck level) above the mess, he found a number of men standing round, a lot of dust in the air; he heard the story—the anchor cable had parted and run out—saw the remains of the cable, heard that shipwrights and cable party would be coming along soon; so he turned away, visited the night heads below the wardroom on the port side, returned to his mess and found the same impression held by others who had gone up and come down to turn in again.

'Some of my messmates had not even woken up and not all who woke appeared to have felt the occurrence of any major importance. No orders were received or address system heard.'

Thompson, still in pyjamas, settled back in his hammock.

In his own hammock outside the Divisional Office, at the after end of the starboard 6-inch battery, Dick Kerr, duty Petty Officer of the anti-aircraft pool (spare hands not required to close up at the AA guns), had been awakened by a sound he'd later describe as 'like a large zinc bath dropping onto the deck of the wardroom bathroom alongside of which I slept.'

Wondering what was going on, Kerr sat up in his hammock, saw others moving about, got up and did the same, heard the bosun's mate pipe 'Magazine Party take magazine temperatures.' An Able Seaman came along and told Kerr that the anchor cable had run out; but someone else said an air bottle in the CO_2 room had blown up.

Kerr finished dressing and hurried off, heard again someone say 'CO_2 bottle has exploded.'

That was the most common rumour, although the presence on main deck of stoker Herbert R. Johnston now did a little to quash it. Johnston had just left the refrigerating room where the bottles were stored, had jotted in the engine room register his hourly readings when he heard a terrific explosion, was reminded at once of the *Vanguard* disaster*: 'I thought we'd blown up. I thought we'd hit a mine, and then I decided that there had been an air-raid, that a bomb had hit the forecastle, so I closed down the machinery, shut the doors and the hatches and went up on the main deck. When I got up on deck the people there seemed to think that there was probably on explosion in the Paint Store, or the

* The battleship HMS *Vanguard*, anchored alongside *Royal Oak* in Scapa, blew up from a cordite explosion on the night of 9 July, 1917, with a loss of more than 700 men. Only one officer and two ratings survived.

Inflammable Store just forward. In the meantime, all very gas-conscious, I decided to go and get my gas-mask.'

On his way down Johnston passed the stokers' mess decks, found men sleeping, a few stirring, most growing irritated at the disruption.

Said a Leading Stoker to some men moving: 'Why don't you lot quiet down so that we can get some sleep.' ('Alas, he was not a survivor,' Johnston would later lament).

Johnston picked up his gas mask, continued forward 'intending to return below to restart the refrigerators.' But now he found a fair crowd about; 'so I decided to hang back a little until they'd thinned out. I did not hurry as I knew every little noise would frighten me the remainder of that watch.'

Amidships, where sprawled the boiler and engine rooms and central stores, taking up huge areas of space, the explosion was felt only slightly, though it awoke many men suddenly. Marine Corporal John Arthur Payton, in his hammock on the port side of the boat-hoist flat, awakened immediately, sat straight up in his hammock, looked at his watch: four minutes past one. Sailors sleeping near him were roused too, asked about the commotion; but only a few turned out, most went back to sleep, as did Payton.

Farther aft, in the Royal Marines' messes at either side of the ship, between 'X' and 'Y' barbettes, men felt the *Oak* shudder, sat up in their hammocks, cast questioning glances at one another.

Under the quarter-deck, in the band locker flat just forward of the portside Marines mess deck, soundly slept members of the Royal Marine band who a few hours earlier had been playing for 'Guest Night' in the wardroom. While the officers had gathered and taken their drinks, the band had played 'The Roast Beef of Old England,' then a set routine, a march, an overture, and a number of selections timed to last throughout the dinner, after which the King had been toasted, the national anthem played, each member of the band given a bottle of beer from the wardroom pantry.

Harold J. Wernham, who played violin and B♭ tenor saxophone, awoke to shouting—'Explosion forward! The heads are flooded! The cable has run out!' And just then he heard a pipe come over the loudspeaker: 'Magazine testing parties close up.' Wernham had no idea what had caused the explosion, just thought to himself, 'Whatever has happened, I shouldn't think that the band would be required at this time of night.'

Before falling back to slumber, he turned to the musician in the next hammock, H. A. G. Kelly, who played cornet and violin, and asked, 'Is it still Friday the thirteenth?'

Kelly rubbed his eyes, looked at his watch, replied 'No, it's now quarter past one Saturday morning.'

A little farther aft, Marine A. R. Jordan, attired only in a khaki drill shirt and wristwatch, was forced out of his sleep by the bos'n mate piping 'Temperature parties to the temperatures of magazines!' Then he heard a voice saying 'That sounds like a depth charge explosion in the Flow.'

Jordan would remember later: 'Taking no further interest, I dropped off to sleep again but before doing so wondered why I had not heard that specific pipe on other nights.'

Marine Sergeant George H. Booth, the duty NCO who had been sitting on the Sergeant's Mess settee, was thrown to the deck by the blast, got up, smelled a whiff of fumes coming through the air intake, hurried onto the Marines' mess deck, then thought of the prisoners, two men locked in the cell flat right forward near the cable locker flat. He headed through the seamen's mess deck to reach them, while in various parts of the ship, others as well, including Regulating Petty Officers John Henry Smith and Walter Phillips, got the same thought, rushed quickly forward to release the men.

Smith was the first to reach the prisoners—it was he who released them—and when seconds later Phillips and Booth arrived, moments apart, they found the prisoners gone, also the sentry; but also the deck plates of the flat sprung, thick yellow smoke seeping through.

Below lay the torpedo warheads and the refrigerating machinery containing dangerous CO_2 bottles. Perhaps, thought Booth, as he gazed at the smoke, one of the warheads had exploded. He took off, heading aft, quickly through the seamen's mess deck, now clearing of smoke.

About this time, near the cell flat, Ordinary Seaman Vincent Maurice Marchant, eighteen, dressed only in vest and shorts, came running up, saw men rushing forward to the cell flat and paint locker. He heard the pipe 'Stokers Fire Party!', an order to deal with smoke coming from below; but not being involved, he rushed onto the upper deck, found the AA twin 4-inch gun crew calmly speculating about what might have happened. One of the crewmen, he remembered, said it could be 'a bomb dropped from a great height.' Then the Master-at-Arms gave orders to clear the scene, dismissing the whole thing as a minor matter: all onlookers were to turn in.

Marchant began to do so, heading for the fore messdeck, but before starting down he noticed something unusual over the port rail: the forward 15-inch guns' white blast bags, which had been taken off and painted the previous day, had been blown overboard and were floating in the sea alongside.

Below armour level, Booth was still running aft. 'Air Raid!' he heard someone shout, saw men hurrying to the air raid space, which was covered by a large armoured door, in the centre of which was a manhole, large enough to allow only one man at a time to pass through.

Continuing on aft to the Marines' messdeck, Booth noticed men still in their hammocks, unmindful of the commotion, or not caring about it.

'Clear the lower deck!' Booth ordered.

There were moans of objection.

'Bugger off,' he heard someone shout back.

In a small locker space about fifteen feet below the waterline, another Marine, Corporal Norman T. ('Taffy') Davies, a Gunner's Mate, was lying in his bunk, after finishing a letter to his wife when he felt the ship shudder, saw cockroaches fall from the deckhead above.

'What the hell is that?' said Davies.

'CO_2 machine blown up,' came an answer from someone passing by.

'I was a little apprehensive to say the least,' Davies would remember. 'But having got this far, I dressed and thought I would get up and have a look to see what was happening. But like all people, you're afraid to show you're nervous. So I headed for the night "heads," the lavatories on the battery deck!'

Before leaving Davies shook a fellow sleeper, Warrant Officer Frank Williams; but Williams, not entirely awake, heard only Davies mutter something about 'a bump forrad,' turned over, went back to sleep, Davies moved out: 'There was a hatchway going up to the 6-inch gundeck, and at the after end of the port battery there was this little urinal, large enough for just two fellows, but there were fifty men lined up. "Oh, Christ," I thought, "I could wait here all night for that bloody lot to finish, two at a time." So I decided to go to the main heads, right forward on the fo'c'sle, right up in the 'eyes of the ship.' Along the way, on the port side of the quarter-deck, saw a friend, the corporal of the watch, said to him 'What the hell was that?'

'We've heard it was a CO_2 machine going up,' came the reply, as farther forward Davies headed, careful as he stepped: 'It was as dark as a cow's guts, contrary to this story about the Northern Lights.' But with eyes accustomed to the dark he saw a familiar shape emerge from the darkness: the drifter *Daisy II*, a Scottish fishing boat taken over by the Admiralty, tied now by bow and stern lines to the battleship's port boom, just aft of the last two 15-inch guns in 'Y' barbette and slightly abaft a second small vessel, a steam picket boat which lay opposite a third vessel, a large motor launch at the starboard boom. Still another small boat, sitting high and dry on the *Oak* (waiting for a paint job she'd never get), was the captain's gig, covered and fitted in chocks on the quarter-deck aft.

The sudden impact of the explosion had rocked little *Daisy*, making her civilian skipper, John C. Gatt, jump from his bunk, climb on deck in his underwear to speak to the Marine officer of the watch.

The *Oak*'s officer saw Gatt first, shouted down to him, 'What's happened to your boiler, skipper?'

This astounded Gatt. 'No,' he yelled back, 'I think it's one of your big guns.'

For a moment the two men stood staring at each other; then the *Oak*'s commander, the second in command, Captain R. F. Nichols, appeared on the scene, looked down on *Daisy*, unaware that by a thread was his life hanging—for the second time in Scapa Flow. A young Midshipman on *Vanguard*, he was living this day only because on the night that battleship had blown up he was attending a concert-party presented by *Royal Oak* sailors on the theatre ship *Gourko* and missed his boat to the doomed *Vanguard* when the show lasted longer than intended. Awakened now on *Royal Oak* by the shattering thuds abaft, he had quickly donned clothes, sprang to the deck, at once noted, as later he'd remember, 'a faint aurora by which I could see the outline of the land against the sky and men moving about the deck, but not distinctly enough to recognise them.' Spotting *Daisy,* he gave orders for her to raise steam, then called for the picket boat's and launch's crews to man their vessels.

Hearing 'Away launch's crew!' piped in the *Oak*, Leading Seaman John Goodlad, coxswain of the launch, who had been moving aimlessly around the seamen's recreation space on the main deck, trying to find out what was happening, headed below deck to retrieve his greatcoat and whistle. John Gatt, meanwhile, had hastened below in *Daisy* to put on his trousers and jersey and to alert his five crewmen—a mate, two deckhands, a cook, an engineer.

Far aft, far from the hurt up front, the *Oak* had shuddered, shook strangely, men pitched from bunks, got up, stood stunned, or slept —did nothing but sleep. In the most remote cabin, next door to his office, Paymaster Lieutenant W. E. Sandifer had been ejected four feet from his bunk to the deck, amid shattered glass fixtures and fittings: 'Still in pyjamas I entered the officers' cabin flat immediately forward of mine and was soon joined by several of the occupants with a general "What the hell was the explosion all about?" Most of them returned to their cabins leaving duty officers to sort things out.'

Sandifer did not share the general indifferent reaction of the officers around him; he quickly slipped into his uniform, put on cap and blue raincoat, and set off toward the wardroom in quest of information.

Another officer, Engineer Commander J. W. Renshaw, the man whom Captain Benn had ordered up to the fo'c'sle, was at this moment climbing to the Admiral's lobby on the main deck after inspecting the steering compartment below the officer's cabin area. Renshaw had not yet received the order from Benn and in the lobby he came face to face with the Rear Admiral of the 2nd Battle Squadron, Henry Evelyn Charles Blagrove, a small but brawny man, with sleek grey hair, piercing eyes, a 'passenger' really on the *Oak*, albeit a very distinguished passenger, who had been jolted awake by a rumbling he thought had come from immediately beneath the afterpart of the ship.

Fifty-two years old, sailoring since the age of fifteen, Blagrove

had been well-known through the early part of his naval career as
a fine athlete—as a young lieutenant he had been the shining light
of the United Services Rugby football team ('Small of stature, he
was amazingly fast and as an insignificant-looking wing,' it would
be said in his obituary which was to come out in five days, 'three-
quarters of his speed was ever a surprise to opponents who had
not known him earlier'). Blagrove had been a Rear Admiral for
only ten months and had not the war broke out he would have
been serving a shore appointment for which he had just been
selected, as Admiral Superintendent of the Dockyard at Chatham.

In the Admiral's lobby of the *Oak*, Renshaw and Blagrove exchanged salutes, and Blagrove in a voice that was calm said, 'That
came from directly below us. Locate what it is, Engineer Commander.'

'I agree, Sir,' responded Renshaw, who turned and walked
quickly away, down to the Tiller Flat, where he found Warrant
Engineer Dunstone already there, of the same mind, both fully ex-
pecting to find the compartment flooded. As Dunstone watched,
Renshaw cautiously opened the watertight door, stood by while
Dunstone opened the sliding door.

Slowly Renshaw descended into the flat, searched, looked
around, found nothing amiss; so he left and waited while Dunstone shut both doors and both officers went to the Admiral,
Renshaw reporting: 'All is in order aft.'

Blagrove was puzzled; but not overly alarmed: with Renshaw
and Dunstone he climbed to the quarter-deck, found his coxswain,
A. W. Scarff, asked him: 'What do you know about this, Coxswain?'

Scarff, who messed opposite the cable locker, replied, 'The explosion was in the centre line of the ship, fore-side of the cable
lockers and the ship is unmoored, Sir.'

For a few moments Blagrove stood chatting with Renshaw,
then he told him 'I'm going for'ard to have a look.' The Admiral
handed his torch to Scarff, both proceeded to the forecastle, while
Renshaw and Dunstone made for the Marines' messdeck.

At this moment, inspecting the vacant Admiral's office flat, and
adjacent compartments, was Lieutenant Commander T. P. Wisden. He had been sitting in the staff office on the starboard side of
the officers' cabin flat when suddenly he had felt the shock, a violent athwartship—side to side—movement, saw books and papers

and other paraphernalia fly to the deck. 'I personally feel that the ship listed slightly to port after the first explosion,' he'd testify later; but now he was just hurrying to the quarter-deck to find out what happened. The quarter-deck staff didn't know, so Wisden proceeded to the Admiral's lobby to make his inspection. Then finding no damage, the Admiral gone, Wisden, like Renshaw and Dunstone, headed for the Marines' messdeck.

Other officers scurried about in haste. At the main switchboard aft a group that included the assistant torpedo officer, Sub-Lieutenant Kenneth Bernard Clayton, and warrant electrician Frank Bulley, were investigating a report by the switchboard watchkeeper who upon hearing the explosion had immediately checked his meters, noted a rise in voltage, which indicated a drop in load. Wondering if the explosion had affected the ship electrically, Clayton and Bulley descended to the dynamo rooms, first to number four, where everything checked normal, then to number three, where again load readings on ammeters agreed with log readings taken earlier, at precisely 1 a.m., four minutes before the explosion. So the blast, whatever it was, had not affected the ship electrically: the watchkeeper's report of a drop in load simply was not borne out by the check on log and ammeters.

To the officers at the switchboard, there seemed nothing at all amiss in the battleship.

Approximately ten minutes had passed since the explosion, and still very quiet lay the *Oak*, yet at Air Defence Stations, a condition which put an abnormally large number of the ship's company of 1200 below the main armoured deck. Not only the crew but part of the Damage Control Parties were sleeping at stations below. And because the ship was due to raise anchor at dawn, more engine room and stokehold ratings also slept below than normal, most sacked out in the battery and mess decks amidships and aft.

As Blagrove and Scarff, Renshaw and Dunstone, were making their separate ways forward, more men began to make trails, singly, or in two's or three's, to the night 'heads.' The sound of men moving, shuffling up and down ladders, muttering curses, mixed with orders piped over the loudspeaker and statements reflecting the general air of confusion that permeated the ship. Men bumped into each other, looked at one another, said nothing at all, or passed on the rumours now going about.

'Compressed air bottle blown up.'

'A bomb's fallen.'

'Explosion in the Inflammable Store.'

'Explosion in the Paint Store.'

'Trouble right forrad.'

'A trawler bumped us—no worry.'

In the Marines' port mess deck, Royal Marine A. J. Wheatland was trying hard to get back to sleep; he lay in the nude, half asleep, so tired from the day's work of loading stores that the loud blast he'd heard had not even registered as an explosion: 'I suppose I was a bit dozed and thought that the drifter *Daisy* had bumped against the side of the ship. She was usually moored on the port side aft below the Marines mess deck.'

To Wheatland there did not appear to be any undue scene of activity about, but the Tannoy System was switched on and he heard a voice say: 'Shall I pipe hands to action stations, Sir?'

There was no answer. The Tannoy went off, Wheatland heard no orders, saw no damage, so dropped off to sleep again, like hundreds of others.

For most not making for the night 'heads,' the main problem remained getting back to sleep. Like many others, L. H. Tunnicliff, who found his mess so hot that he slept in the nude, had heard the anchor cables roar, jumped from his hammock to don clothes but then got the order: 'Everyone turn back in your hammocks. Gunners party take temperatures of magazines!'

'So I did so,' Tunnicliff would remember, 'I thought it must have been an explosion in the CO_2 Store where most of the cases went early on' (referring to the ship's stores he'd been detailed to load in the darkness a few hours before). 'Ratings were running around but I had no time for conversation with them.' Tunnicliff turned back in.

Which is what the Boy Seamen in the 6-inch gun casement were doing right about this time. One of them, Boy First Class Douglas Newton, only sixteen, who had never liked the keen discipline aboard the *Oak,* hated being forbidden to talk to older ratings unless he was working, who had been lugging cans of Carnation milk to a hatch up forward, all through the afternoon of the 13th, was now trying to sleep, trying to dismiss the explosion as a near miss from an aircraft; while farther forward, in the Boys' mess, other lads were turning back in, after their duty Petty Officer (shouting 'What the hell was that?') had got them up, then decided no cause for alarm.

On deck, Boy Edward R. Britt, among others, had had no chance to turn in. At the time of the explosion he'd been closed up as a look-out at the Air Defence Position, had felt the ship give a shudder, but reacted as though nothing at all had happened—'I had just been to sea for a week onboard this ship in very heavy seas and noise or shuddering of the ship just seemed to be natural. After a chin wag with the ADP crew, it was decided that the cause of the explosion or noise was the forward anchor cable running out—the bottlescrew stop had not been applied correctly.'

By now, 'Taffy' Davies was well forward, walking the fo'c'sle, heading for a hatchway down to a night 'head,' when just abaft the barbette of 'B' turret he heard people up on the fo'c'sle working: 'I couldn't see a bloody thing, heard talking and giving orders, and clanking of metal, thought I'm not going to go wading through that shower; I was not very anxious about going down below again, I must admit, and so I took out a Craven A, went inside the screen door to light it, then stood on the upper deck thinking "What the bloody hell is all this about?"'

A fellow came up, said 'What the hell is happening, Royal?'

'I dunno, Stokes,' Davies said. 'I heard there was an explosion down in the CO_2 machine.'

'There bloody well wasn't,' said the stoker, 'because I've just come up from there to find out what's wrong.'

Nearby in the recreation space, Ordinary Seaman Philip Arthur White, a member of the Air Defence Watch and a crew of the port pom-pom, an eight-barrelled anti-aircraft gun, was trying hard to relax, felt, like others, that 'the Commander and all those people in charge would sort out what that first explosion was.'

But White was worried: lying on a mess table in the rec space just before midnight, more than an hour before the explosion, he had awakened suddenly 'with a tremendous feeling of apprehension and panic,' and as he'd say years later, 'a premonition that something terrible was going to happen: I was shaking, in a cold sweat, akin with fright. I somehow shook this off and carried on sleeping but it was an uncanny experience which I have never experienced before or since.'

Captain Nichols, who had now joined Captain Benn up forward, could see by the light of the aurora that the Blake slip stopper on the port cable had parted and the cable had run out to a 'clinch.' He chatted briefly with Benn and, satisfied that the *Oak* was not listing, nor settling down by the bows, both officers climbed down the after forecastle hatch, aft of 'B' turret on the way to the cable locker flat two decks below, still feeling no uneasiness about the safety of the ship, unmindful of the countless little dramas being played out throughout her.

In the Sick Bay, on the starboard side between 'A' and 'B' turrets, attendant Reg ('Lefty') Bendell, who had slept through the explosion, was being prodded awake by a voice pleading for him to wake up and mend a cut knee. Bendell felt no urgency but raised himself up, stretched out his six foot three frame, began to dress the small cut on the sailor's leg, casually asked him where the cut came from. The sailor said there had been an explosion—it had sent him flying from his hammock and the ship was sinking.

Bendell dismissed this as nonsense, and when moments later he heard it whispered that a carbon dioxide gas bottle had gone up, he shrugged off the sailor's warning, saw no reason why he shouldn't go back to sleep. He told the sailor to see the Medical Officer in the morning and headed back to his cot, moments later was dozing again.

Just forward of the 6-inch gun deck, in the small supply and writers mess, Leading Supply Assistant Frank Gordon Sims, who on the morning of the 13th had taken a party of sailors to a store depot ship to collect meat and butter and, dead tired, had turned in early, about ten o'clock, had felt panic on hearing the explosion —'as all know that in a battleship you are virtually sitting on an ammunition dump.'

Perhaps, he thought, another ship had bumped alongside 'because the *Oak* shuddered slightly.' He was dressed in pyjamas but did not get up, instead called to his mate, L.S.A. Hyde, asked him what he thought the trouble was.

'Oh, go to sleep,' replied Hyde.

'Presumably,' Sims would recall, 'he went on sleeping, because I never saw him again, although he was a very good swimmer.'

Lieutenant Commander Roper, the *Oak*'s Gunnery Officer, now responding to the 'Temperature parties!' pipe, forming a magazine temperature party to check against the possibility of explosion, was the same officer who on the day war had been declared, had mustered his men, given them a pep talk with the opening words, 'Well, lads, this is what we have been training for, and now we are to put it to the test.'

Eleven more days and Roper would be dead.

In a hammock in the passage outside the starboard seaman's mess, Leading Seaman William P. Casey, awakened by a 'terrific jerk,' had sat up, puzzled: 'Everything was normal, the fans for ventilation and the electric motors were running, the lights were on—it was all a mystery.' Then after a few minutes Casey heard from his chum, John Harty, with whom that evening in the Royal Hotel in Kirkwall he'd had a couple of drinks: 'Come on Tim, let's go and find out what's happened.'

Casey swung from his hammock, dressed, and with Harty he climbed to the Torpedo Flat: 'When we arrived there it was very hazy with what seemed like a thin mist of blue smoke. The flat was filling up with men and there was a peculiar smell. Everyone was asking, "What is it?" A Chief Stoker came aft from forrad and we asked him. He said it was "a CO_2 gas bottle exploded down in the fridge compartment." Then Leading Seaman Draper came along and said that the heads up forrad was in a terrible state, the deck was bucked, doors off and the urinals smashed.'

Like many others Casey was only half-dressed, prepared for nothing like this, wearing socks, trousers, jersey, a pair of fleecy-lined slippers just received from his wife ('I felt proud of them; they must have been the best on the lower deck'); the thick stocking-shaped scarf that had come with the slippers he'd given to another friend, Harry Farmer, with whom he used to work opposite and who before going on the 8 o'clock watch had said to Casey 'That's a lovely scarf, we can share it when we are on the watch.'

Casey and Harty retraced their steps to their mess, followed by others, who hung about in a group, talking about all the fuss, and after a while Casey announced he was turning in—he had to be up at six, so needed his sleep.

He'd survive, but see neither scarf nor Farmer again.

In the officer's cabin area there dozed a reluctant guest, chief cook to Admiral Forbes who had missed the boat to *Iron Duke*—when on the way back to Scapa Pier from an afternoon in Kirkwall his bus had been halted by a conductor trying to collect the 6d fare from two of *Oak*'s stokers, slightly intoxicated after three hours of beer drinking in Kirkwall. The stokers had spent all the money they'd received that day—pay day on *Royal Oak*—and were still arguing with the conductor when Warrant Officer Frank Williams in his own special small bus had pulled up behind the stopped vehicle, on investigation had found the cause of the delay, paid the stokers' fares himself.

The cook's bus pushed on but arrived too late to make the tender to Forbes' flagship; so Williams had taken the cook with him on *Daisy*, now rocking with men in good cheer, singing the usual naval songs, one in particular, 'There's a tidilly ship on the ocean so blue, she's steaming by night and by day (the *Oak* was sailing at six the next morning) . . .' and finishing up, 'Roll on the *Nelson*, the *Hood*, this one-funnelled hook pot is getting me down.' ('And there was the moaning,' remembered one of the riders that day 'What the Captain and the Commander were called dare not be put in writing'), Williams arranged with the *Oak*'s officer of the watch to make a signal to *Iron Duke*, letting them know the cook was aboard; whereupon *Duke* signalled back they'd send a boat over in the morning.

'If the bus hadn't been held up, the chief cook would have caught his own boat,' as Williams would later complete the story. 'As it was, it wasn't to be.'

For want of a shilling, the cook would die.

Paymaster Sub-Lieutenant G. R. Harrison, staying up late to open on this Saturday, his birthday, a present received from his wife, on holiday in Kirkwall, was censoring letters, tinkering about with a camera in his mess with some other officers.

'I awakened some of the men who had not heard the explosion. I had the present in my pocket, and as we had entered the actual birthday I began to open the parcel, and then somehow changed my mind after taking off the string. I walked up to the deck, taking the present with me.'

His fellow officers would die. Harrison would live.

When Nichols and Benn reached the cable locker flat, they found that Ward had been joined by Renshaw and Dunstone, plus half a dozen other officers, including Senior Engineer Officer Clark and Warrant Engineer Whitebread. A man in a smoke helmet, on the way down to investigate the Inflammable Store, brushed by the officers, who now entered the locker flat, looked around, walked forwards to two horizontal hatches, opened them, peered down, heard the unmistakable sound of pure air escaping freely, hissing loudly from the Store's ventilation pipe. At this moment Chief Stoker Farr came up to Benn, reported that the compartment immediately abaft the Inflammable Store, the CO_2 room, was intact —dry and closed up. And so, as Benn would later explain, to the Board of Enquiry, 'the very strong force of opinion formed by myself, my Engineer Commander, the Senior Engineer, Lieutenant Moore, and my Damage Control Officers, indicated that the damage was in the very fore part of the ship and we were all of opinion that some explosion must have occurred in the Inflammable Store from internal causes.'

It was assumed that an explosion had caused the Store to flood —when in fact Commissioned-Gunner James T. Pearce, the Duty Officer, who had just completed a round and was passing through the Sick Bay flat on his way back to the Gunnery Office when he heard the explosion, ordered the Store flooded when the duty ERA told him the blast had originated in the Store.

'It never seemed a minor explosion to me; I thought the Inflammable Store had gone up,' Pearce later would say.

So they had localised the trouble, at least thought they had. Benn considered giving instructions for closing any doors that might be opened—he knew that half the vertical doors in the ship were closed for air defence purposes; but it never occurred to him to close anything more 'as I realised,' he'd later say, 'we had everything closed except those particular doors and hatches which were necessary for communications.'

The ship's trim had not been affected, the lights were still on, and Benn felt in fact rather relieved that if there had been an explosion in the Inflammable Store, water was coming in.

'We have everything closed here,' he remarked, 'don't open up anything more.'

Not for an instant did Benn consider the possibility of attack by

Motor Torpedo Boat, surface craft, or submarine without warning.* The *Oak,* he knew, leaked constantly, some of her ventilating trunks had no valves in them, fractures in various trunks would flood adjacent compartments, and more than once, Lieutenant 'Pony' Moore, his ventilation and watertight compartments officer, had confided in him the thought that the *Oak* would not stand up to one torpedo under her bottom (earlier that very day Moore had remarked to Frank Williams, while the two casually had strolled the quarter-deck, that if he had a German submarine he'd 'put a torpedo into half-a-dozen big ships of the fleet, then scuttle and surrender'). No need whatsoever, thought Benn, to order men to battle stations—in line with Article 112 in the Damage Control Handbook:

When an attack is known to be imminent, the ship should be brought to the battle state immediately. At other times, the ship should be maintained as close to the battle state as possible, due provision being made for the comfort and health of the personnel, the care and maintenance of the ship, and the requirements for training and instructions.

With nothing apparently to fear, Benn gave orders to start the salvage pumps, prepare to open and examine the damaged compartments; and with that, the officers in the small group around him began discussing the type of pump to use.

'Start "A" Number 15, 350-ton pump,' ordered Warrant Engineer Edward Whitebread to Chief Stoker Farr.

Since the explosion, almost twelve minutes had passed. At no time was any action taken to close scuttles, watertight doors or deadlights; no air alarm was sounded, indeed no precaution of any kind was taken. Wide open were a large number of scuttles, or portholes, which had been fitted with light-excluding ventilators, to allow fresh air in; not waterproof, they were intended only for use in the safety of harbour.

Like a sleeping giant the *Royal Oak* lay. The torpedo had struck her starboard anchor cable, splintered her bow; but she

---

* 'My reason for holding this opinion,' he'd later tell the Board of Enquiry, 'was that I was anchored in the main fleet base. A point which is worth bringing out, when the Commander-in-Chief was in harbour he invariably detailed ships for AA Guard but not for any other Guard.'

bore no sense of wound. Her shaded anchor lights still burned, her guns, though quiet, pointed ever-menacing barrels seaward.

It was 1.15 a.m.

In the aft engine room of *U-47* Obermaschinists Gefreiter Herbert Herrmann and Willi Loh stood at tube five waiting for the firing order from Endrass. On the bridge the towering column of water had been seen. But that was all; no sign of any real explosion, the silhouettes of the two ships, designated only 'northern' and 'southern' by Prien, still stood out against the bleak hills, neither vessel looking at all disturbed.

Three 'eels' had been fired, two definite misses, only the third had exploded, and that well up front, on the bows of the farther 'northern' ship, as Prien, mistaken, had thought: he suspected no hit at all on the nearer, 'southern' ship. It was as though the *Englisch* still slept, not aware even that they were under attack: no searchlights scanned water or sky, no signals made, from either ship.

Prien raked the sea with his binoculars. Endrass hunched over the aim optic, again took the range, sent down the firing instructions, the orders the same as they had been in the forward torpedo room 'Flood Number Five!' 'Number Five is getting flooded from Tank Number One' 'Number Five is Flooded' 'Open outer door' 'Open outer door' 'Outer door is open' 'Number Five is ready.'

'*Los!*'

'Number Five has fired,' said Herrmann, then 'Torpedo has left tube. Torpedo is running.'

'Close outer door!'

'Outer door closing.'

'Outer door is closed.'

'Tube is secured.'

Torpedo fired from stern, Prien would jot in his log.

Loh and Herrmann could hear the torpedo running: but again no hit: so 'eel' number four had missed.

Four shots, three misses, only one hit. It was inconceivable to the men on the bridge that a submarine could fire four torpedoes at a stationary target, see only one hit, even that take little effect, more astonishing that no alarm had been given.

U-47 was like a boat taking target practice; only the 'targets' were ships of the Home Fleet.

'The English had not yet done anything,' as Hänsel would later say, 'so we turned around and attacked a second time.'

'Reload the tubes,' Prien ordered, as the slender prow of his boat moved closer on target.

Preparing for another fan of three, from tubes one, two, and five, the hands in the forward room pulled down the chain hoist from overhead, pushed the long 'eels' into the waiting empty tubes. As soon as the first tube had been reloaded, word was passed to the bridge.

When all three tubes were ready, Prien ordered an attack broadside on the nearer of the two vessels. *U-47*'s bow pointed forward once more. Again, for the third time, Endrass bent over the aim optic, again took the measure of the sleeping giant, again the orders to fire, tube doors swung open, 'eels' jumping out.

Three torpedoes from the bow.

5

The Gates of Hell

In *Royal Oak* in the cable locker flat there stood the senior officers, still waiting for word on the cause of the explosion but comforted now by a sort of gratification that the long spell of quiet had augured well for their ship—when suddenly, at 1.16 a.m., the quiet was shattered: the thunder of another explosion, more forceful than the first, flung men upon men, pushed shoulders and arms up against the small compartment's steel sides, poured looks of fright into widened eyes.

The *Oak* shuddered; after a short interval, about one or two seconds, perhaps three—exactly how many no one ever would agree—there came another explosion, then another, each equally violent, booming fatal thumps down the starboard side, between 'A' and 'Y' turrets and taking immediate and catastrophic effect: the ship lifted, then settled back, the officers stared with horror, countenances smitten by the revelation that the impossible was happening.*

Lights flickered, slowly faded, fans stopped humming, power failed, putting the broadcasting system out of action, too late already for Captain Benn or Commander Nichols to command 'Abandon ship!'

'Clear out!' Benn shouted as in the darkness men tottered, made for safety, heading aft, along the port side, on decks fast-tilting, so soon heeling over to starboard.

'Get up on the fo'c'sle!' Benn shouted.

* The claim of 'sabotage,' totally without foundation but still clung to by a small fraction of *Oak* survivors, is based mainly on the fact that civilian workers had loaded stores all through the 13th and the explosions occurred, as Alexander McKee implied in his book *Black Saturday*, 'from the direction of the storerooms and outside areas where stores had been put.' As borne out by the new evidence, this is misleading, the explosions striking abreast or about the boiler, dynamo, and engine room.

There was a sudden rush for the forward hatch.

'Steady, steady,' someone urged coolly.

'No panic!' exclaimed Benn, who remembered the *Weymouth,** at once felt the *Oak* had been torpedoed—although 'I had nothing to guide me in that respect—it was only an impression.'

The list increased, a warrant officer turned to Renshaw, asked, 'What is to be done?'

Renshaw, who was following Benn, replied, 'Nothing can save her now.'

In a moment, Benn, Nichols, Renshaw and other officers and men staggered onto the fo'c'sle and 'B' gun deck nearby. They could see, anyone could see, the *Oak* was going over; she lay, even now, at a fair angle—ten to twelve degrees—in minutes she might sink. Officers and seamen frantically began heaving over the side, for swimmers to grab, heavy Carley floats, oars, empty petrol drums, 'church deals'—long wooden planks put down for church services—and anything else they could find.

'I was quite convinced the ship was going over—she was going so quick,' Benn would tell the Board of Enquiry. He moved quickly aft, met men coming up onto the fo'c'sle, ordered them to get out the Carley rafts. But, 'by then there was very little time to do it.' The rafts were simply too heavy; they didn't just slide over the side, as ideally they should have, but rested in chocks out of which they had to be lifted. 'The men made up their minds that their only hope was to go over the side,' said Benn.

Commander Nichols made for the 'B' gun deck, to ring the signal house on the flag deck; he told them to make a general signal on the projector to send all boats; but the reply he got back was that it was too late, impossible without power: all power had failed.

Commander Gregory rushed to the boat deck to see if there was any hope of getting a cutter or anything else over the side. There was not; he scrambled aft, was thrown against a motor boat, thickly slimy with oil fuel.

'I crawled to the after ladder and so down to the quarter deck, where by now there was a considerable quantity of smoke or fumes.'

At this time Renshaw, stepping aft along the port side and past

---

* Benn had seen the British cruiser *Weymouth*, the ship astern his, torpedoed in World War I near the Austrian naval base at Durazzo.

'B' turret, then onto the quarter deck, perceived in the darkness
the dim form of Blagrove, the Admiral's mouth partially agape,
his face wearing the piteous expression of disbelief.

'What caused those explosions do you think?' asked the Admiral.

'Torpedoes, Sir,' replied the engineer commander directly.

'My God,' gasped Blagrove, who turned away, towards the
bridge, and melted into the darkness.

Across the decks crashed columns of water shot up by the three
torpedoes—'first spray and then a big shower,' remembered Leonard Soal. Sub-Lieutenant Anthony Henry Pearman, standing on
the afterpart of the compass platform, saw the water shoot over
him, then stared in amazement as a sheet of orange flame flashed
from beneath the deck and curled around the starboard side of the
funnel casing, then up the casing.

The ship listed immediately. Thick black smoke rolled over the
after port of the ship. The odour of burning cordite fouled the air.
Bulkheads shook, decks collapsed, balls of fire roared from forward to aft, hungrily searching the open air. Everywhere cries of
horror. Men blown through doors, from hammocks, up hatches,
out scuttles, flung from ladders, swallowed alive by flames—all this
within the first sixty seconds of the last torpedo.

In some parts of the ship, secondary lighting and power came on—
amazingly, some men remained unaware of the impending disaster. On the lower deck, nicely settled in his hammock in the passage outside the seamen's mess, Leading Seaman William Casey
felt at first a 'shuddering dull explosion' that seemed to come from
underneath:

'It lifted the ship out of the water and then she settled down
again on an even keel. I sat up at once as did the rest of us. Some
got out of their hammocks right away and got dressed and were
off, but once again everything became normal—ventilation shafts
and the electric motors were going, lighting was normal and we
were talking about it in our hammocks. Someone wondered if it
was the starboard 6-inch magazine that had blown up.'

Casey now heard another explosion, then another, the third,
then from under the deck a rush of water, like a sea breaking
on board, water crashing through the light-excluding ventilators—

thin plywood things fixed by butterfly nuts in every porthole on all decks (except the Admiral's office flat deck right aft which lay very close to the water).

Casey jumped from his hammock; and not waiting to dress or get his money belt with his pay in it he took off. The midship hatches, he remembered, were closed 'for safety reasons.' Many watertight doors were closed. So he ran forward, to the cross passage abaft 'A' turret, then he crossed to a hatch at the fore end of the lower deck which led up to the Sick Bay and torpedo flats.

Casey reached the hatch but found a queue of desperate men shouting, pushing to get up the hatch, the one open at the fore end of the lower deck. 'Everyone was scrambling up the ladder as quick as they could, as if going to action stations.'

Casey had no choice, waited his turn, made it up just before the heavy door slid over with the heel of the ship, completely sealing the fore end of the lower deck. Then he ran, scampering for the hatch leading to the fo'c'sle abaft 'A' turret at midships, heading through the Sick Bay—not noticing the sick berth attendant, Reg Bendell, who had been blown out of his hammock, sent dazed to the deck.

Bendell felt the ship's heel with increasing velocity, heard someone yell to clear out, as he groped for a jacket, felt for the pay in a pocket, then with Sick Berth Petty Officer Henry Main he tried to reach the upper deck by a ladder near the Sick Bay. Up the now steeply angling ladder they scrambled, but found the sliding armoured hatch closed. For their lives, they pushed, but the hatch would not move, not even budge. So Bendell and Main gave up, began to head aft, only to find sheets of flame pouring toward them from the vents of the cordite store below. The flames missed Bendell and Main but caught several others, turned them into human torches.

In the confusion Bendell lost contact with PO Main. He stumbled into the pantry of the petty officers' mess, heard crockery breaking all about, found a porthole, saw the sky, no land: but the sheer delight in seeing the stars would be something he'd never forget.

William Casey, meanwhile, found he could not open the manhole cover of the hatch leading up to the fo'c'sle deck abaft 'A' turret; it was closed tight. Desperately he banged at the clips. They wouldn't budge. So he turned aft, ran through the armoured door into the port 6-inch battery—when 'a blast of very hot air caught me and took me about nine feet backwards.' Casey steadied himself, headed aft, climbed a ladder into the galley flat; as far as he can remember he was on his own going up:

'When I got up to the flat I went to the midship ladders leading up to the boat deck just before the funnel. There were a lot of men coming up from the starboard battery. One ladder led to starboard, the other to port and everyone was going up the starboard ladder. Rather than wait, I went up the port one.

'It was hard work climbing it and when I got to the boat deck I decided to go to the port side of the ship—all the others were going to starboard. I climbed the deck to the port seaboat which was turned inboard and stood by the side of it wondering what to do. I looked around, and saw no one. The fo'c'sle seemed deserted, likewise the port side of the boat deck. I looked up at the spotting top on the fore mast and I could see it moving to starboard against the starry sky, and with that I decided to get off the ship.'

Most men, and boys, had yet to escape their messes. Frank Williams, who long had forgotten that 'bump forward' described by Taffy Davies, was jerked from his slumber by the new explosions, thought at once that 'something was really wrong—probably German aircraft bombs.'

Williams jumped from his bunk, slipped on his jacket and slippers, was too excited to remember to put on the new gold wristwatch his mother had bought him in Wallace's in Victoria Street in Douglas: 'Then the lights went out, pitch black and three decks down from the upper deck. I got out of my cabin, promptly fell over a large wooden box in the passage. Everyone else had already gone, felt my way to the small hatchway door and up through that one, two more small hatches to go, still pitch dark and about two minutes left. By this time the ship was listing considerably so it became obvious that things were serious.'

So serious that at this moment, unknown to Williams, in the darkness on the lower deck, in passages and cross-passages, hundreds were losing their way, stumbling into dead-ends, running into each other, in panic crying to get out, slipping or falling on inclining decks, groping forward on hands and knees, many burned but forgetting their wounds, struggling only to be free.

In the Boys' Messdeck on the lower deck the boys' instructors were trying to keep the youths from dashing out.

'Stand fast and don't panic!' yelled the instructors.

'Keep calm, lads. Don't lose your heads!'

Most obeyed. Most died.

Frank Williams had found another hatch, heard voices at last, climbed up through the hatch, through another, then joined about twenty Marines and a warrant officer striking matches, looking up a hatch which would bring them out onto the open deck; there was just a small manhole open, in the centre of the hatch, space enough to allow one man through at a time.

'The next one through, open up the hatch,' yelled Williams, meaning the main hatch cover; and when someone did, all climbed through.

They could see the quarter-deck clearly, now heeling enough to know, said Williams, that 'the poor lady was gone.'

Elsewhere, unbelievingly, many were headed down, deeper into the ship, after jumping to the conclusion that the *Oak* had been attacked by bombs; they were doing what they had been taught to do in an air attack—'get under armour.'

Ordinary Seaman Leonard Soal would tell the Board of Enquiry, 'We had the orders to go down below.'

Others, hearing no command to abandon ship, just waited: they needed an order, received none, moved only when told 'Save yourselves!'

The ship's heel was increasing; common sense said to go up, and most did, or tried to, forgetting about discipline, dashing from messes any way they could, up ladders, through doors and hatches, on inclining, shaking decks, trusting only their sense of direction. Many would never remember their escape routes out.

The ship's postman, Royal Marines Corporal Herbert Pattison, was now in, by his own description, 'a dream world'—he'd 'lost all consciousness of my actual surroundings'—remembered climbing up, repeating to himself, 'I've got to go on for ever and ever,' when suddenly he stopped, thought 'What's the use? I might as well stay here.'

He leaned against a bulkhead, then 'suddenly I imagined I saw a very bright light and a picture of the head and shoulders of my wife. With this, again without being conscious of my actual surroundings, I said, "I've got to go, I've got to go" and I pressed on.'

Pattison finally reached a door leading aft, got hold of a blackout curtain, pulled it to one side, felt the cold night air 'and my mind cleared instantly.'

Still in number three dynamo room Assistant Torpedo Officer Clayton and Warrant Electrician Bulley, now joined by the dynamo watchkeeper, felt the new explosions, all thinking the first unmistakably well forward, the second abreast the boiler rooms, the third close to number three dynamo room but forward of it, near the starboard wing engine room; they looked up, saw orange-coloured flames licking over the edge of the dynamo room hatch—like 'looking into an oil furnace,' remembered Clayton—and then they saw the forward bulkhead, between the dynamo room and the wing engine room begin to bulge inwards. Steam began to escape, smoke seeped from the rivetted joints. After a moment of indecision all three scampered up the ladder. Halfway, the lights failed; but by the time they reached the top the flames had vanished from the hatch.

They stumbled onto the Marines' messdeck, the *Oak* now listing about 25° to starboard; and in the next few seconds, as they ran through the deck, they saw choking fumes boil all over the place, hammocks like flaming cocoons with Marines still in them. Clayton, Bulley, and the watchkeeper stopped in their tracks, tried to smother some flames with blankets but they could not; they were driven off by the flaming cordite, smoke, choking nitrous fumes, and oil gases spread by fuel driven out of the bunkers.

More flames shot in, through the door in the foreward bulkhead at the starboard side of the mess; so they ran on, Clayton to squeeze through a porthole and land on a blister before being tossed to the sea. Sergeant G. E. T. Parham opened his eyes in horror to see 'a ball of fire which came from forward along the boat hoist flat and hit eight Marines who were on the deck; they were all badly burned.'

Marine A. R. Jordan, his left arm burnt from flames curling round his hammock, used his right arm to desperately shake the Marine in the hammock next to his. Jordan had assumed the man was still asleep but then he looked in and 'found he was burnt black from head to foot and so assumed he was dead.

'Nobody on the messdeck seemed to know what was happening

but a Corporal Jordan, no relation to me, was telling Marines to get below through a hatchway under the armoured deck, because we assumed it was an air raid. Other Marines were going forward through the Stokers' messdeck and others were calmly getting dressed. Something in my mind told me to get in the upper deck and directed me aft towards the quarter-deck.'

In pitch darkness Jordan made his way through the various flats to the port side, climbed over upturned lockers, then up the captain's ladder hatch to the quarter-deck, in time to see people lining up across the tilting deck to lower themselves on a single rope to *Daisy*. Jordan didn't like the idea of waiting, made his way farther aft, dived into the water, swam to the drifter, climbed aboard just as he heard a further muffled explosion in the ship, which Jordan assumed was internal, for gazing at the boat, he discerned no flash or fire.

Many took cover in alleyways. Sergeant George Booth, while trying to help Marines, suddenly looked forward along the port passage—and this saved his life, for he saw heading directly towards him a sheet of flame, bright orange outside, intense blue inside, like fire from a blowlamp. Instantly he backed behind a steel wall, then spotted 'men in their hammocks being engulfed, then . . . carnage.' Marine Corporal J. A. Payton watched in horror as 'balls of orange fire appeared to come through the deck and spread towards midships, leaving thick smoke and Marines sleeping to starboard amidships burnt in their hammocks.'

Ribbons of fire twirled and whirled, then rolled through the messes. Lieutenant M. H. Benton, looking through a half opened screen door, saw 'red flash which literally filled the starboard side of the Marines' messdeck.' Benton ran aft, found a porthole in the Admiral's pantry, jumped or dived through it into the sea: he'd never know how he reached the water.

Most had no chance to get out, the flames swirling about, back and forth, catching them about waist-high, or before they had time to jump from their hammocks. Those who did make it to their feet had flames clinging to thin undershirts and shorts, some driven so crazed that they ran directly into the flames. Booth gripped one man, seared by flames, and a part of the man's flesh came off, revealing bone.

Running aft, Clayton and Bulley looked back at the Marines' mess, saw the blazing streaks gone; the flames had escaped through the port battery into the open air of the quarter-deck, leaving behind only the faint red glow of things smouldering.

Paymaster Lieutenant William Sandifer, standing aft of the Marines' mess, felt hot air fumes blow his cap off. Quickly he snatched it up, made for the quarter-deck, where he found a few officers trying to launch the captain's gig sitting on chocks right aft. The *Oak* was by now heeling increasingly to starboard, the deck so slanting it was impossible to stand upright: hundreds of hands reached out for steadiness. 'There was a surge of ratings from up forrad toward the port gangway ladder—probably as a result of *Daisy* having detached herself. I was among the early arrivers on the platform of the ladder—then at an angle of nearly 45°. Though still fully clothed—uniform, cap, and blue raincoat—I dived—and surfaced. It took time to disengage myself from all except uniform and shoes. There were many men in the water—most shouting agonised appeals to *Daisy* to stop and pick them up. Then voices gradually declined as they sank. I was spared the embarrassment of being clung to by any drowning man.'

Still in the battleship were two-thirds of the ship's complement, struggling desperately to get out.

Petty Officer Dick Kerr, fire at his back and coughing heavily from cordite gas in his lungs, threw all of the weight of his fifteen and a half stone at an exit door leading to an officers' bathroom, intending to get to the main door, then out into the port battery. 'Here you are, lads, in here,' Kerr called out, feeling relief when the door opened; others followed him into the dark bathroom but suddenly flames blasted in—'fire seemed to be eating the air.' Coughing, struggling desperately to get out, the men made it to the main door but couldn't get it open.

'We're done, it's stuck,' said someone, seeing that because of the list, the door's handles had become wedged inside the framework.

'I could see and feel the inferno outside through the cracks in the door and it was creeping in the exit door behind us, the handles each side of the door were terribly hot and I kicked the door in desperation to try to loosen it so as it could be opened. I tried and tried again to open it and when it seemed that I would have to give up as I was suffocating with fumes the door gave and I opened it.'

'Come on lads, it's opened,' yelled Kerr, but he looked and saw nobody, heard only the coughing and 'somebody running around in a bad way shouting "OK, OK". There was also terrible screaming from somewhere in the starboard casemates. I knew it was no good going back as my strength had almost gone and I tried to go out into the red flame but had to step back into the bathroom again, but I had to do it I thought, better than being caught like a rat in a trap. I had to take a chance so I staggered out through that awful inferno into the port battery and almost fell as my legs seemed helpless. A hammock which was slung up saved me and I pulled myself along rather than walked and fell over the armoured doorstep at the end of the port battery, but my luck held as my hands felt the guardrails and chain around the hatch outside the officers' heads.'

Realising now that he was in the quarter master's lobby, Kerr staggered to the screen door, fell forward through the black screen used to darken ship, and found himself on the quarter-deck.

'Thank God,' he said.

Still below, around a door leading aft from the Marines' mess deck, a crowd of about twenty were trying to loosen a clip so they could open the door and reach the officers' cabin flats. No matter how hard the men struggled, the door would not open.

Finally, musician H. A. G. Kelly, the Marine band's leading violinist, screamed, 'Stand back you bastards, and let's get the clip off this door!'

Kelly's friend, Harold J. Wernham, who was standing nearby and heard Kelly scream, saw the clip knocked off, the door open at last, everyone run through.

The *Oak*'s list to starboard increased steadily, but then, at about 45°, the ship suddenly 'hung'. Beneath the quarter-deck, amidships, an officer hurried up from aft, struck a match, and in the faint glow the men noticed the hatch leading up to the deck. A group reached it, but none could stand upright, the list so bad that they had to crawl up the deck to the port side; they climbed through the guardrail, found themselves standing on the ship's side, in water lapping over.

Inside the sinking vessel, flames still erupted everywhere. F. J. C. Hobbs, the engine room CPO, who'd left his mess after the first explosion to visit the night 'heads,' was standing with his back toward a hatch leading down to the officers quarters when a sheet of flame rolled up through the hatch, caught him in the back, struck another rating, who'd been standing facing the hatch, full in the face.

'At that moment'—he would never forget it—'the explosion blew me through the screen door leading to the quarter-deck where I laid semi-conscious!'

Gunnery instructor James T. Pearce, on hands and knees, was struggling to regain his balance. He'd been supervising the AA arrangements when the very first explosion had occurred, had gone to the Gunnery Office to issue keys to the gunners mates for taking the temperatures of all magazines, was standing outside the office waiting for the return of the mates with their reports when the next blast knocked him down.

'My first impression was of Nero burning Christians,' he'd recall: he rushed up the ladder to the 4-inch gun deck, felt more explosions and 'when I got to the deck the ship was already heeling.' He saw men running, spotted a signal bosun, yelled out to him:

'Hoist the Ensign, set light to the Confidential Books and get out quickly.'

The bosun just kept running.

Sliding armoured hatches, taken off their security clips at 9 p.m. and lowered a little way on the assumption that in the event of a sudden alert they could be closed in a few minutes when everyone had reached their action stations, locked hundreds in. At the back of 'A' turret on the port side, Corporal George Harold Woolnough saw from one half-open hatch a man's face and hands sticking out. He heard a voice below: 'I cannot move him. He is jammed in the hatch.'

Woolnough knelt down by the hatch, tried to move the heavy inch-and-a-half thick armour plate, but could not. In a rolling sea these hatches would slide just a little, no more than allowed by the play of the wire strops holding them. But now, with the list of the ship, the strops broke under the strain, sending the huge slabs athwartships.

'After that,' said Woolnough, 'the ship started to list a lot more than she had already done. Finding I could be of no assistance by the hatch I went over the port side.'

Sergeant Booth, who by now had made his way to a cross passage between two mess decks, found a hatch he knew led up to the quarter-deck, joined a number of injured attempting to get up the ladder, now helped them as the *Oak* continued to heel to star-board. Underneath the hatch cover lay another sliding door, closed like the others by pulling on a toggle attached to a wire shackled to the door. But the heel of the ship was too much.

Booth remembered: 'It was then the armoured door slid across under its own weight and cut two men in halves, the lower part of their bodies in falling pushed back the men lower on the ladder onto the mess deck.'

Near another hatchway, one to the quarter-deck, just aft of the forward 15-inch gun turrets, Warrant Telegraphist Hughes-Rowlands stood near the foot of the officers' ladder, calmly light-ing matches, directing men to the hatchway.

'Easy, lads,' said the old fellow. 'Steady there. Easy now . . . easy . . .' as younger men streamed past him.

Hughes-Rowlands would die—as would Marine Corporal H. D. Jordan, who instead of scampering from the heeling ship when he had the chance was now supporting a hatch on his shoulders to allow other men to pass up.

Near the refrigerating access hatch, just below the upper deck, H. R. Johnston, the watch-keeper on the refrigerating machinery, climbed through to the deck just in time: 'It was plain the ship was rolling over. I saw a lieutenant go over the rail near the high angle guns and slide down the ship's side into the steam launch or picket boat. She was tied to the lizard of the port lower boom and due to the listing ship she had swung in alongside. I followed the lieutenant into the boat. After a moment or two on her, I heard four more explosions from forward to after at about half second intervals.'

On the twisted and shattered quarter-deck stood the Captain's Maltese Steward, Petty Officer A. Camenzuli. A few minutes ear-lier he had seen an explosion in the boys' mess deck and when he had run back aft to see the stewards mess in flames. Now near the officers' ladder to the quarter-deck he slipped then came suddenly upon Admiral Blagrove on the port side, heard him 'giving orders, telling chaps to jump farther forwards because they were hitting themselves on the rails.' Camenzuli spotted a lifebuoy hung on the quarter-deck rails, grabbed it, ran to the centre of the slanted deck with the buoy in his hand.

'If you wish to jump with me, I have a lifebuoy,' he said to the

Admiral, who was alone—after sending his coxswain ahead to tell Benn to abandon ship.

'Don't worry about me,' Blagrove told Camenzuli. 'Jump and try to save yourself.'

The deck's lower rail lay level with the sea and Camenzuli just slid into the water on the starboard side. He swam for a minute and turned to see 'the ship turned altogether—two 15-inch guns in "Y" turret broke away and swung round. After the guns gave way a big flame came up through the officers' deck ladder and I saw no more.'

Finding himself in the gunroom below 'X' turret, Stoker H. P. Cleverley, groping about in the dark, looking for a way out, felt suddenly cold air streaming through a ventilator. 'I think it was plywood or something because I went through it. I didn't hit the deck or guardrails, but dropped straight into the water, and "X" turret was over the top of me.'

On the boat deck nearby, Boy Douglas Newton, who'd been thrown out of his hammock in the 6-inch gun casement and had pulled himself up when he sighted a 'reddish orange flash coming from the starboard side aft,' was now lying on the deck, face down, feeling the heat from the flash pass over him; he got up, in the dark ran forward, climbed the ladder leading to the galley flat, hearing 'a lot of panic and shouting,' then finally up another ladder to the boat deck; he went, making for the port side, preparing to dive from the sinking ship.

Staring across the port bow, Taffy Davies was looking around thinking, 'Christ, what am I going to do now?' He could see the outline of the cliffs, even though it was dark, and being a good swimmer thought 'right, that's where I'm going.'

In his mind he had no doubt the *Oak* had been torpedoed: the explosion had first rocked the ship to port, he'd remember, 'which always convinced me from the start that it was external. When I was in the *Hood* in '35 we were out at sea, out with the *Renown* buggering about doing exercises, and the *Renown* tried to cross our stern, and she misjudged it or we misjudged our speed, and the *Renown*'s bows hit us right on the starboard side aft, on the starboard quarter. I was reminded of that as this thing hit us, the way she shuddered.'

Before moving an inch Davies just stood on the heeling deck, 'for a couple of seconds, working on my old man's basis, if you want to run, stop and think first. I thought it's going to be bloody cold in that water, then heard a voice on the fo'c'sle say, "Make yer way aft to the *Daisy II*!" I walked along the upper deck, across the boat deck, and when I got to the ladder up from the quarter-deck, the ladder had gone.

'A Maltese PO on the boat deck, his leg injured, was calling out to Mary, I helped him down to the quarter-deck, could see that the hatch onto the Marines' messdeck, which was normally closed, was open, I could see flame and smoke. I walked over to the portside guardrail, saw fellows who, contrary to what my old man had taught me, were going to the side and jumping straight into the bloody water. I saw one fellow dive in and then swim straight round to the *Daisy* which seemed to me to be a very shocking waste of energy.'

Davies, like going down a steep cliff, walked down the side of the ship, now heeled more than 45°, stepped onto the slippery blister, and hauled himself onboard *Daisy*—still tied to a bollard on the *Oak*'s quarter-deck, joining about a dozen or so other survivors already in the tender.

'I never got my feet wet,' Davies would remember years later.

One of the first things Davies noticed was a man of about fifty, an *Oak* seaman, standing in *Daisy* puffing a pipe—'looking quite unconcerned about the whole business, as if it was a Sunday afternoon and he was contemplating his rose garden.'

Inside the sinking ship, hundreds were struggling furiously to get out. In the torpedo flat, Chief Petty Officer Writer Stanley W. H. Thompson suddenly came level with a ladder sloping almost horizontal. No one else seemed to consider this a way out, but Thompson decided to crawl on it and found himself in the galley flat: 'I sat down and slid on the steel deck down the slope to the foot of another ladder, went up this one and came out on the upper deck between the funnel and the bridgework. I again slid down the sloping deck and reached the guardrails which were in the water. Some ratings were attempting to lower a boat which appeared to have jammed and I called to them to get swimming quickly as it was obvious further delay in getting clear would be too late.'

Thompson didn't wait. He dived in, and fearing the suction he swam from the ship as fast as he could.

Most of the hatches were now battened down, doors shut tight, exits blocked. 'The whole starboard mess deck was alight and what men could get out of their hammocks seemed to be jumping down into a fire hole,' remembered Marine A. J. Wheatland. 'My next thought was to go forward and try to get out amidships but the way seemed to be blocked and the only exit for me was a porthole. Wheatland, very slim, just over ten stone, found one open, slipped through, discovered he was standing on the side of the ship and didn't know what to do next. He spotted the *Daisy*, now loaded with men, saw the 15-inch guns of the *Oak*, of either X or Y turrets, twisted right out of shape and thought, 'Christ, it must have been some explosion to have done that.'

Suddenly a man crawled up next to him. 'Come on mate,' said Wheatland. 'We'd better get off this tub fore she goes under and takes us with her.'

The two ran down the side and into the cold (about 50°) water.

Up the decks, all ever-inclining, men were inching their way, grabbing whatever they could to steady themselves, or perching on the port guardrails, finding it hard to believe the ship was sinking. Philip White, who had had that premonition, who on hearing the series of explosions had rushed desperately with others to escape the rec space (the push of bodies had made the inward-pressing door almost impossible to open), now saw others going over the side and knowing that this is what he would have to do, he felt for his boots which he'd have to remove (he'd just had them soled and heeled by the ship's boot repairer) and thought this 'rather a waste of money' as he crawled sitting-down fashion down the *Oak*'s side, passing sailors coming out of portholes who, like him, were soon sliding over weeds and barnacles. Finally White bounced off the rolling chocks, the wooden stabilizers extending fore and aft, and then he was in the water.

Clinging to the port guardrails was Captain Benn, who could see that the ship had now heeled over to more than 90°. For a moment or two he just sat on the rails and had 'a good look at the ship he was losing.' Then he walked along her side and into the water and began swimming.

Commander Nichols, about to do the same, saw men falling down past him. He slipped, clutched the rails, saw that 'the keel of the ship was well over my head and falling on top of me. At that moment some force threw me straight up the side of the ship.'

There came 'a blank' as he hit the water—'I don't remember what happened.' But in a moment he was swimming with scores of others.

It was an uphill walk to the port guardrails. Frank Williams, making it, turned round for a last look, saw the hatch he had come through ten seconds before now under water, remembered: 'I dived into that awful cold sea.'

Another of those climbing up, Leading Supply Assistant Frank Gordon Sims, who'd been blown up a hatchway—'by force of wind,' he'd explain later—noted that 'although it was dark, it was surprising how clearly one could see. There were many men swimming in the sea or clinging to pieces of wood which had apparently been thrown overboard by those who were on the upper deck at the time of the first explosion. I heard one of my young messmates screaming that he could not swim.'

Sims himself was not a good swimmer; but the instinct for survival drowned out his fear. He saw that the picket boat was still tied up to the end of the forward boom; so quickly he edged his way along the sinking *Oak* and slid down the rope. 'As soon as I was aboard the picket a seaman cut the rope attaching it to the boom because it was being hauled up because of the list. Those on top paddled with their hands to get away from the *Oak* as it was certain she would heel over.

'The only man I recognised was clinging to the side of the picket boat; he was a seaman who used to help in the storerooms and he was pleading to be got aboard the boat because he was unable to swim because he had broken his leg. This of course was impossible. The boat was crowded to capacity and nearly all the survivors made their way to it. The boat began to rock badly, backwards and forwards.'

Heading for the launch lying at the boat boom starboard side, Ordinary Seaman Vincent Maurice Marchant, who had made his way up from the lower mess deck, after being almost carried up the succession of steel staircases by the pressure of men dashing to reach the upper deck, somehow got into the launch. 'The boat boom dipped into the sea pulling the boat rope attached to the bollards bar taut and dragging the launch under,' he'd remember. Marchant shouted for a knife; but no one had one; so he dived over the side and struck out for shore, fearing the launch would roll over and drown everyone on board.

The last to leave were diving in, some jumping, some sliding, others tumbling into the oil-slick sea. Victor Ayles, who following orders had been making his way to the upper deck and was hurrying aft, had reached the quarter-deck when he was thrown over the side 'and all I can remember seeing were flashing lights until I hit the water.' George Booth, who'd also escape, remembered jumping about in the *Oak*, missing his footing, falling on a ladder and 'the next sensation was as if I was tied to a great ball, then oblivion.'

Many waded off the ship into the sea, like people on a beach stepping into the water; but most jumped or were flung in, or slid in, tearing their bodies on barnacles. Boy Edward R. Britt, on the crazily tilted B Gun Deck, heard them screaming. 'Maybe that was the reason for me not moving. Scared? I don't know. I was not panicky. I had my full head on me. Then the last I remember was another explosion and I was in the sea, blown in by the blast or pushed in I don't know; but once in the sea I was completely at ease—although smothered in fuel from ruptured oil bunkers.' (Except for the inner tanks in 'A' boiler room, which had been in use, the bunkers had been 90 percent full.)

Charles Cartwright, the Chief Engine Room Artificer, walking barefoot down the ship's side, 'thinking that I was the last and only walker on a wide track,' was knocked over, he'd say later, 'by a post entrant from behind who, in his panic, elected to choose the same path as I had. With the impetus gained by the collision I rolled quickly, hurled into the churning sea caused by the ship's turning over. I struck out with arms and legs and eventually I surfaced. Whether I went under the ship, around it, or where I went from there I don't know and never shall.'

Douglas Newton, the boy who had hated lugging those cans of Carnation milk, also found himself on the ship's side. He slid down, ready to scramble over the anti-submarine blister and dive in, then looked around and saw sailors sitting on the blister, removing boots and trousers. One of the sailors, Ginger Lestor, who was calmly putting on a coat, saw Newton's look of amazement, and told the boy 'It's going to be cold in there.'

At this instant Newton spotted another boy, Matthew Shilling, from Manchester.

Shilling was rubbing his hands.

'Fourteen days leave after this,' said Shilling, grinning.

'Then he shouted, "Taxi!" and jumped in,' said Newton, who did the same, taking to the water just before the bilge, swimming under the oil, making for the picket boat.

Dick Kerr, one of the last to leave, was about this moment walking down the ship's side. He had taken his jacket and trousers off and hung them over the rails (reminding him of the war song 'Hanging out the Washing on the Siegfried Line'), and trying to forget the four shillings in silver in his trousers pocket he stepped into the water and kicked clear with his feet (only to find out the next day that he'd sprained his left foot in the process). Fearing suction, he swam clear as fast as he could; and about this moment he heard a terrible grinding.

It was *Daisy* sliding off the *Royal Oak*'s bilge.

Fearing the *Oak* was now going over, terrified she'd lift *Daisy* with her, men in the tender were screaming 'Cast off, skipper! Cast off!'

From the sinking *Oak*, however, a few others, still sitting on the battleship's side, were screaming 'Don't cast off!'

At just this time, swear Taffy Davies and Henry Pattison, they heard an officer still aboard the *Oak*, holding onto the starboard quarter-deck guard rail, shout 'Wait for the order to abandon ship!'

Said Davies later (contradicting many published reports), 'There was no cutting away of cables. It didn't happen. Skipper Gatt walked from aft to the wheelhouse, without hurrying—coolly phlegmatic—and I heard him say, "Cast off!" And they cast both the headrope and the stern rope without difficulty, and when they cast off, it looked as though that had been what was keeping the *Royal Oak* up because as soon as they'd cast off within a matter of seconds, she turned over. *Daisy* would have gone down with her.'*

Daisy slowly went astern and stopped.

On the *Oak*, as she was turning, John Goodlad, the coxswain of

---

* Actually, Gatt had intended to cast off earlier, when the *Oak* first began to capsize, but the ship's anti-torpedo blister had come up under *Daisy* and he feared the drifter would turn over. He did not 'seize an axe' to sever the mooring ropes, as Alexandre Korganoff stated in *The Phantom of Scapa Flow*; nor did he swear, 'like a trooper,' as the same author maintained. Dismissing this as melodramatic nonsense, Gatt said: 'I started my career as a boy and I finished as the skipper of my own boat and in all that time a swear-word has never passed my lips and I have never taken a drink in my life.'

the launch, who had been about to go for his greatcoat and whistle on hearing that first explosion, who had attempted to go straight for the launch when another explosion had stopped him and he saw the ship commence to ship water 'like a sea breaking on board,' was now in the launch, still at the starboard lower boom; but he was terrified: he and the others manning the launch could not cast off from the boom, for the *Oak* was turning over on top of them, tossing metal from her foretop into the launch; then the foremast itself toppled across the launch: men ducked, dived overboard, and then, between the launch and the ship's side, the launch's funnel slammed down. The boat sank, a boat which could have carried three hundred survivors.

Ordinary Seaman Ivor Henry Pagett, among those on the capsizing launch, had looked back and 'saw the bridge and everything was coming on top of me and that it was impossible to clear the launch in time; so I jumped into the water and the launch went down with the ship.'

Survivor W. Nichols, who had dived into the water immediately after the last explosion and had clambered into the launch, had found himself partially sucked *inside* the funnel. As later he'd write for the Board of Enquiry, 'The rush of water in the funnel drew me into the funnel (head and shoulders). I got clear. There was no rush of steam and water out of the funnel or explosion.'

At this moment, another swimmer, N. Larzell, turned, thought he saw the *Oak*'s quarter-deck 'exploding into the air.'

Other swimmers looked up, saw 'A' and 'B' turrets swing round and 'fall into the sea.'

Frank Sims looked back, saw 'a massive explosion in the after part,' then 'a red glow and the 15-inch guns seemed to curl up and then she turned over quickly with minor explosions.'

H. P. Cleverley, swimming about fifty yards off the starboard side, unmindful of the burns on his feet and legs, paused with others long enough to look back at his ship. 'We watched the ship roll and go down. I recall nothing unusual, except bangs, and rumbles from inside her.'

A skimming dish (small motor boat) flew off a broken deck and floated up to Able Seaman Victor Ayles, who quickly climbed aboard it, and just as quickly left it, as water poured through the floorboards. For the second time Ayles abandoned ship: he swam for a catamaran broken away from the battleship 'and I sat on that for a while with a number of other ships' company, trying to pick up people in the water, shipmates covered in oil, some almost unrecognizable, badly burnt.'

H. J. Instance, his hands badly burned from cordite flames, had been swimming for about 100 yards when suddenly from a floating spar he heard someone call out. Instance swam ahead, caught hold of one end, from the other, heard someone ask, 'Who are you?'

'Leading Seaman Instance and ain't I bloody well burnt.'

The fellow at the other end of the spar identified himself as Lieutenant Anthony Terry, and together they made for *Daisy*.

Herbert Johnston, swimming along with his waistbelt between his teeth so he could get his boiler suit off, thought that if he didn't get away the three pounds in the belt's purse wouldn't be of any use to him; so he dropped the belt and stroked for a lifebuoy on a rope tossed from *Daisy*.

An Edinburgh lad, Able Seaman John Murray, saw a large can floating towards him, grabbed it, a few minutes later found an upright Carley raft and clung to that until yanked from the water by helping hands in *Daisy*.

'There is no doubt,' Murray would later declare, 'that the skipper of the drifter was the hero of the affair. I saw him leaning over to the water and hauling man after man into his boat. He seemed to have the strength of ten men. It was just as if he was pulling fish over the side, and all the time the *Royal Oak* was taking a bigger list.'

The *Oak* didn't go right away, not yet; like a great wounded bear ready to take the final plunge—'she made a huge splash and sigh combined, the sigh being escaping air, I can hear it now,' recalled Frank Williams, a good swimmer who struck out with others to get clear of the ship.

At this moment F. J. C. Hobbs, who had slid over the ship's bottom, his ears and hair burned and 'minus my pyjama trousers and shoes, leaving me almost naked,' felt the ship shudder 'and I was being sucked under the water but managed to struggle and swim away from the ship.' Hobbs looked back: 'I saw the ship roll over to starboard, her port propellers were visible; after about three minutes she seemed to stop on her starboard side. I saw the port boat boom which had boats tied to it was almost upright and men who had got into the boats were now dropping into the water as the boats just dangled in mid-air and I am sure that many of these men never survived.

'As I swam from the ship, I did not see any other men I knew but was grabbed by a rating who pulled me under, perhaps trying to keep afloat; but he released his grip on me. I couldn't help him as I was almost exhausted myself due to the oil fuel which I had taken in during the struggle to keep afloat. All I could hear were shouts of "Over here!" and shouts from *Daisy II*—"We are over here!" I swam towards the sound from *Daisy*.'

Suddenly on *Royal Oak*'s upturned stern there played a light—a probe by a searchlight from *Pegasus*—revealing figures walking on the ship's bottom. Seeing this from the crowded picket boat, Stoker Johnston, who thought the *Oak* now 'like an upturned gigantic plate,' was reminded of the classic photograph of the sinking *Bleucher* during World War I.*

About 150 yards away, Stanley Thompson, floating about, looked back, also saw the *Oak* bottoms-up: 'I could see figures walking on the ship's bottom, having I suppose walked against the turning-turtle of the ship.'

Lieutenant Commander Gregory, thrown into the water, climbed onto the ship's bottom, onto the bilge keel where with three other men he remained for some minutes. 'During this time the ship remained steady, settling very slowly,' he'd live to say. 'I walked some way forward but the hull appeared intact. I took to the water about 0140 by which time there was about 8 feet of the blister still under the water.'

Everywhere men were swimming, some shouting, a few even singing, *Roll out the barrel*—'a form of reaction to the shock,' Frank Williams gathered. None wore life jacket—none ever had been issued. Most said nothing, just watched the ship roll over and go down. 'The only words I remember,' said Stoker H. P. Cleverley, 'were from an upper deck lieutenant who said "Let's keep together and make for the shore." Most of us started in the general direction of the cliffs, but only a few made it. I eventually reached the beach and got a few feet from the water, then I blacked out.' Still in his left hand, Cleverley would find later, was

* This spectacular photograph, taken from a British cruiser, showed the German battle cruiser going down in the North Sea, in the Battle of Dogger Bank, the crew scrambling for their lives to topside.

a box of matches he had grabbed instinctively after the second explosion, after the blast had sent him to the deck.

For a few seconds more the *Oak* showed her bottom, men jumping, diving, sliding away.

Taffy Davies, staring out from *Daisy*, remembered feeling terrified the *Oak* was going to blow up—'I had heard of a reputation of British ships for blowing up when like this. But she didn't. She just went down quietly.'

L. H. Tunnicliff said, 'It was so cold and dark. My first thought was the ship is coming over on top of me; so I just swam until someone shouted, "She has gone." I rolled onto my back to rest a while as I seemed to be full up with water and black oil. I remember no more until I was being brought round on the deck of a boat, which I found out afterwards was *Daisy II*.'

Her death throes over, Drake's Drum gone, the *Oak* plunged beneath the water—a tomb for more than eight hundred men and boys, fifteen fathoms down, at Latitude 58° 55′ 42″ N, Longitude 2° 58′ 54″ W, to lie with her old adversaries of Jutland. It was about thirty-three minutes past one, twenty-nine minutes after the first explosion, seventeen after the last.

In the distance, on the drifter HMS *Mist*, patrolling the inside of the boom at Hoxa Sound, Able Seaman George W. Fisher, who normally helped man the 15-inch shellroom on the *Oak* but had been assigned temporarily to the *Mist* and was glad of it (the *Oak*'s history of mishaps made her a 'jinx,' he believed), said the battleship 'was visible to us as she was sinking, being lit by a probe searchlight of HMS *Pegasus*.'

The *Oak*'s stern was up and showing her under-water paint. Then the light snapped out. 'We never left our patrol area to go to *Royal Oak*'s aid,' said Fisher, but the little boat tried to fire its distress rockets to no avail: the Very's pistol failed to fire no matter how hard the crew tried. Seeking replenishments, the men hurried in frustration to the ammo store, only to find it locked, the key not on hand—the last man to use it had failed to turn it in; so they could only stand and stare in the direction of the lost ship; they could not even make contact with base, for the local station that Friday the 13th had closed down for the night at 10 p.m.

In the crowded picket boat—she had a life saving capacity of 59 but had more than 100 on her deck, in her cabin and fore peak—

sailors three deep were hanging on, some to old motor tyres hanging over her side; others were using ripped-up floor boards to paddle her away. Some were using their hands. One man clinging to the side was pleading to get aboard. His leg was broken. He could not swim. But by now the boat was beginning to rock, backwards and forwards, heeling from one side to the other, the freeboard getting lower and lower, shipping water on the lower side.

Amidships, to keep her on an even keel, the chief buffer was holding two boys and shouting: 'Lean to starboard!' 'Lean to port!'

Someone ordered those on deck to get inside the cabin, to make room for more; and some did, while others, Philip White among them, declined: 'I didn't think this was a terribly good idea because I could see that the thing was going to turn over any second.' White stayed at the stern, handing out life-jackets to swimmers alongside, the first life-jackets they'd had that night.

Dick Kerr, clinging to the picket boat's side, heard someone start a song in the now dangerously overcrowded vessel—'Down Mexico Way, South of the Border'—and, he said, 'we all joined in until it was interrupted by still more men trying to get into the boat, poor devils, they didn't have the strength to hang on over the side owing to burns and the boat started to heel over which made everybody on her deck dive off.'

Any second, the men feared, and she'd topple over under the weight of so many.

Suddenly a voice cried out of the dark, 'Help, I can't make it!'

Kerr, powerless to help, called back, 'Come on, only a few more yards!'

And the voice said, 'I can't do it!'

'Come on,' said Kerr, 'a few more feet!'

Smothered in oil fuel, the man made it, was hauled on board—just as others were making plans to leave.

'I'm going to swim to Kirkwall,' said one of the engineering officers before he took the plunge. James Pearce, who in jumping into the water from the *Oak* had landed on his bottom, sustaining injuries to his buttocks and a leg, also left the picket boat, head first, intending to make for shore: 'When I entered the water quite a lot of men who were hanging on round the picket boat followed me, and periodically I called for a united shout for help. We came up against oil fuel and could not get through it and I had to alter course. From then on I lost all sense of direction.'

Now the picket boat, the little coal-burning steamer, which had no steam, lost her stability completely, due to the heavy numbers on her. She capsized, turned completely over, tilting first to port and then to starboard, and throwing from her deck and sides men like fish tossed back to sea.

Douglas Newton, swimming for his life, remembered seeing 'one or two men drown from panic.'

White could hear the muffled screams from inside the cabin he had refused to enter. He swam for the upturned hull, wrapped himself around the propeller shaft. Two men came up behind him, he edged farther forward; but the stern began to slide under, throwing them all back into the oil and water. Disoriented, not knowing which way to swim, they spied in the distance the lights of *Daisy II*.

'*Daisy, Daisy*,' there went the cry.

In the dark, doing the breast-stroke, minus his pyjama trousers but too frightened to feel the cold, was Frank Gordon Sims, who had managed to jump clear of the turning picket boat.

Kerr was watching the boat go down. 'I could imagine the scene in the fore peak, boat upside down, loose gear everywhere, anchor, grapnel, brooms, ropes, etc., and those men struggling to get through that small hatch, my God.'

Then somehow the picket boat righted herself. One swimmer, Robert Hayhoe, an engine-room artificer on the *Oak*, swam back, climbed in; but once more the boat heeled over. Hayhoe managed to swim free, later making it to a cliff (where he was to hear a voice calling: 'You're all right now, laddie.')

The Pearce group was still swimming on, the struggle grew desperate. 'Our shouts for help got weaker and weaker as men died,' Pearce said, 'and eventually I was the only one left to shout and at the end of my tether I was picked up by a Scottish lad in a skiff from a drifter that was on its way to the scene of the disaster.'

Others, less fortunate swam about in the dark. Most could see each other, for 'when one's eyes became accustomed to it,' remembered Lieutenant Commander Gregory, 'it was comparatively light; men swimming could be seen for about seventy yards.' But for most there was just loose oars, empty petrol drums, broken or torn Carley floats to grab onto.

'O God, what have I done to deserve this,' Douglas Newton heard someone crying.

Then Newton saw suddenly rise from under the water the *Oak*'s gig. He helped eight men get onto her but none could get inside, for the light little boat still wore her cover. Then the gig turned over, tossing the men back into the sea. A few grabbed life lines dangling from her.

Newton would remember: 'Some men were crying, some singing hymns and some singing 'Daisy, Daisy' to call *Daisy II*. I was feeling done in but I found the strength to keep another tall bald man afloat until *Daisy* pulled us aboard.'

Kerr was trying the dead man's float to keep himself above water; he was alone, he'd pen later, on a 'wide, wide sea,' expecting to be picked up by a boat but there was none to be seen. 'I tried to swim to the cliffs but small waves seemed to hamper me as each time I struck out I got a mouthful of water. I stopped swimming, preferring to paddle around rather than swallow salt water. I turned to my right and then saw two white lights in the distance. I thought it was a rescue boat coming, and I waited and waited but they didn't seem to get any nearer to me. Two men paddled past me and disappeared into the darkness on a piece of wreckage. I found by breast-stroke swimming in the direction of the lights I was not affected by swallowing water and the tide seemed in my favour so I kept going and after what seemed hours I reached the lights which were the anchor lights of a big ship with a trawler or drifter alongside.'

Kerr had reached *Pegasus* and the drifter was *Daisy*, putting her survivors aboard.

Frank Williams could not find *Daisy* but he could see cliffs, about a mile away, and suddenly he remembered a cleft he'd seen the afternoon before when in one of the *Oak*'s boats he'd been out exploring with Commander Nichols 'with a view to making some sort of road to the top of the cliffs.'

Williams made for the cleft, using a steady side-stroke; but after a minute of this he came upon an upturned boat with some thirty men clinging to it: 'The boat was holed, so no point in righting it. The men were singing and I joined them in both singing and hanging on.'

Farther away, treading water alone, Stanley Thompson decided not to try for shore, which he thought well over a mile, probably two, away; when suddenly a long heavy plank nudged against him. 'I locked my arms around it and shortly after another man joined me and held on the other one. I told him I thought if we hung on the boats from the fleet should be along soon and I will not readily forget my feelings when my companion said, "No luck there, they went out this morning." We were then joined by a man with a beard who took up his place in the middle of the plank. Not much was said and we gave a shout now and again but gradually odd lights that had been visible on the water and on the distant shore disappeared. After a short while the bearded chap in the middle suddenly said, "So long chaps," put up his arms and sank and did not appear again.'

'Why did he do that?' Thompson asked.

'God knows,' his companion replied.

The next thing Thompson knew was a voice saying 'Let go mate, you're all right now.'

Feeling his hands prised from the plank, Thompson told the men in the boat, in *Daisy*, that there was another man on the plank.

But there was no one else.

Sergeant George Booth came across a swimmer. They knew each other.

'Let's swim for the shore,' Booth called out.

'I can't' came the reply, 'my arm's gone.'

Then Booth heard him say, 'Cheerio, General (Booth's nickname).'

And his one-armed friend sank out of sight.

In this way would life ebb or go on, men die or live to tell their story.

William Casey, wearing only a singlet and shorts, bumped into a length of wood, hung on, floated about. 'I saw someone near me and I shouted out to him that I had a spar and he came over, but we had nothing to say to each other and to this day I do not know who he was.'

Frank Sims was trying to stay alive. He began to lose breath and falter, turned on his back, dog paddling, was at last pulled aboard *Daisy*, his stomach filled with oil fuel.

Vincent Marchant, eighteen, of Doncaster, who, remembering *Courageous*, had bounded from his hammock, ran to the upper deck after the first explosion, and after the last had stripped, tied a safety belt around his waist, and dived into the water, now saw searchlights playing over the surface, hundreds of heads bobbing in a blanket of oil.

'My eyes started to smart and the faces of all the men swimming in the water turned a greasy black. I was caught in a searchlight for several minutes and saw that two of my pals were swimming alongside me. Later, however, they had cramp and disappeared. A small boat passed near at hand with someone on board shouting for survivors. I "ahoyed", but they evidently did not hear me and the boat disappeared into the darkness. I swam and swam for I don't know how long, but I must have gone about a mile and a half when I felt the rock under me. I scarcely remember what happened after that. It was like a nightmare.'

He just had a vague recollection of climbing up the sheer face of a cliff about twenty or thirty feet high, ahead of another figure climbing behind him, who suddenly slipped and crashed among the rocks below. 'He must have been killed or drowned. I lay down on the top of the cliff and lost consciousness.' (Covered head to foot in thick oil fuel, Marchant lay for two hours, too weak to crawl, until found by a search party, stripped of his clothing, rubbed down with blankets, given a large dose of brandy, carried to a waiting car, and rushed to Balfour Cottage Hospital in Kirkwall—suffering from oil fuel poisoning and lacerations.)

Unlike many others, Alfred Wheatland had decided to swim in the direction opposite to the cliffs—'because I knew that if I went to the cliffs I would never be able to get out of the water. I decided to make for one of the small islands, then I caught sight of a launch about fifty yards away. I called to it and they came over and pulled me out of the water.'

It was one of the launches from *Pegasus*, with three or four survivors aboard.

Philip White discovered that the man with his eyes a few inches above water with him was Richard Gregory, the ship's navigator. Almost indistinguishable to each other, the two had been floating about in the oil fuel when 'somewhere, from nowhere,' White would remember, 'a whaler, a 32-footer, appeared, apparently from the aircraft repair ship *Pegasus* near us. I heard a voice say "Here's two more," and remembered being yanked out of the water onto the bottom boards of the whaler.'

Everywhere oil. The vast, irritating foul-smelling liquid got into men's eyes and stomachs, into nasal passages; or into their flesh burns; it mixed with the harsh saline sea, made men puke or whimper in discomfort. Without life jackets, they had only debris to keep them afloat—that and the depth of their will to live.

Some, unable to stand the pain, resigned to die, let go their grips on whatever it was that was keeping them up, slipped quietly beneath the sea.

Others were just plain lucky.

Boy Edward Britt, who at first had remained on B gun deck, watching others go over the side, then saw them sliding, heard them screaming when their bodies tore on the barnacles on the ship's bottom—later to find himself either blown or pushed into the oily sea—clambered aboard a Carley float and survived.

William Sandifer, exhausted and floating on his back, bumped into a lump of wood, grabbed it, shared it with another officer who swam up, until picked up by *Daisy*.

Frank Williams, in the group of about thirty still clinging to the upturned boat, too far from the main party of survivors to be picked up by *Daisy*, after an hour struck out to find the tender, did find her, directed her to the others: 'I have never been so cold before or since,' he'd say years later. 'The cold seemed to have got right inside my bones somehow and *Daisy*, with nearly 300 of us aboard, couldn't help to warm us.'

An unknown rating, rescued by *Daisy*, jumped overboard three times with a rope's end to save other men; while others on the drifter fished some unconscious from the water. George Booth felt a pain under his right arm—a boat hook had caught him—the next thing he knew he was being hauled aboard, heard someone say, 'Christ, he's alive.'

Musician Harold Wernham caught hold of a rope dangling from *Daisy*'s side and was pulled aboard.

'What was tragic on several occasions,' remembered Henry Pattison, 'was where there would be a group of three or four men in the water hanging on to some floating debris and they would let go to reach for the lifebelt we had thrown and one would just suddenly sink below the surface of the water and not come up again.'

The small boat, about a hundred feet long, seventeen feet wide, bounced over the sea, drunken with the weight of men thinking mainly now of keeping warm. 'We packed ourselves like sardines and huddled together to try and keep each other warm, as many of us were almost naked,' said F. J. C. Hobbs.

'Oh! Christ! Why doesn't someone come and help us,' cried one man, looking out for a ship. 'They must know by now that the *Oak* has gone.' But no ship came. 'There was only darkness and cold and death,' remembered Taffy Davies.

'And when skipper Gatt decided that *Daisy II* was dangerously overloaded and he made his way to the *Pegasus,* I remember the heartbreaking, gut-rending misery we felt when we heard men still calling for help and imploring *Daisy* not to go; and this was more than two hours after the *Oak* went down, and still no help had arrived.'

H. R. Johnston, pulled aboard, hurried down a small hatch forward 'and pulled some canvas over me.' Boy Douglas Newton, who saw a dead man on the deck grating, climbed down to the boiler room, found most of the men smothered in oil fuel—they cried out when touched.

One helper pulled a head only from the water, went almost berserk, had to be restrained—he 'had to be knocked out,' said A. R. Jordan.

William Casey, newly arrived, cast around, saw men everywhere, down the fish hold, around the funnel, the rigging, in the engine room, the galley, all over the place, spotted one man in particular, 'a chief stoker, the flesh on his face had melted, his nose was a long snout and his chin looked as if he had a beard, and all he wanted was a smoke and no one had one to give him.'

Taffy Davies came down. 'I know it's a bloody silly question,' the stoker said to him, 'but have you a cigarette?'

'As a matter of fact, I have,' said Davies, who reached for his packet of Craven A's, lit one, gave it to the stoker, who took a puff, and passed it on.

6

Escape

When Marine Bandmaster 2nd Class William Owens had opened his eyes upon the foul-looking, foul-smelling world of oil and water that so viciously had curled around him, he had struck out swimming, like others struggling to get free, was soon three hundred yards astern of the foundering *Oak*, in company with another swimmer, pyjama-clad (sure sign of an officer, thought Owens; who else wore pyjamas?), and there came from this man, whom Owens would never again see, excited motions to look at something yonder: a strange object in the water. And so Owens had turned his head, scoured the bay in the direction the officer had signalled and there, a few hundred yards off, on the desolate starboard side of the drowning hulk of the once mighty *Oak*, he had made out the shape of a conning tower—a conning tower rearing miraculously in Scapa Flow!

A U-boat for sure. Owens had no doubt, and later, on a bulkhead of *Pegasus* he'd draw for witnesses the outline of the impudent thing he'd seen, the way it was. A conning tower! He was emphatic, and because his companion never was traced, he, Owens, would remain the only British eyewitness to the invader.

And when at that moment Owens had glanced upon the conning tower, the Germans in it had been staring back, Prien and the four others, in the best experience of their lives, sharing an excitement that had drenched, like a giant wall of water, the little boat. In amazement they'd seen it happen, had surveyed for an instant the results, glorious to them.

After three tense minutes comes the detonation on the nearer ship. There is a loud explosion, roar, and rumbling. Then come columns of water, followed by columns of fire, and splinters fly through the air.

The impact of the torpedoes had seemed to the Germans more

than enough to destroy the battleship. 'The explosions appeared extremely loud,' said Dziallas. 'This made us suspect right there that the forward ammunition chamber had been hit.'

Inside the boat, all three hits had been heard—'they were enormous explosions,' said Spahr—the mood had been quiet, subdued, the crew expecting a counter-thrust; but there was in the boat 're-lief and pride,' said Herrmann: 'At last a success which could hardly be equalled. You don't feel the impact, only the explosion; but as soon as the explosions occurred we headed out. There were handshakes and smiles, but everybody stayed quietly on his battle stations on the way to the exit and listened to reports coming from the bridge.'

Prien didn't stay to watch his victim heel or 'hang' or turn bottom but left almost immediately, steering a route for Kirk Sound via Skildaenoy Point. The machinery responded beautifully; but of a sudden Hänsel thought he perceived a ship signalling—a destroyer, he thought, possibly giving chase, probably signalling 'What ship?'

Hänsel conveyed his fears to Prien, and the skipper peered through his glasses. He couldn't change his tactics, couldn't submerge then surface to sneak out later, run the risk of being picked up on Asdic sound gear; he had to be careful to avoid any change in the line of his wake.

Presently Prien said to Hänsel, 'She doesn't see us at all.'

Spahr, below, who heard this comment through the voice tube, kept busy with his sea chart—there was a boat out there somewhere, either a destroyer or a patrol boat, he was convinced; but no time to worry now, time only to retreat: 'We had to leave against the current which in Kirk Sound was already running at about 10 nautical miles per hour. With full steam ahead we made for the Sound.'

Deciding to play out his hand and remain surfaced, Prien called down the voice tube for more revs. 'Emergency full ahead! Everything you've got!'

Then, according to Prien, the harbour sprang to life.

Destroyers are lit up, signalling starts on every side, and on land 200 metres away from me cars roar along the roads. A battleship has been sunk, a second damaged, and the other three torpedoes have gone to blazes. All the tubes are empty. I decide to withdraw, because: (1) *With my periscopes I cannot conduct night attacks while submerged.* (2) *On a bright night I cannot manoeuvre unobserved in a calm sea.* (3) *I must assume that I was observed by the driver of a car which stopped opposite us, turned around, and drove off towards Scapa at top speed.* (4) *Nor can I go farther north, for there, well hidden from my sight, lie the destroyers which were previously dimly distinguishable.*

In no other part of Prien's log would so much controversy be evoked as here. Two cruisers, *Rawalpindi* and *Voltaire*, did lay at anchor at Scapa that night, in Hoxa Sound—Prien would say later he saw them 'sleeping at anchor'. But no evidence was presented to the Board of Enquiry to indicate that either ship made signals. Admiral French did send his destroyers out. But by the time they arrived *Royal Oak* was gone, *U-47* had made her exit—never was there a race between the U-boat and her pursuers, not a depth charge was dropped on *U-47*, and the only searchlights burning that night shone from *Pegasus*—onto the sinking *Oak*, not the fleeing U-boat.

The vessels Prien mistook for destroyers were simply patrol boats, the two at Hoxa and Hoy booms—'they were maybe even fishing boats,' as Spahr would later admit.

But of the difficulty of getting out there could be no doubt, for ebbtide was running, fear of dying was real, of the submariner's death—suffocation or drowning in an 'iron coffin.' If necessary, said Hänsel, *U-47* would fight her way out: 'The aft torpedo was ready, and in the forward compartment one tube was still loaded.'

At high speed both engines we withdraw.

Twice Prien called down for 'ten more,' meaning ten revs on the diesels, enough for a knot or so more.

Then down the voice tube he told Spahr: 'If you hear a terrible amount of noise, you'll know we're running right through a broken-up blockship.'

A change in tactics, Prien knew, would make him vulnerable to searchers. But now, approaching Kirk Sound, he talked to Endrass, decided to avoid the shallow north channel through which they had passed on the inward journey, chose instead the southern channel in the same Sound, in which it seemed reasonable to assume the water would be deeper.

Everything is simple until we reach Skildaenoy Point. Then we have more trouble. It is now low tide, the current is against us. Engines at slow and dead slow, I attempt to get away. I must leave by the south through the narrows, because of the water. Things are difficult. Course, 058, slow—10 knots. I make no progress.

Prien was wrong: he had the current, he didn't have to fight it—the Tide Tables for the night of 13 October show he had a strong outgoing tide; but manoeuvrability was difficult; he faced a twisting channel between the broken portions of the blockship *Minich*.

At high speed I pass the southern blockship with nothing to spare. The helmsman does magnificently. High speed ahead both, finally ¾ speed and full ahead all out.

On land a few lights gleamed in the blackness; on passing the blockships, said Dziallas, the men noticed 'something strange happening, presumably between the coasts and the searchlight batteries some lively signal communication began. They were using Morse lamps. Unfortunately, we could not decipher it. To us this still seemed perfectly normal after what had happened in the bay. What we could not understand, however, was that they were scanning the sky with their searchlights. The searchlight beam was always directly over our boat in the air space. Apparently the British were scanning the air space looking for enemy aircraft; they probably took the noise coming from our engines for that of aircraft engines.'*

Free of the blockships.

According to Spahr: 'We got around them, never touched them, and now we discovered we had normal passage.'

But then: Ahead a mole! Hard over and again about.

A small anchorage, unprotected, empty of ships, had suddenly jumped from the north side of the tiny island of Lamb Holm, inviting danger by ramming, moving Prien to command instinctively, 'Hard rudder to starboard!' which turned the nose of the boat in a free channel.

The boat slashed past the mole and then, said Spahr, 'Searchlight beams suddenly began scanning the sky. We assumed their monitoring devices had picked up our Diesel noises because we

* The British survivors, almost to a man, maintain they saw no searchlights scanning the sky or signal communication of any kind. They were probably right; the searchlight batteries were not active. In the excitement, the Germans may have confused the beams from *Pegasus* for beams from shore-based searchlight batteries.

were sitting exactly under the beams. But the British were looking for aircraft, not for a submarine.'

After 3,000 metres of fast and steady manoeuvring, the North Sea loomed clearly ahead.

And at 0215 we are once more outside.

U-47 had forced its way free, almost two hours after stealing in. 'We're through! Pass the word,' said Prien.

They were safely out, unscathed, without leaving a trace; a tremendous shout carried through the boat, drowning out the heavy beat of the engines.

Prien bent to the voice pipe.

'A battleship is sunk, another ship is damaged, and we got away!'

Everybody was shouting. 'We all embraced,' remembered Lüddecke, who, in a few minutes, like the other crewmen, would be given a moment on the bridge, a chance to breathe freely, to reflect on the deed, marvel at the great feat accomplished.

'When I came up there they were pointing behind us and said to me, "Back there, that's Scapa Flow!"'

Lüddecke cast a hurried look aft. 'But all I saw were searchlight beams scanning the night sky.'

From beneath the floor boards in the forward torpedo room a crate of beer was dragged out.

'Just to have escaped that hell made them all happy,' said Dziallas.

Everyone downed a bottle—'toasting each other,' said Herrmann. 'There was a lot of laughter and smiles. But we still had a lot of work to do, stow away all the weapons, ammunition, clean up the boat generally, dismantle the charges, put them away in their metal containers, stow away the empty cannisters of the torpedo detonators.'

Prien ordered a new course, due east 180°, to get into deep water, perhaps catch a ship inshore.

I still have five torpedoes for possible attacks on merchantmen.

The watch saw no ships; and finally the bay of Scapa Flow vanished from the sea.

The glow from Scapa is still visible for a long time. Apparently they are still dropping depth charges.

Prien ordered the boat down, first to a depth of sixty metres, then onto a south-easterly course, back to Germany and home.

On Sunday, the 15th, *U-47* surfaced at dawn, listlessly moved upon the water, then with haste submerged and lay low, after coming across a swift British unit, a minesweeper or submarine chaser.

'I happened to be on watch on the bridge and at once gave the alarm,' remembered Spahr. 'So we submerged, steering toward the bottom and turned off the engines. Utmost silence in the boat. Then the British started to rake the ocean with depth charges.'

Thirty-two depth charges were definitely counted.

Random charges, they were hurled aimlessly down, they gave no cause to worry.

'No damage to us,' said Spahr. 'We surfaced at dusk and continued our journey. Then (about 9 p.m.) we heard for the first time, listening to the German news, that the ship we sunk was HMS *Royal Oak*. They were just repeating the British news'—telling all Germany what soon all Britain would know.

> The Secretary of the Admiralty regrets to announce that HMS *Royal Oak* has been sunk, it is believed by U-boat action. Fifteen survivors have been landed.

There was no mention of a second ship, the 'northern one' Prien thought he had damaged in his first salvo. He felt sure he had seen two funnels on her (probably the one of the *Oak* and the one of *Pegasus* blending, though distant, as two), and since on last report he had heard *Renown* was not at Scapa, he guessed the other ship to be *Repulse*, like her sister ship *Renown* a two-funnelled battle cruiser, 32,000 tons unladen, one of the best known names in the British arsenal, a prize even greater than *Royal Oak*.*

For a moment Prien wanted to make for the Firth of Forth where he thought the English might be towing the wreck; but nothing came of it. He went below, where the air still smelled of

---

* *Repulse* had been in Scapa, as revealed by the reconnaissance photographs taken on the 12th. Prien did not see these pictures but German intelligence, having seen them, and having received Prien's radio report, jumped to the conclusion that the U-boat commander was correct, thus putting *Repulse* and *Royal Oak* in the world's headlines, when in fact *Repulse* lay at Rosyth that night—not to sail to disaster until 10 December, 1941 when with *Prince of Wales* she was attacked and sunk by Japanese bombers and torpedo planes near Singapore.

oil and sweat and where the crew was still enjoying the exhilaration set loose by his announcement.

In the operations room at the *Toten Weg*, the officers and men who were following the movements of Dönitz's small fleet of underwater weapons, shifting pins and tiny flags round a big map of the world, had been on the 14th still out of touch with *U-47*, had heard the startling news from Radio Monitoring, which had picked it up from a BBC announcement.

The naval hierarchy was ecstatic but refused to confirm it: 'We must wait for a report from whatever German units may have been involved.' But in the Operations War Diary for the 14th news of the raid on the British anchorage began to dominate.

> *North Sea:*
> The British radio reported the sinking of the *Royal Oak* by a submarine.
> Radio traffic within the area of the British Home Fleet indicates movements in the area of the Orkney Islands.
> At 0310 on 14 Oct. Commanding Admiral, Scapa issued an urgent radio message to all vessels, which seems to indicate a special incident in his area.
> Commanding Admiral, Home Fleet and a number of destroyers were at sea off Scapa and Rosyth on 14 Oct.

Dönitz, informed at once, feeling reassured, despite the lack of confirmation, must have possessed a feeling of relief when he penned in his own diary:

> Receipt of the news that *Royal Oak* was sunk by a submarine—no indication of place. About 370 survivors. It must be caused by *U-47*.

At the same time, in a new item on the 14th, while the hours passed without word from *U-47*, the War Diary was growing less cautious.

> *Special Operation 'P':*
> Submarine *U-47*, Commander. Lieutenant (s.g.) Prien, pene-

trated during the night of 13 Oct. into Scapa Flow and torpedoed the *Royal Oak*.

The sinking has become known up to now only through a Reuter report from Great Britain. The Admiralty ascribes the loss to action by a German submarine. It is definitely assumed that submarine *U-47* succeeded in entering Scapa Flow Bay as planned. The submarine *has not yet reported*; her position, therefore, is unknown. It is possible that she actually found only the *Royal Oak* in Scapa and that she is still in hiding there. It would be particularly tragic if the air reconnaissance flown at a comparatively low altitude over Scapa on 12 Oct. were the cause of the British Home Fleet leaving Scapa in the expectation of a large-scale attack, so that submarine *U-47* thereby lost an unusual opportunity. Further news will have to be awaited. It is already certain, however, that the sinking of the *Royal Oak* entails not only a serious material loss but, in addition, a tremendous loss of prestige to Great Britain, the effects of which cannot yet be visualized. In view of the extraordinary importance which must be attached to the still unfinished operation of submarine *U-47*, strictest secrecy has been ordered concerning the position of the submarine and details of the operation.

To Dönitz in the *Toten Weg* late on the 14th Prien radioed his first message since the raid. *Der Löwe* would have to be pleased:

Operation carried out as planned. Royal Oak sunk: Repulse damaged. Please send particulars about route back to base for 16.10 evening, for I no longer have data on this subject.

In Germany, Radio Monitoring was picking up brisk radio traffic on all waves: the Germans knew for instance that the netlayer *Guardian*, which had disappeared from radio monitoring for some time, had received orders to return to Scapa. And when at last Dönitz heard from Prien himself, he instructed *U-47* to return at once to Wilhelmshaven, later, penning with pleasure in his diary, 'This message confirms the happy result of an operation planned a long time beforehand: the penetration of a submarine in the bay of Scapa Flow. It is a remarkable feat on the part of Lieutenant Prien, commander of the *U-47*, and of his crew.'

The War Diary now reported with pride: '*U-47* on return passage from Scapa,' and then there followed a confident long statement on the hopes and expectations for the war at sea:

North Sea:
Submarine *U-47* reports operation in Scapa Flow carried out as planned: sinking of the *Royal Oak* and damage inflicted on the *Repulse*. A glorious success and proof of the outstanding operational efficiency of our 'young' submarine men. The damage inflicted on the *Repulse* is confirmed by air reconnaissance: the battle cruiser is lying in dock at Rosyth. It has been requested that air forces be sent out against the *Repulse*. The loss of the *Royal Oak* and the damage to the *Repulse* are particularly hard blows to Great Britain at the present moment—shortly after the British Prime Minister rejected the German peace proposals—especially as she was in no way willing to conduct the war by using all available resources and accepting great sacrifices. This success greatly impairs British prestige with the neutrals and increases respect for German power. In the German nation it enhances respect for the Navy and awakens affection for the 'young' German submarine arm, in the same way as the successes of our submarine warfare against merchant shipping. The military effects of the success of our submarine arm and air forces on naval warfare in the North Sea cannot yet be fully visualized.

Realizing the serious danger to her heavy ships in the North Sea area, it must be expected that England will withdraw them completely from the North Sea and North Sea bases and use them, in conjunction with the aircraft carriers, for safeguarding her trade routes in the Atlantic. For the North Sea she will rely on those forces which are primarily suited to fulfil the tasks of naval warfare arising in this area, that is to say submarines, destroyers under cruiser escort, PT boats, planes, and minelayers. It may nevertheless be assumed that, even in the future, the British Admiralty will not be willing to carry out a strong offensive, in view of the fact that any naval warfare which extends beyond the vicinity of the coast involves operations by the forces in question. From this arises not only the possibility but also the obligation on the part of Naval Staff to apply all available combat facilities with the utmost vigour.

For Dönitz the way seemed glory paved. The toll on enemy ships was mounting, more than a dozen ships brought in as prizes, almost 100,000 tons sunk by mid-October. West and north-west of Ireland, west of Scotland, throughout the central part of the North Sea, the eastern part of the Baltic, his small fleet of fighting boats was moving the British and French to exasperation. Between the 12th and 14th *U-48* (Herbert Schultze) had sunk by gunfire the British steamer *Heronspool*, 5,200 tons, the French tanker *Emile Niquet*, 14,000 tons. On the 15th, while the War Diary was gloating over the sinking of *Royal Oak*, Dönitz could ponder with satisfaction a shower of good news:

Radio Monitoring reveals further successes by our submarines; a British steamer reported the *Bretagne* (10,108 tons) to have been torpedoed 120 miles south-west of Ireland; the steamer *Caramea* (8,457 tons) chased by a submarine, the steamer *Sneaton* (3,337 tons) fired on by a submarine, the British mailsteamer *Lochavon* (9,205 tons) sinking.

As instruments of war, Dönitz held his U-boats with growing esteem.

U-47 had surfaced to make better speed and presently the watch spied in the distance the mast of a steamer: a Norwegian which turned out to be the *Meteor* carrying passengers to Newcastle-on-Tyne. She saw the U-boat, stopped at once, but when the submarine's radio room reported wireless traffic, Prien ordered a salvo fired—in a moment, however, was allowing the vessel to proceed, when the radio operator retracted his report: the steamer had not made any signals.

On the 16th *U-47* submerged on Dogger Bank, after sighting three successive floating mines from an unknown minefield; Prien ordered the submarine to make her way slowly back, then round ten that evening he rose to periscope depth, saw through the scope another mine, waited half an hour, then surfaced.

'The sun was shining,' said Spahr. 'We could take a position line, and then rested on the bottom. We resurfaced late in the afternoon, when the sun stood at 10°, and we could take the second position line. With those two lines we had a good location, which helped us pass the barrier gap Route I through our western wall.'

U-47 was going home, a new emblem painted in white on the starboard side of her conning tower. On the long approach to Scapa, comic papers had been read by the crew, including one showing a bull, 'Harry Hotspur,' pawing the ground, nostrils smoking. On the return, Endrass had got the idea of adopting the bull—the 'Bull of Scapa Flow'—for *U-47*: he made a picture of the animal, cut out a large pattern from paper, and a working party painted it in white, surprising and pleasing Günther Prien.*

And around the grim scene of the disaster, two days earlier, deathly silence, huge patches of oil fuel, like a disease, a macabre dark blanket, floating over *Royal Oak*'s final resting place. After the *Oak* had gone, after *U-47* had withdrawn, long hours after the invader had turned her long, sharp stern to the sea once more, there had stirred little boats, vessels of all shapes and sizes, cruising wearily about the still, black water, life lines dangling, but with no lives to save, just the floating dead to haul in. An aeroplane droned overhead. Several small motor boats, *Muriel, Chaucer, Sybil*, a floating canteen, *The Scarlet Thread*, sailed silently upon the bay, *Scarlet Thread* ironically, to take from the brackish liquid the floating body of the *Oak*'s canteen manager.

Chaucer plucked two bodies from a little cove, the corpses so covered with thick black slime that they could barely be got on board. 'As far as we could see,' *Chaucer*'s bowman would say, 'they were just lads, and fully dressed, all but boots and caps, and they must have been on watch at the time. We moved over to a pinnace belonging to *Iron Duke* and turned the two bodies over to the pinnace, and then went and made fast to the boom of *Pegasus* till daybreak.'

The seaplane tender swarmed with pitiful bands of shivering, coughing, wincing men, teen-aged boys, in pain or aching from cuts and bruises: they were all dehydrated, some suffering from fractures, forty per cent from burns, they were all cold, most freezing, rubbing bloodshot eyes, holding hands to peeling skin: almost four hundred survivors, some deposited by *Pegasus*'s boats, most, three hundred and eighty-six, by *Daisy* about 3 a.m. on the 14th. Making for the warmth of engines and boilers, they had removed the few rags that clung to their bodies, stood naked

---

* This emblem later was adopted by the entire 7th U-boat flotilla.

behind each other, rubbing the oil from the backs in front with water and cotton waste fed to them by *Pegasus*'s crew.

'Captain Benn was there—he told us to get ourselves warm,' Douglas Newton remembered. 'We were collected in batches of eight and bathed in shale oil and then washed with soap and water. I was wrapped in a blanket and put in a hammock.' The crew of the tender gave freely of their clothing, their bunks; they offered hot rum and hot cocoa, poured tea, helped the more badly burned to the Sick Bay.

Dick Kerr, trembling and shivering with cold and shock, was looking at his hands and arms for the first time since the lights on the *Oak* went out 'and the hands looked like raw meat with a sheet of skin hanging off of each. One rating stripped my underclothes off and then rubbed me down with towels, another gave me a tot of brandy, and then another tot and another but it didn't stop my shivering. They laid me onto a bed on the deck and covered me with blankets and hot water bottles but I couldn't throw off the awful shivers, it was terrible, the chap who rubbed me down brought me another tot and told me it was half past three, so I must have been in the water over two hours. The Surgeon Commander saved from *Royal Oak* (G. L. Ritchie) was doing everything he could for us all and how that man worked.'

The canteen swung open: cigarettes, chocolate, anything wanted, free of charge. But not all had the strength or disposition to take what was offered. Sergeant Henry Pattison, for one, just sat in one of the gangways on the deck, leaning against a bulkhead. 'This was the first time that I had been unoccupied since the second explosion aboard the *Oak* and I suppose the horror of the whole event must have hit me, because my body was shaking visibly from head to foot, every few seconds, with violent shudders for a period of about half an hour, before I had control of myself again.'

Others in the excitement showed fright in their faces, still shaken from the experience: H. R. J. Johnston recalled 'one messmate who was horrified because he couldn't remember his official number.' Other survivors tried to calm him, while others lay trembling violently in hammocks in the mess deck, naked or clad only in underwear; and then for a moment for some there came the same fear that had leapt out at them on the sinking *Oak*, they fled, fear leaping out again.

William Casey remembered: 'We had been down there (in the engine room) about half an hour having a smoke given to us by the crew and talking about the sinking when someone mentioned a torpedo hitting us—with that we were out of the engine room in a flash and up on to the mess deck.'

Like animals pursued, chased by the thought of it happening again, they ran, found that the alarm was false, and turned back slowly, angry but subdued, resolved to take comfort wherever they could find it. 'The ship's company were very good to us,' said Casey 'and one of the ratings gave me his hammock to turn into and there was plenty of hot cocoa. There were a lot of people who were very badly burned, one in particular an old shipmate of mine in the *Revenge*, Harry Instance, whose face and hands were terrible. You could see the bones in his hands and head, not a hair to be seen, he was terrible to look at.'

Many of the survivors, in pain, cuddled up in bunks, looking deathlike in sleep. R. A. Rowley, a member of *Pegasus*'s crew, stared hard all around, macabre sights everywhere; yet at times, he'd confess, he could not help but feel amused—at the picture of *Royal Oak* officers dressed in ordinary sailor's clothing.

All through the early hours of that Saturday after the disaster the survivors had pressed hard questions upon each other.

'Everyone talking at once,' remembered Frank Williams. ' "Is so and so safe?" "Saw him in the water but don't think he's here." "How did you get out?" and so on and so on. Speculation as to the cause of the disaster was of course a main topic but all anyone could think of at first was mines or bombs. I remembered "Pony" Moore's statement of the same evening and wondered if he could be right and a submarine had got in. In a short space of time the commander sent for me and took me in to see our captain who was also saved. I could tell them nothing at all, in fact felt a little ashamed that I knew so little. It wasn't until I saw the captain that I knew there had been four torpedo hits and that it was quite certainly a submarine attack and not mines or aircraft.'

Not everyone was so certain. Mostly the talk was of sabotage. How could a submarine have got into Scapa Flow. *A submarine? Scapa Flow?* The stores from Scapa Pier—they'd been hoisted inboard from a boat and taken below, but it wasn't the regular storeship; there was something odd about that. Couldn't fuses have been set? Couldn't high explosive devices have been inserted in the crates by enemy agents operating in Kirkwall?

'Another opinion,' said A. R. Jordan, 'was that after the first explosion something happened at a magazine when the temperature was being taken. This could have caused the second and subsequent explosions. Others stated the explosions were caused internally and did not come from outside the ship. Another theory was that the ship picked up a string of mines while at sea the day before and these caused the explosions.'

Came Sunday morning and upon awakening Newton thought the sinking was all 'a dream I had had'. The smell of roast beef cooking for *Pegasus*'s Sunday lunch helped support the thought. Perhaps he'd be able to forget it all. But he glanced at the eyes of those around him and saw that it had been no dream. 'I searched for my mate, Joe Riley, but I didn't find him. The hangar was full of men badly burned.'

Pegasus weighed anchor and transferred the wounded to a hospital tender; and as each man was helped or was carried in, he gave his name, rate, and official number to the Corporal of the Gangway.

'I was put into a small cabin on the upper deck which had four bunks in it,' said Dick Kerr. 'It was nice and warm in there and I am glad it was as I only had a blanket draped around my naked body. In the cabin were men I could not recognize owing to their burns and they could not recognize me as I didn't know until a week afterwards when they showed me my face in a mirror that all my front and top hair was all burnt off and my face and ears looked like the crackling off of roasted pork.'

When the *Oak*'s Sick Berth Attendant Reg Bendell was brought in, suffering from shock, he was helped into a bunk and 'it was funny,' said Kerr, 'to see us trying to help one another, giving one another drinks, lighting cigarettes, or trying to pull one another's blankets up round our shoulders with our hands raw.' The tender pulled up to a hospital ship, HMS *Abba* and there sisters, nurses and stewards sprayed the men's burns with tannic acid, dressed the wounds, put mouth feeders to swollen and blistered lips; many of the survivors wore bandage masks with two holes to see through and a slit for the mouth.

The other survivors, more fortunate, were transferred to an

armed merchant cruiser, the former Lamport and Holt liner TSS
Voltaire, anchored off Flotta at the other end of the Flow. Henry
Pattison remembered: 'Along the way, a young Sub-Lieutenant
asked us to kneel and pray, for thankfulness, which we did.' And
in the cruiser, every survivor was offered a tot of rum, issued with
jerseys, overall suits, long underpants, socks, and gym shoes: by
the time William Casey got to the counter, the ship had run out of
footwear; 'but there was plenty of rum to drink.'

A big bag of mail arrived for the *Oak*'s company. 'It was pitiful
shouting out the names and so many not claiming them,' said Pattison. Long hours of waiting passed, boats coming and going, nes-
tling against the cruiser, some bearing the bodies of the dead
pulled from the water for survivors to identify before burial in
Scapa cemetery the next day. Meanwhile nobody could leave;
there was talk of a 'Board of Enquiry' and while the Admiralty
was out looking for a committee, the men had to be content with
concerts, whist drives, a few light moments: Stanley Thompson
remembers walking down the grand staircase to the liner's dining
room; he still had oil fuel in his ears but he heard loudly the roar
of laughter that went up at his appearance, as the sailor's duck
suit given him on *Pegasus* 'must have been the smallest size in
stock and was a foot short in the legs and the arms only reached
my elbows.' But mostly the survivors just wandered around, exploring the ship, grumbling about not going back to Portsmouth.

'No one had any money,' said Casey. 'They would not let us
have any subs and with no cigarettes, trouble was brewing. The
Padre was constantly with the men trying to pacify them.'

Fear like the oil that had been wiped from them, still clung to
their bodies; it had got into their pores, could not be shaken off.
Before taking a nap in a cabin, Herbert Johnston opened the porthole, had to overcome an impulse to put a life-jacket on—he just
left it on top of his pillow.

Sunday passed peacefully; in the morning small sheets of *Voltaire* stationery were passed among the survivors and for the
benefit of the Board of Enquiry they sat to write answers for a
questionnaire: 1. (a) Where were you at time of explosions 1, 2,
3, 4? (b) What did you see? (c) Where were the explosions?
2. Can you throw any light on whether there was any flash, splash,
bulge in the deck or hole in the deck? 3. How did you get onto the

upper deck and when? 4. Did you see any hole in the side or bottom of the ship?

Then on Monday in the cemetery at Lyness the dead were buried, near the British who had perished in *Vanguard*, near some Germans as well, who had died in the great scuttling of the First War; and in an ill-fitting array of hand-me-down garments, mostly drab boiler suits, an odd assortment of foot gear—many wearing one black leather shoe, one white canvas shoe—the long sad files of survivors trekked, behind others carrying wreaths, a few ratings with rifles. A bugler played over the graves.

And then, the next morning, about ten o'clock, again the survivors felt the threatening, badgering persistence of death revisiting, for suddenly there sounded the 'Red' air warning. In the first air-raid of the war over Scapa Flow four Junkers 88's mistook *Iron Duke* for the *Repulse* Prien claimed to have damaged. A flurry of bombs dropped on either side of *Voltaire*, three about thirty yards from the port side, two just off either bow. One, hitting the water near *Iron Duke*'s port engine room, split open her port side; another flew over her quarter-deck, landed almost beneath the ship, shook her from stem to stern, sending Admiral Jellicoe's old frock-coat flying from its case—and 'over my shoulders,' as one officer of *Iron Duke* would maintain years later (claiming, predictably, some 'have greatness thrust upon them').

On a little drifter plying the Flow, a boat named *Horizon*, which had set out from Lyness, sailors heard the roar of the bombs, turned eyes skyward, felt helpless, did the only thing they could think of: hastily stripped the Union Jack and a White Ensign from the coffined bodies of two sailors, Dunk and Chappell, picked up at St Margaret's Hope.

From one of the portholes in the *Abba* Reg Bendell was watching for his chums lying in cots, was giving a running commentary as bombs hit the water or flew over the *Duke*'s quarter-deck; every gun in Gutter Sound was answering back. The Germans didn't bomb *Abba* but they began their air dives over her, said Kerr, using the hospital ship as a screen against fire from British dreadnoughts. Bendell's description was too much for the men lying down. 'What with our nerves being in a terrible state and him excited,' Kerr would remember and write down, 'well, the sister soon stopped him and made him get into his cot; she then went around and closed all the deadlights onto the portholes.'

George Booth, fished from the sea by *Daisy II,* who had boarded *Iron Duke* to collect the *Oak*'s mail, was watching with astonishment as the sound of the German engines swelled to a roar. With mailbag in hand, he abandoned ship, began to swim frantically; he kept his grip on the sodden bag and stared up to see the shore gunners send one Junkers down, then witness the *Duke* heel to port and settle into shallow water. A fishing boat scooped Booth from the sea, took him to Flotta, where by coincidence a group of survivors from the *Oak,* men and boys who had been suffering from a bad state of nerves, had been landed shortly before for a walk—'to give us the happy feeling of being on land again'—remembered F. J. C. Hobbs. Watching *Iron Duke* get hit, they lay on the ground, cowered in peat diggers trenches as bombs and shrapnel cut the land and water around them.

A Junkers spun down in flames, fell near the hospital ship: not far to go for the injured German pilot, who was helped in, his burns and broken ribs treated, later to go to Invergordon hospital along with the British injured of *Royal Oak.*

In the afternoon the *Oak* survivors returned to *Voltaire.* 'There was hell to pay,' said Casey. 'Everyone demanding to be sent to Portsmouth where they could hold the Enquiry if they wanted to. Word soon went round that the captain was on the telephone talking to the Admiralty in no uncertain words.' It was Benn. 'This raid completely ended any good which had been done to officers and men,' he'd later tell the Board of Enquiry, 'and with the exception of a few officers they became quite demoralised. The *Iron Duke* was sinking, and I was determined that my men should not suffer the same fate in the *Voltaire.*' He beseeched Admiral French for a minesweeper to take the survivors to Thurso on the Scottish mainland. French agreed, sent over the *Hebe,* which that afternoon took some three hundred survivors to Scrabster, from where by bus they continued to Thurso while the local committee of the Service Men's Canteen, working with the Town Council, was organising a complete canvas for accommodations in private houses. The whole of the little burgh threw open its doors.

Meanwhile on *Voltaire* about forty men, delayed on Flotta, were suffering through another 'Red' air-raid warning. The Germans inflicted no further damage but the muffled thunder of the engines was enough of a fright laid on and by the time the remain-

Triumph in Berlin

In Hitler's personal Focke-Wulf-Vogel, Prien is interviewed on his way to the Tempelhof and an audience with the Führer

Congratulations from Grossadmirals Böhm and Raeder

Berliners were electrified by Prien's exploit

(*Top*) Flowers for the crew and (*below*) flushed with victory, *U-47* crewmen (in round sailor caps) were chauffered through the German capital

ing survivors left the next morning, aboard the *St Ninian*, they were reduced to a pitiful state: on their last night at sea no one could persuade them to lay down anywhere but in the passages near the ship's gangways.

How much more could they take without the means to strike back? Not much, it seemed; yet the solemn threat of death kept shadowing. For after two nights the survivors boarded a special train for the long ride to Portsmouth barracks.

As Frank Williams would write it up later: 'I shared a compartment with four other Warrant Officers and a journalist from the *Daily Herald*. The journalist whose name I now forget had been with us at Thurso interviewing whoever cared to talk about the personal angle. He and I got on pretty well together and he had wangled a passage on the train and joined up with us. The train left Thurso about 8 p.m., dark of course. We played cards for an hour or so, then lapsed into desultory conversation.

'At some time or other the journalist (David I think) said, "You chaps have had a pretty fair basin-full lately, torpedoed, sunk, swimming around and then bombed. All we want now for a real write-up for the *Daily Herald* is a train smash." We told him what he could do about his train smash and went to sleep as best we could.

'At 1 a.m. the train stopped for some reason, waited about five minutes, then started again. We had reached probably about twenty miles an hour or less when sure enough there was a crash. We had run into some stationary coaches on the line, our engine was pushing us from behind and consequently the first coach on our train took the blow and was damaged. Though nobody was hurt badly, one chap had jumped out and busted his ankle. We sorted ourselves out with the help of matches (the lights having failed) and David opened the door, leapt down onto the track and was gone into the dark just like that, saying something about a story for his paper. In a very short space of time the damaged coach was uncoupled and we were off again. David had found us again; he had found a small station back on the train and somehow phoned his paper with the story—a keen type, David!'

'So ended the unhappy story of the *Royal Oak*.'

By now Britain and the world had heard of the Royal Navy's second big loss of the war. On Saturday, the 14th, the first news-

papers had bannered the news. ROYAL OAK SUNK BY GERMAN SUB-
MARINE: OVER 1,000 OFFICERS AND MEN ON BOARD, read the
startling headline of *The Evening News* of Portsmouth, the city
where the ship had been commissioned, where she had been
manned. 370 SAVED FROM ROYAL OAK, boomed the headline in the
Sunday Graphic, and halfway down the front page, the subhead
'How Germany Heard the News,' above the story of the BBC announcement.

In most accounts there were few details, just the official Admiralty statement, followed by a brief history of the ship, her cost
to build (£2,500,000, another £1,000,000 for her refitting),
then the first short list of survivors. Paymaster Seymour's was the
first name announced, followed by fourteen others: Holligan,
Dunstone, Higgins, Rowland, McCabe, Harmer, Smith, Crichton, Martin, Scovell, Hine, Cleverley, Stares, Woods. More lists
followed, in later editions, and gradually bits and pieces of sor-
rowful news stumbled into print: 140 Portsmouth men lost, 91
Marines dead; whole towns and cities in mourning—in little Ha-
vant sons in five homes gone, from Eastney, Gosport, Emsworth,
Chichester heartbreaking stories of men and boys who had 'made
the supreme sacrifice.'

Small groups of people, women mainly, many with prams,
stood silently or quietly talking to one another, whispering news
of husbands, sons, or brothers gone. Many got out last letters received, or showed names on fatal telegrams. All took the news
bravely. 'It's terrible losing Ron,' typically said the Portsmouth
sister of lost Marine Ronald Thomas Parker, 'but I've heard of a
woman round here who has been left with six young children and
another with four. So many are young men whose wives are going
to have babies. It's so sad for them.' Mr and Mrs Thomas Spelman of Chichester heard of the death of their only son, Thomas, a
Boy, only eighteen, on their 20th wedding anniversary, also Mr
Spelman's birthday. And at the Royal Naval Barracks, where the
lists of survivors were posted, friends and families crowded round
to anxiously await the posting of more names; even when the rain
fell they waited, thirty more names on the second list, ninety-eight
on the third, fifty on the fourth, and so on, through eight separate
lists, the last on Sunday, a stoker, Sydney Henry Cook, the last
survivor named.

The train from Thurso rolled into Portsmouth, and the survivors told their stories to a press anxious for anything to fill in the scant Admiralty statement. 'They say things run in threes, and we had our share,' proclaimed Leading Stoker Kenneth Hickman of Gosport. 'We were torpedoed, then we had an air raid, and finally we were in a railway accident.'

Boy Telegraphist Ernest F. Upham, told the story many would recount as long as they lived, 'We were asleep when the first explosion occurred. It woke us up, but we turned over and went to sleep again. When the other explosions followed we quickly turned out and went to the boat deck. The ship was heeling over, and we slid down her sides, sitting on the blister to take off our boots and trousers.'

Upham's chum, Signaller Boy George Trewinnard anxiously joined in the telling: 'I struck out and was swimming for about two and a half hours before being picked up by a naval motor boat.'

Over and over, from survivor after survivor, the details emerged, trickled onto the journalists' notebooks: 'The lights went out . . . the ship heeled over.' 'I clung to an oar . . . somebody put a rope around me.' 'It was awfully cold . . . I reached a rock; I climbed onto the rock and was there for about twenty minutes when a boat came and picked me up.'

But why? How could a U-boat get so close? How could it get into Scapa Flow? 'Inexcusable,' the *Scottish Daily Express* called the disaster: Scapa Flow was Britain's main naval base, 'the most important stretch of water in all the oceans. If any of our harbours should be impregnable, this one should be. Yet a U-boat enters the harbour, and, with due deliberation, sinks a British battleship. And then, apparently, goes home! Magnificent seamanship by the submarine's commander? No doubt. But the defences of the Flow should be safe against the finest sailor.

'It should be impossible for an enemy craft to creep into the harbour in the wake of a minesweeper, as this one may have done. It should certainly be impossible for her commander to know so much about the disposition of defences that he can pilot his ship through them unscathed. The Scapa affair is a disgrace. In war there must be accidents and there will be disasters. But this disaster is inexcusable.'

Across Britain other newspapers echoed the same sentiment. 'How on earth could such a thing happen?' asked H. C. Ferraby, naval correspondent for the *Sunday Express*. There still had been no detailed statement from the Admiralty, the silence giving life to a rumour that the phrase, 'it is believed by U-boat action' was put out to cover a disastrous air defeat. Ferraby deduced that the lateness of a full Admiralty announcement meant the sinking occurred during the night. 'When more details are available we shall, certainly, find that the *Royal Oak* was a victim of submarine attack,' he guessed, correctly. 'And in view of her construction we may expect to learn that more than one torpedo was put into her.' Then finally, two days later in the House of Commons Winston Churchill rose to clear up the mystery:

'The battleship *Royal Oak* was sunk at anchor by a U-boat in Scapa Flow approximately at 1.30 a.m. on the 14th instant. It is still a matter of conjecture how the U-boat penetrated the defences of the harbour. When we consider that during the whole course of the last war this anchorage was found to be immune from such attacks on account of the obstacles imposed by the currents and the net barrages, this entry by a U-boat must be considered as a remarkable exploit of professional skill and daring. A Board of Enquiry is now sitting at Scapa Flow to report upon all that occurred, and anything that I say must be subject to revision in the light of their conclusions.

'It appears probable that the U-boat fired a salvo of torpedoes at the *Royal Oak*, of which only one hit the bow. This muffled explosion was at the time attributed to internal causes, and what is called the inflammable store where the kerosene and other such materials are kept, was flooded. Twenty minutes later the U-boat fired three or four torpedoes, and these, striking in quick succession, caused the ship to capsize and sink.

'She was lying at the extreme end of the harbour, and therefore many officers and men were drowned before rescue could be organised from other vessels. The lists of survivors have already been made public, and I deeply regret to inform the House that upwards of 800 officers and men have lost their lives. The Admiralty immediately announced the loss of this fine ship. Serious as this loss is, it does not affect the margin of security in heavy vessels, which remain ample.

'Meanwhile, an intensive search of the anchorage has not yet yielded any results. It is clear, however, that after a certain time the harbour can be pronounced clear, as any U-boat would have to rise to the surface for air or perish. All necessary measures are being taken to increase the precautions which in the late war proved effectual. For the rest, I must await the report of the Board which is now examining the event in full technical detail.'

The opposition, in the person of A. V. Alexander, was restrained and sympathetic, yet there was some thought that perhaps the House ought to know whether at the outbreak of the war a systematic survey of the harbour defences was carried out to ensure the anchorage was safe.

'Also,' asked Alexander, 'can we be assured now that during the whole period since that survey there has been maintained properly at all times the boom defences required?'

Churchill replied yes, the boom defences had been kept up. He said nothing about the eastern entrances, where there were no booms. 'But there is an enquiry which will not take very long, and I would like to have the advantage of reading the report before I go into the details of this disaster.'

Another member of Parliament, Sir A. Southby spoke up. Was the German submarine actually sighted inside Scapa Flow? Could Churchill assure the House that as soon as the report was received he would give the House information from it 'consistent with the national safety?'

'I did not say the U-boat was sighted inside Scapa Flow,' answered the First Lord of the Admiralty. 'But I gave the information in our possession. When the enquiry is completed I shall be very glad to answer some other questions if they would add to the information of the House.' Southby was not satisfied. Is the claim made by the German High Command that they command the North Sea false? Yes, it is false, said Churchill: 'There is, of course, a most effective control of all contraband and of all commerce entering Germany. The North Sea is patrolled effectively, so that they can derive no advantage whatever from ocean-going commerce.'

Churchill said nothing of the U-boat threat against British commerce, and Southby did not press him for a reply.

While the British Parliament was meeting, the German Navy was celebrating. On this very day in Wilhelmshaven, the crews of every ship at anchor were lining the rails to honour the successful invader. On her flagpole the wind tugged the ensign of the *Kriegs-*

marine; and in the conning tower, wearing leather jacket, black woollen jersey, his familiar white peaked cap, Prien gazed foreward over the spray deflector, saluting smartly, his officers behind him; while on the decks in columns of two there stood his crew, loosely at attention, listening to the cheers of sailors aboard ships and the clash of steel produced by shipyards on shore, a loud raucous blare that sent from man to man among the crew the happy joke: 'That's them making our Iron Crosses!'

7

Board of Enquiry

On Wednesday morning 18 October in a rude corrugated iron shelter at Scapa Flow—the Paravane Shed—the Board of Enquiry, comprised of Vice-Admiral R. H. T. Raikes, Captain G. C. Muirhead Gould, and Admiral Sir Reginald A. R. Plunkett-Ernle-Erle-Drax (who for a period in the early 30's as Commander-in-Chief of the America-West Indies Station had had Admiral Blagrove as his flag captain in the cruiser *Norfolk*), met to commence its investigation into what would become, in time, the most controversial sea disaster in the history of the Royal Navy.

For more than thirty years, under terms of the Official Secrets Act, the proceedings conducted by these three men would remain closed to public scrutiny, giving rise to charges in some quarters of the British press that in the locked files of Whitehall there remained hidden away the perfidious details of a sabotage plot too scurrilous ever to be admitted by the Admiralty.

Such might have appeared to be happening, for on that autumn day in 1939, as the Board was about to convene, just a glance at the gleaming uniforms of the senior officers seemed to foretell an event of extraordinary importance. Even the Germans, as though prescient, appeared primed for the great affair, for hardly had the Board members (up by train from Whitehall the evening before), begun to weigh the evidence when another 'Red' air raid warning sounded, delaying the opening meeting. It proved a reconnaissance flight only—no new bullet holes were added to the rusty ones already in the old shed's roof—and when the drone of enemy aircraft faded from earshot, there began at once the delicate mission of trying to determine, in the Admiralty's own words (1) Whether the *Royal Oak* loss was due to action by an enemy submarine and if so (2) How the submarine was able to enter Scapa

Flow and how this could be prevented in the future; (3) What occurred during the subsequent sinking of the ship.

For six days, beginning at Scapa and ending at Thurso on the 24th, the Board, in committee and subcommittee, studied the evidence, compiled reports, questioned a long parade of witnesses, including Admiral French, who was directly responsible for the defence of the base, a crushed Captain Benn, whose ship so suddenly, so unbelievably, had been taken from him; Commanders Nichols, Renshaw, Gregory, and others; skipper Gatt; Thomas McKenzie of Metal Industries Limited, whose report had forewarned of the possibility of the disaster; the deckhands off *Dragonet*; a dozen or so others, a few Leading Seamen, a few Ordinary Seamen—about three dozen witnesses in all, officers mostly, men whom the board felt could best supply the details it needed to get at the truth.

In anguish, they gathered, in embarrassment, disbelief; it showed in their faces. They had been caught unprepared, stood helpless in the grip of a horrible fact.

'Will you please tell us what you consider caused the loss of the *Royal Oak*?'*

Admiral French listened to the question, must have felt a flash of horror that it even was being asked. In his mind this day there still existed a possible doubt that a U-boat had entered the Flow, had attacked the great battleship—because it had not yet been established that *Royal Oak* had been sunk by torpedoes. On the morrow he'd recruit divers from *Iron Duke*; their report, he felt, would make submarine action clear. So he answered the question directly:

'A submarine that fired four or five torpedoes.'

There were no journalists to perceive the features of those present, no one to regard the tone of the questions or answers; thus there is no way for us now to discern the dejection that must have marked the witnesses' countenances. The questions and answers bore only an expression of the determination to carry on.

Admiral French was asked, 'May we have your opinion please as to what entrance the submarine probably came in at?'

* In only rare instances is it possible to tell who on the Board asked the specific questions. The official transcript names only the witnesses and presents the questions and answers.

'I should say at Hoxa boom when the gate was open at some time.'

'Do you think the submarine got out again and if so, how?'

'There is absolutely no evidence anywhere that a submarine has got out of the Flow, only the evidence that so far we have completely failed to locate it. There is one position which has been depth-charged but has not been properly examined by divers.'

'In what depth of water is that?'

'About fifteen fathoms, I think.'

'Do you feel confident you would have had a report if a submarine had passed out after sinking the *Royal Oak*?'

'No. I think there was a period of about two to three hours after the sinking of the *Royal Oak* when a submarine might have got out without being observed.'

'Where would you expect her to go out in that case?'

'The Kirk Sound.'

'Taking into consideration that the Germans now know they can get a submarine in, how many of the different entrances do you consider to be impregnable at the present time?'

'My opinion is that Skerry Sound is impregnable and I also consider that East Weddel Sound and Water Sound are impregnable at night, unless it is very light, due to navigational difficulties. I do not consider that any of the booms are impregnable due to the side gates, which consist merely of a gap. Kirk Sound is definitely not impregnable, although extremely difficult due to the strength of the tide.'

Admiral French was right about the U-boat, right about the divers' report, wrong about the entrance (he had, he would later tell the Board, 'thought that following another ship through the gate was much the easiest method of getting into the Flow.'). As for Kirk Sound, he said, 'It would be an extremely fine feat if a submarine commander tried to come through that sound.' He was right about the exit; but more than this, his testimony showed, conclusively, that no British destroyer gave chase to Prien: *there is absolutely no evidence anywhere that a submarine has got out of the Flow, only the evidence so far that we have completely failed to find it.* So the 'sighting' of a pursuing destroyer by the Germans on the bridge of *U-47* was fanciful imagining under the pressure of fleeing.

As the testimony further unfolded, it became clear that not only was Scapa Flow not impregnable but it was in fact perhaps one of the most vulnerable places to enemy attack in all of the British Isles. Faced with the knowledge that a U-boat had got in, Admiral French soon was expressing dissatisfaction with almost everything about Scapa's defences. Blockships alone would not do for the eastern gaps—'we must have lookouts, searchlights and guns at all four entrances.' Close the gap at the western end of Switha boom, he told the Board. Close both ends of Hoxa boom—'the small boat traffic there is practically negligible.' Even so, the present boom at Hoxa is too far to seaward, he complained: in bad weather the buoys would almost certainly break away. Better to place it from Roan Head to Neva Skerry to Uppertown where it might stand up to gales. It would take three months to move the boom and 'It is also unfortunately a fact that the new loop minefield is going in precisely the place I suggested the boom should be laid.'

'Did not the boom lie satisfactorily from Hoxa Head during the last war?' French was asked.

'I think it was a much lighter boom,' he replied.

'We have heard a story that the telephone line from Kirkwall to the South Island, passing across Holm Sound, broke down about 0200 on the 14th October. Is that correct?'

'All I can say is I immediately sent a destroyer to investigate and they found nothing.'

'Is the cable still broken down?'

'I was told at the time that it had broken down for two hours and then came on again, but I know for a fact that the cable is broken down at the present moment.'

'What patrol vessels were operating on the night of Friday, 13th October, and where were they?'

'There were patrol vessels at Hoxa and Hoy booms. No others.'

The Board was probing for weaknesses in Scapa's defence organization.

'From the manner in which the attack was made it would seem that the submarine was steaming northwards along the west coast of Holm. Does this suggest to you that one entrance is more probable than another on that account?'

'Personally I do not consider that it shows that. I think that the necessary information had been obtained by a reconnaissance plane and that the submarine therefore attacked the biggest ship in the Flow.'

French next described the action he had taken after receiving *Pegasus*'s signals about the *Oak*: he had ordered all boats and drifters to be sent, made a general signal to raise steam with the utmost despatch and ordered the destroyers out to search for a submarine.

The questioning moved to the placement of the nets.

'Have you ever heard doubt expressed as to whether the Hoxa boom could keep out a submarine with certainty, even though the foot of the net is some 35 feet from the bottom at high water springs?'

'I am afraid that I must acknowledge that I thought that the foot of the net was much closer to the bottom because I had been told that the nets had been cut to fit the depth of water and I naturally assumed that they were right on the bottom. I have gone through the technical course, where I was given to understand that the double net at any rate was submarine proof.'

'It had been suggested to us by Vice-Admiral Horton* that there should be little difficulty in taking a submarine underneath the present net. What action can you suggest to deal with this possibility?'

'I see no reason why the net should clear the bottom by more than a few feet. The best protection, I think, is loop minefields.'

French went on to agree that Scapa's defence should be bolstered with Asdic or echo-sounding apparatus, either ashore or afloat. The Asdics needn't be placed outside the entrances, he said, just so long as they covered the booms; and, on being questioned, he answered there should be a boom at Kirkwall. He had tried to lay one with indicating nets but the strength of the tide had prevented it. He had only one minesweeper for sweeping the approaches to the port. He had no Asdic ships, no gun defences, apart from 4-inchers in a few guard ships. He had asked for more patrol vessels—he wanted two at each boom—but never got them. It would be an 'absolute catastrophe,' said French, if owing to German action any neutral ships in the port of Kirkwall were damaged or lost.

In effect, French was saying the Admiralty had not listened to his pleas. He had seen the *Scott* survey and 'I reported that in my

* An experienced submariner in World War I, Horton later in World War II became Admiral Sir Max Horton, and from November 1942 until the end of the war Commander-in-Chief, Western Approaches.

opinion there would be no difficulty for a submarine to come in by either of these two sounds (Kirk and Skerry) at slack water.' The other two eastern sounds he thought impassable to submarines 'on account of the natural navigational difficulties, assisted by block-ships that were placed there.'

To anyone reading the transcript, the tragic irony by now be-comes obvious: by and large the British considered the boom defences the weakness at Scapa, the eastern Sounds impregnable, while the Germans, thinking the opposite, believed the booms impregnable, the unguarded, eastern Sounds the weak points. But more than this, it is obvious that the barriers protecting Scapa Flow were mainly psychological, constructed not of real steel, thick netting, hard blockships, but of threads, imaginary ones, woven out of the belief that what never before had happened never could happen, just *because* it had never happened. Scapa Flow was the best base on the North Sea that could be found; but it could 'never be made definitely impregnable to a determined submarine officer,' said French. Cromarty, Rosyth, or any other North Sea base could be made more secure than Scapa for the Home Fleet—because 'in the past we have always relied on the psychological effect of the varying tides of the Pentlands, which, as a matter of fact, are not so big a bogie to those who know as people make out.'

Captain Robinson, the Extended Defence Officer stationed at Stanger Head, added his testimony to this effect, asserting that in his opinion none of the three main entrances was impregnable. At Switha a vessel up to 160 feet in length, about 10 feet draught, could pass between the boom end and the Flotta end *at low water*; around the Flotta end of Hoxa boom most small vessels could proceed at all states of tide; and at Hoy boom small vessels could pass between the boom end and Scad Head (Hoy end). Further-more, said Robinson, the boom gates were left open longer than could be considered safe. Drifters guarding the gates did not take sufficient precautions to make the entrances absolutely safe: they had no hydrophones or Asdics, sometimes there was only one drifter to do duty at both Hoxa and Switha; and on several occa-sions rockets and flares fixed to booms to warn of disturbances fired prematurely due to movement of the booms from the tide.

Thomas McKenzie, Metal Industries' chief salvage officer whose report of 20 May warning of the openness of the Sounds to submarine attack had been largely ignored by the Admiralty, now found himself face to face with the generally unseen men of Whitehall, officers to whom he could rightly have waved the prophetic statement he had made five months earlier, the one containing the words:

> It is fully recognised that the navigation of the Sounds, even now, presents difficulties, owing to the strong tidal streams and the existing obstructions, but it is safe to assume that an intrepid submarine officer, in war time, would take risks which no discreet mariner would think of taking in peace time. The possibility of a hostile submarine entering Scapa Flow, if the Sounds are left as at present, cannot therefore be excluded, and the fact that any such craft successful in passing through one of the Sounds could be within torpedo range of capital ships in 15 to 30 minutes, makes it of vital importance that the Sounds should be efficiently blocked.

The Admiralty, having not heeded McKenzie's forewarning, was not about to disregard him now: the civilian testified at length about the gaps he knew. Ahead of the *Soriano* in Kirk Sound he'd taken the anchor of the *Soriano* and stretched it right inshore until his tug was aground, he told the board, 'but I would not say it was absolutely sealed.' Then ahead of *Thames*, between that ship and Lamb Holm a vessel could pass. There was plenty of room—width and depth enough. The tide ran strong, up to ten knots, 'but there is a slack water of 15 minutes.'

'Then for the defence of that passage I take it we rely on the tide rather than on the complete blockage?'

'Yes, I think that is right,' said McKenzie.

Pressed for further details, he mentioned Water Sound, told of two blockships, one whole, one in pieces, to the north of which he'd sunk a concrete barge, the *Naja*; but ahead of her, he said, lay a fairly good passage, about 200 feet wide, 18 feet deep at high water. 'That passage I recommended should be blocked in my report about nine months ago. The tide there is about six knots.'

'What is the period of slack water?'

'About one hour.'

McKenzie went on to say how he thought Skerry Sound safe;

the sunk *Cape Ortegal* was doing the job. East Weddel and Burra could keep out a submarine but the passage between Hoy and the end of Hoy boom was about 500 feet wide, about 30 feet deep: 'The ordinary mail steamer to Stromness goes through that passage every night.'

'Are there obstructions further out to prevent a submarine reaching this gap?'

'I think there is no obstruction at all.'

'Is there a channel a submarine could come through?'

'Yes, through Hoy Sound.'

'Do you know why nothing has been done to close this gap?'

'I cannot say I know that. I think it was left open with a view to having a passage for steamers operating inside the Flow and save opening the gate so often for small craft passing back and forward.'

'Is it your opinion that a submarine could quite easily enter through Hoy Sound?'

'I think a submarine could. The passage is much easier than Kirk Sound. It is regularly navigated by Coast of Scotland steamers with a draught of 16 feet.'

Asked for his suggestion for making the various entrances he described absolutely safe, McKenzie had no doubt: 'I have a ship now for putting in the gap ahead of the *Thames* in Kirk Sound which I will be sinking on Saturday or Sunday, and to make it absolutely safe it might be advisable to put a small ship ahead of the *Soriano*; and I think I would say the same—a small ship ahead of the concrete barge *Naja* in Water Sound.'

The ship McKenzie had been given for Kirk was the *Lake Neuchatel*, requisitioned by the Director of Sea Transport on September 15th after Metal Industries, acting on behalf of ACOS— the headquarters organisation of the Admiral Commanding Orkney and Shetland—could find no other.

Since the start of war, the price of blockships had been ever-rising, making bartering an agonising chore. One vessel, the *Capitaine Damiani*, had been detained at Marseilles for use as a blockship in Kirk Sound but because of bickering over price it had got no farther than the French port. Another vessel, the *Cape Ortegal*, also had been considered; but the owners had placed on her a very high price—an 'absurd price,' said the Admiralty—and she was eventually sold for use elsewhere.

A third candidate, the *Virginias*, had foundered in a Greek port on her homeward trip, was finally replaced by the *Lake Neuchatel*, which was then docked at Cardiff. She had been intended for Kirk but she wasn't ready. As Admiral Forbes would explain to the Board,* 'She sailed from Cardiff on 22 September for Rosyth to be prepared, and left Rosyth for Scapa on 14 October and arrived on 15 October with a view to scuttling on 20 October. The *Royal Oak* was sunk early on 14 October.'

When next McKenzie was questioned about his recommendations for Hoy, he was quick to condemn the security of Scapa's front door.

'The Hoy entrance would need a very big ship to block that, but it might be possible to put another boom across there. Hoxa boom from my knowledge of the weather conditions usually encountered during the winter at Scapa will not stand the winter and in its present position it will be impossible to repair any damage for weeks on end. My personal opinion is that a boom from Neva Skerry to Flotta and Neva Skerry to Roan Head to Uppertown would be much easier maintained. A double boom from Hoxa Head to Flotta would be less effective and very difficult to maintain. You would only be able to approach the boom from one side if the wind was in a certain direction.'

The Board did not yet know through which passage the U-boat had entered and left; they knew only that Kirk Sound seemed to present the least difficulty; the Germans could have slipped in submerged through the Hoxa gate while opened, under the Hoxa boom, through the gap at the Flotta end of Switha boom, through the gap at the Hoy end of Hoy boom, on the surface or trimmed down, even through the difficult to pass opening in Skerry Sound on the surface, or other gaps in East Weddel and Water Sounds—

---

* Not in person, but in a written statement he submitted from *Nelson* explaining that he was unable to attend the Enquiry but accepting full responsibility for the presence of *Royal Oak* at Scapa and for the number of patrol craft left there from those available for guarding the entrances to the three bases at Scapa, Loche Ewe, and Sullom Voe; Forbes made no attempt to call the Board's attention to his possible Fleet-saving move of taking the big ironclads to Rosyth. Much has been written about a blockship arriving at Scapa on the 'very day' *Royal Oak* was sunk, but Forbes' statement makes it clear that even had the *Lake Neuchatel* arrived on the 14th, one day before her actual arrival, it would have taken almost a full week to get her ready for blocking the Sound. Worth noting too, and almost always overlooked, is the fact that there were *two* navigable channels in Kirk Sound. Finding one impossible to enter, Prien might have tried the other.

on the surface: the board in its summation would later admit the possibility that officers who had studied the problem before the disaster were thinking of keeping out a *submerged* submarine, and these officers 'lacked expert knowledge of the probable draft of small German submarines, or the possibility of their scraping along the bottom of a channel.'

Was it a submarine? Could there be any doubt? Late on the 20th, the third day of the enquiry, the divers would present proof of holes in the starboard side—definite sighting of plating blown inboard, edges bent in: what else but holes caused by torpedoes? But the Board made no effort, none whatsoever, to enquire into the rumour, the 'buzz,' of sabotage then going about—that the shipped stores may have contained explosives. A careful reading of the transcript indicates that from the moment of the tragedy the Admiralty believed nothing but torpedoes had sent *Royal Oak* down. Most questions, therefore, trailed over details, concentrated on the heel and 'hang' of the ship, the actions of officers and men when the explosions occurred, the Admiral's movements, the state of the defences, and so on. Only occasionally was there asked directly the question which in later years would stir so much bitter controversy.

'Had you any means of ascertaining what caused the explosions?'

The query may have caught by surprise Sub-Lieutenant Kenneth Bernard Clayton, coming after a simple one about when the lights went out. But Clayton fielded it quickly.

'My impression was that the second, third, and fourth explosions were caused by torpedoes on the starboard side, because I definitely felt that no large magazine was exploded.'

At another session, confirmation was sought from Captain Benn.

'Have you any personal knowledge of whether there were columns of water that might have indicated torpedo explosions outside?'

'Only from what I have heard afterwards,' Benn replied. 'I have subsequently been told, although I did not notice it myself when standing on the forecastle before going below, that the forecastle deck forward was quite wet. The whole of what I saw of the rest of the upper deck was quite dry afterwards. Further information I gained from men whom I questioned is that a spout of water was seen to go up with the first explosion; also that the second or third explosion drenched the air defence position which is on the foremast above and abaft the compass platform. Leading Signalman Fossey gave me the information about the first explosion.'

'Do you know if there are any witnesses who said afterwards that they had seen the track of a torpedo or a conning tower, or anything that might indicate the presence of a submarine?'

'No one has stated that they saw the track of a torpedo. Marine Owens, I have been given to understand, when swimming away from the stern of the ship in company with an officer whom he could not recognize, stated that he saw the conning tower of a submarine and pointed it out to the officer. This officer cannot be traced, but when asked by Lieutenant Keen to draw what he saw he produced something on a bulkhead which showed the shape of a conning tower of a submarine.'

'Can you express any opinion either from the spread of the torpedoes or from the distance to the shore as to how far the submarine was when she fired?'

'I do not think it is possible to express an opinion on this because, so far as I can understand, the ship has been found to have sunk with her head in such a direction as to have exposed her starboard side to attack from anywhere inside the Flow to the southward.'

The questioning of Captain Benn lasted longer than any other witness, ranged over a dozen subjects, from the state of preparedness of the *Oak,* the way she was darkened, her watch and lookouts, the way he left the ship, the rescue work. No, he had given no orders for closing the starboard scuttles after the first explosion and knew of no other orders being given: he was able to do nothing effective to try and save the ship. If the ship's company had been issued with life jackets stowed in messes, lives would have been saved—if the lights had not gone out, if half of the vertical doors had not been closed for air defence purposes, if the horizontal hatches had not slammed shut by the force of explosions and list, if there'd been enough boats and Carley rafts to accommodate the whole of the ship's company, if the rafts had not had to be lifted from chocks, if they'd been stowed in accessible places, instead of out of the way positions amidships.

'The combined effect of all these,' said Benn, 'leads one to the opinion that a large number of men never got out of the ship.'

But, 'I am afraid that the real loss of life on this occasion was caused by no real alarm being raised after the first explosion, and on account of the second explosion men jumping to the conclusion that the ship had been attacked by bombs, and a great number of them, I believe, then tried to do what they had been taught to do for some time, that is get under armour.'

Personally, Benn had witnessed no panic: 'With regard to the ship's company generally, I heard no shouting and I have no recollection of seeing any officer or man running. It was all extraordinary quiet.'

'Can you estimate even roughly how many men were not saved who were in the water when the ship sank?'

'No, Sir.'

'What SOS signals were made from the ship?'

Benn replied: 'The Commander ordered a signal to be made to *Pegasus*. When I got to *Pegasus* some time later and I had consulted with one or two officers I felt very strongly of the opinion that the ship must have been torpedoed. I had an immediate signal made to ACOS to inform him of my opinion so that counter action could be taken at once. This was followed by an amplifying signal and by a further signal.'

In fact, no fault of Benn's, but the fault of a lack of power, no SOS signals were made from the *Oak*. *Pegasus* was alerted but not by signal but by shock waves carried through the water by force of the explosions: *Pegasus* crewmembers heard bangs on the side of their ship, heard a quartermaster order 'Away all boats' crews'; then later, at approximately thirty-five minutes past one, or two minutes after the *Oak* went down—as later testimony by other officers would bring out—*Pegasus* made a visual morse signal to the Flotta Signal Station: SEND ALL BOATS, then a half hour later a further signal: ROYAL OAK IS SINKING AFTER SEVERAL INTERNAL EXPLOSIONS. Even then Admiral French was not informed.

The first suggestion that enemy action had been taken, according to later testimony by Commander Heath, Operations Staff Officer to the Admiral, 'was a message from Captain Benn which reached the Admiral within one and a half hour of the *Royal Oak* sinking.' So only then were all boats and drifters sent, a general signal made to raise steam with the utmost despatch, three destroyers sent to depth-charge the invader. What invader? By this time, Günther Prien was gone. In Roskill's official British history of *The War at Sea, U-47* 'by 2.15 a.m. was out in the open sea again.'*

Commander Nichols, present while Benn testified, added little; he'd seen nothing of the actual explosions, knew only that *Royal Oak* did not 'blow up.' Prien was wrong.

'Have you formed any definite opinion as to what caused the explosions?'

'Only from evidence based on hearsay,' said Nichols, 'and from the fact I am convinced that no major magazine blew up. It is conceivable that a 4-inch magazine might have blown up but I think it highly improbable. From the intervals between the explosions, torpedo attack appeared probable.'

'Is there any magazine anywhere near the Inflammable Store?'

'No, Sir.'

Nichols told how he'd gone onto 'B' gun deck after the fourth explosion, hailed the flag deck, told them to make a general signal on the projector to send all boats, only to get back word that power had failed.

'Had you a rocket on the bridge ready for firing, or Very lights?'

'I cannot say, and unfortunately it did not occur to me to order their use.'

'Can you say what visual signal from ships in harbour would have been regarded as an urgent distress signal?'

'There would have been nothing more than the normal international signals for a ship in distress.'

'Were any such signals made from *Pegasus*?'

'I saw none; but I knew she made a general signal to send all boats to *Royal Oak*.'

'Did *Pegasus* promptly switch on a searchlight and was it helpful?'

'I saw her burning a searchlight very soon after I was in the water, but it was of no assistance so far as I know.'

So ran the questioning, switching rapidly from subject to subject and sometimes taking a wrong turn, as when after being ques-

---

* Roskill's next statement: 'Meanwhile inside the Flow it was realised that a U-boat had probably penetrated the defences, but a search by every available vessel revealed no trace of her,' infers the search began *before* the U-boat escaped, which in fact never happened. Prien was too quick, the British too stunned, too confused over where in the huge anchorage to even begin to search.

tioned about the height of the lowest line of open scuttles, Nichols suddenly was asked whether he ever considered the desirability of being prepared for torpedo attack when at anchor in harbour.

'Not in our main naval base, Sir,' he responded in astonishment.

There was no deliberate attempt to fix blame, dig into the possibility of personal negligence. This was not the purpose of the hearings—it was an 'enquiry,' not a trial; and yet some of the questions touched on the idea of responsibility. Commander O. M. Frewen, Senior Naval Officer and King's Harbour Master, denied for instance that he was personally responsible for the closing or defence of any of the harbour's entrances; his job, he said, was only to point out to Admirals Forbes and French 'which gaps in my opinion are dangerous.'

Asked if he'd made any written report on the subject, Frewen said no, the matter already was in hand when he was appointed; but he ventured to state that in view of the open space south of *Thames* in Kirk Sound, he wouldn't have thought a submarine would have bothered anywhere else, 'as there would be sufficient water at that high water, as it was high water springs in both East Weddel and Water Sounds.'

'What action is being taken now to deal with these two passages?' Frewen was asked.

'So far as I know, none,' he answered.

It was Frewen who in June had taken Admiral French out and in again through both Skerry and Kirk Sounds in a boom defence picket boat; then in September a Metal Industries tug had passed straight through Kirk Sound near *low water* on the way to relieve a ship grounded on one of the northern islands; the tug was 'not reported by anyone,' said Frewen.

So the vaunted belief in Scapa Flow, impregnable Scapa Flow, was shattered. Witness after witness said it: a U-boat could have got in through that gap, that opening, those openings, round that boom, under that net, in the dead of night, at high water, at low water. The most impassable of gaps could be navigated. With difficulty true, but the gaps could be navigated—by a *daring* submarine commander.

Would Karl Dönitz have sent to Scapa Flow anyone not daring?

By the time skipper Gatt was called, there was no question of whether a submarine had got in but how—how had the Germans done it, and through what entrance, from what special knowledge picked up before the war?*

Gatt was asked, say the minutes of evidence: 'I believe you can give us information about German trawlers coming in the Flow.'

'Yes,' answered Gatt. 'The German trawlers came in a lot through here in winter time instead of going through the Pentland. They generally came in at Hoy Sound and went out at Holm Sound.'

'What size are these German trawlers compared with ours?'

'There are one or two in Aberdeen. They draw about the same draught—about 15 feet.'

'Are you telling us this from hearsay or from your own knowledge?'

'From my own knowledge.'

'Have you seen these German trawlers?'

'I have never seen them personally.'

'What makes you say they constantly come through here in the winter time?'

'I have heard it spoken about in Aberdeen—that the trawlers are well acquainted with coming through here.'

Once Gatt himself had been through Holm Sound, in the trawler *Crevette*, he said; he was a deckhand on her.

'Can you tell us of anyone who would be able to say they had seen a German trawler going through it?'

'No, Sir. Maybe one of the fishermen could. It is mostly herring fishermen here.'

'As the wrecks are lying now—would you say you would be able to take a trawler through this passage?'

'Yes, I believe I could. There is only one way left that I know—between one of the ships and the yacht which is sunk.'

'At any time?'

'No, just at high water.'

The enquiry wore on, the Board pressing for facts, lacking information about where the explosions had occurred. Wasn't the *Oak*

---

* The most oft-repeated story, totally without foundation, denied by Dönitz and other German planners of the raid, has a certain Alfred Wehring, a German World War I naval officer, turning up in Kirkwall and opening a small watch repair shop before the war, using a short wave sender hidden in a cupboard of his home to tap out details of the flaws in the eastern defences of the Flow. Some accounts, equally erroneous, have even had Prien picking up 'The Little Watchmaker of Kirkwall' off Orkney after sinking *Royal Oak* and taking him back to Germany.

'bulged' to pre-explode torpedoes? The blisters had not done their job; the torpedoes had struck vulnerable parts of the ship, below the starboard bulge—or above it (the diver's report would prove the bulges ineffective).

Engineer Commander Renshaw, questioned, said he could give no facts, only theories—'my theory is that the bottom was inadequately protected. Great care had been taken to protect the sides of the ship, but the same care had not been extended to the bottom. I think the explosions occurred at the point where there are only two skins.'

Captain Benn, recalled, agreed: the explosions, he thought, occurred beneath the bulge or beneath the bottom of the ship 'and the reason is that according to accounts, flash was very generally seen in the region of the engineers central store hatch and on the boat hoist flats, which are in the centre of the ship. Both hatches would have been open or partially open.' On the contrary however most of those questioned believed (correctly) that the oil-heavy ship, lying deep at anchor, had suffered wounds to her side, above the bulge.

In their statements scribbled on *Voltaire* a few survivors had written that they'd actually sighted holes. Ordinary Seaman Ivor H. Pagett, declared he 'Saw hole in foc's'le starboard side' (although later, on direct questioning by the board, he'd say only 'it looked to me like a hole, but I would not swear to it'). To Leading Seaman A. Radford there had 'appeared to be a hole in the port side in bulge abreast mainmast,' and W. Nichols wrote how from the water he had 'an impression that as she turned turtle that there was a jagged hole in the keel of the ship about 30 feet from forward. The hole being about 15 feet long and in the beam of a searchlight from the other side of ship from me it appeared to be a shallow hole.'

Where had the explosions occurred? Almost every witness was asked this question, almost all gave a different answer. For example Warrant Electrician Bulley, who couldn't give the place of the first explosion, thought the second 'well forward,' the third 'further aft, about the boiler-room,' and the fourth 'very close to No 3 dynamo room, but forward,' while Lieutenant Commander T. P. Wisden thought the second explosion 'abreast of "Y" turret on port side of quarter-deck,' the third and fourth 'amidship,' and a fifth explosion 'probably abreast or just forward of "Y" turret.'

The time between explosions also figured in the enquiry, as further proof of U-boat attack, for if it could be shown (as it was shown) that there'd been even timing, between blasts, a torpedo salvo would be indicated. Most witnesses testified, as did Wisden, that it was 'a matter of a few seconds only between the second, third, and fourth explosions.' Unlike him, most did not believe there'd been a fifth explosion.

And as those precious minutes had ticked away after the first explosion? If they had been spent differently, might the disaster have been avoided? If the light-excluding ventilators, used for the sake of habitability, had been closed? Water already was pouring into the ship; before it reached the portholes the sea had smothered the mess decks.

However, the Board found, *closing* of the portholes might have caused the *Oak* to sink more slowly, heel over less violently in the first five or ten minutes after the series of explosions:

We are of the opinion that an order to close all maindeck scuttles after the first explosion would have been a wise precaution, but this is influenced by a knowledge of after events. At the time, the Captain considered that the explosion was internal and local. We do not consider that this action would have saved the ship, even if the scuttles had been closed in time. Otherwise we consider that Captain W. G. Benn and his officers did all that was possible to save their ship. Captain Benn remained in the ship until the last possible moment, until in fact the ship left him, and his behaviour was in the best tradition of the service. We deplore the death of Rear-Admiral H. E. C. Blagrove, a serious loss to HM Service, which was due to his refusing the lifebuoy that was offered to him and spending all his time in helping others to save themselves.

Those beams of timber seen floating past the starboard bow—did they have anything to do with the attack? No, ruled the board, explaining its decision by the fact that recently a number of telegraph poles had been washed up on the shores of the Flow and may have floated off again on the high tide of the night: 'Also a certain amount of timber, shores, etc., may have dropped out of, or been blown out of, the ship's forward compartments by the first explosion.'

The report made by the three *Dragonet* crewmen of possible submarine movement on the night of 11 October? The Board questioned the crew, dismissed the report: the stream was simply running very strong to the westward that night, ships going through were swept down towards *Dragonet*:

> The reports that propellers were heard from the gate vessel at Hoxa on the night of October 11th and that the boom was disturbed or moved, are held to have no significance. The latter was due to bad weather while the propellers' noises were probably caused by our own ships passing the gate. Though it is possible that the submarine entered the Flow prior to the night of 13/14 October this is not considered likely.

There'd be no scapegoats, no laying bare the sins of the Admiralty—the war effort could only be hurt by this—but the final report of the Board, only now made public, more than thirty years later, leaves little doubt about where the fault lay. Noting the absence of patrol craft, guns, searchlights at the eastern Sounds, the Board concluded that:

> the risk of an enemy submarine entering by the eastern Sounds, which the Admiralty itself had considered to be very slight, was accepted by the Commander-in-Chief, Home Fleet, and Admiral Commanding, Orkneys and Shetlands.

Regarding blockships, the Board said, 'We are left with the impression that the problem of blocking the eastern Sounds, before the war, was not handled as adequately as its importance deserved.' Had the Admiralty not wavered in its decisions 'the last ship would no doubt have been sunk in Kirk Sound before October 13th instead of after.' Yet the Board did not wish to imply that the Admiralty decision of May was necessarily wrong. The real fault:

> The variety of views as to what was required—Commanding Officer, Coast of Scotland's report early in 1938, his second report in March, 1939, the Admiralty's view after seeing HMS *Scott*'s survey in May, 1939, and Commander-in-Chief, Home Fleet's view in June, 1939, after the Admiral Commanding,

(*Top*) Prien and his wife leaving the Hotel Kaiserhof during his stay in Berlin to meet Hitler.
(*Below*) Past adoring crowds on the way to meet the Führer

Prien's feat enhanced the Navy in the mind of Hitler

Empfang (reception) for Prien by the Führer. A page from a captured Nazi scrapbook, kept for propaganda purposes

MPFANG DER U-BOOTBESATZUNG PR

EIM FÜHRER — 18.10.39 (39300)

In the Chancellery, Grössadmiral Raeder at right

Receiving the *Ritterkreuz*, Knight's Cross of the Iron Cross

Prien after the raid

Orkneys and Shetlands, designate, had carried out his experiments, all gave different estimates of the requirements.

The Board declared, in other major conclusions drawn from its final report:

Various officers were responsible for various sections of the defence but no one officer was responsible for the whole of it.

The Admiral Commanding Orkneys and Shetlands might have done a great deal more to make the base secure by taking up fishing craft locally and getting the Admiralty to send up crews, asking for guns and searchlights, providing coast watchers.

The Admiral Commanding Orkneys and Shetlands, has not got sufficient patrol vessels. There are about 40 drifters under his orders manned by civilians but when asked to assist with the patrols the crews were not willing to do so. Had they volunteered, or had there been means to compel them to assist, the situation as regards patrol craft would have been very different.

The Admiral Commanding Orkneys and Shetlands, had to take over a defence scheme that was inadequate and unsatisfactory in many ways. It had however been given much thought, it had Admiralty sanction, and was known to be limited to some extent by the unavoidable absence of certain necessary items such as loops and asdics.

The Admiral Commanding Orkneys and Shetlands, had been there only a few weeks, his Chief of Staff Officer arrived on 13 October, he and his staff were constantly harassed by current administrative work, and he had no anti-submarine officer on his staff. Practically all his staff are retired officers, some of whom have been retired for a number of years. The Chief Staff Officer had the additional duty of Maintenance Captain which would certainly occupy the whole of his time.

The enquiry was over, the grumbling however was just beginning. For there was the doubt, talk of sabotage would grow and fester. 'Who Really Sank the *Royal Oak*?' newspapers and magazines would headline long after the war. And '*Royal Oak* Scandal,' and 'Who was to blame?' '*Was* it a submarine?' For years every survivor would be asked this last question. Coxswain Scarff would tell the press years later he was 'kept away' from the enquiry because of his views. 'After it happened the captain asked me what I thought and I told him it was sabotage. He told me to get off the bridge.' Others would complain it 'didn't feel like torpedoes,' or asked, 'Why didn't the Germans aim their first torpedo amidships where they knew the magazines were?' The stores—they had been on dockside stencilled *Royal Oak*, giving advance warning to potential saboteurs.

Who sank the *Royal Oak*? Günther Prien sank the *Royal Oak*. Who was to blame? The Board of Enquiry had said it: the Admiralty was to blame; Scapa's commanding officers were to blame; human complacency was to blame.

And in Germany, the very moment the board was meeting: jubilation. The Nazi press was getting out its boldest headlines. FURCHTBARER SCHLAG FUR ENGLAND—Terrible Blow for England. ROYAL OAK UND REPULSE IN DER BUCHT VON SCAPA FLOW TORPEDIERT screamed the headline in *Der Angriff* of the 18th.

On the inside pages of this Nazi organ, from onboard *U-47* pictures of smiling, smoking sailors, a beaming Prien, the Reich's first hero, the 'brave and brilliant' Günther Prien, to become the 'Bull of Scapa Flow.' The news was all good. *Das siegreiche U-boot—the victorious U-boat* had penetrated the secluded home base of the British fleet, destroyed not one but two great ships, each a *Schlachtschiff*, a battleship, *Repulse* a 32,000-*Tonnen Schlachtschiff* (when in fact of course *Repulse*, not even at Scapa, was a battle*cruiser*).

In Wilhelmshaven when *U-47* had put in on the 17th the crews of every German ship at anchor packed the guardrails, stood cheering, waving in deference to *U-47,* its proud achievement: here was proof that once more, as it had been two decades before, the U-boat was a force in war against Britain.

'We had to ride at anchor for a while,' remembered Stoker Werner Lüddecke. 'Because the reception had not been readied, and our C-in-C, Commodore Dönitz, had not yet arrived. When things were finally all set, we were received with music entering the sluicegate. There were hundreds of sailors up there, cheering us. We had to go through all sorts of things until finally, with the band on board, we got into port, and then all that hand-shaking, again and again, and we had a drink and another drink, and in the end we were all quite drunk.'

When finally *U-47* made fast to her jetty, the top senior officers, including Raeder, Admiral Saalwaechter of Navy Group West, and Dönitz, stepped onto the submarine's narrow deck. A look of pride sat upon Dönitz's face. He bore a love for his U-boats, a deep and sincere fondness for the men who served in them: he was 'Papa Dönitz' to the crews, who felt near him, were the realization of his hopes; and now, as he perceived what *U-47* had done, he gazed upon the crew with tender thoughts, listened with deep satisfaction as Raeder announced that Prien had earned the *Ritterkreuz*, the coveted Knight's Cross of the Iron Cross.

Dönitz, said the *Grossadmiral*, was hereby promoted from *Kapitan zur See* to Admiral, made officially Flag Officer, U-boats (*Befehlshaber der Unterseeboote* or *BdU*); then every member of the crew was given the *Eiserneskreuz*, Iron Cross, Second Class, told they were to fly that same afternoon to Kiel, then on to Berlin to meet the Führer, witness their captain receive from the Leader's own hand the first *Ritterkreuz* of the war given a naval officer. 'The Navy, as well as the entire German nation, is proud of you, my gallant submarine men,' said Raeder to the crew.

In Berlin the press jumped on the story, interviewed not only Prien but almost every member of the crew, for they were now all national heroes—these 'boys of eighteen, nineteen, twenty,' as the American correspondent William Shirer would write in his diary after the afternoon press conference at the Propaganda Ministry on the 18th.

Prien is thirty, clean-cut, cocky, a fanatical Nazi, and obviously capable. Introduced by Hitler's press chief, Dr (Otto) Dietrich, who kept cursing the English and calling Churchill a liar. Prien told us little of how he did it. He said he had no trouble getting past the boom protecting the bay.

Shirer got the impression, though he admitted Prien had said nothing to justify it, 'that he must have followed a British craft, perhaps a minesweeper, into the base. British negligence must have been something terrific.'

That it was. But here was an opportunity to be seized. With each statement made, from whatever source, the story flowered, success at Scapa giving German propaganda the opportunity wanted to ridicule the British, boost German prestige. It wasn't so long, after all, since the twentieth anniversary (June 28th) of the Treaty of Versailles. The Third Reich had come a long way: Britain was impotent, Germany strong, the press seemed to be saying —'our weapons are stronger than those of any other country.' This hostility in tone and attitude coloured every description of the incident at Scapa. The Germans burst with pride, thrilled with every account of the dangerous feat. Boasted the *Boersen Zeitung*, for one:

> This represents another bitter lesson for those English circles who believe they can wage a war of starvation against Germany without much risk. In the great war our U-boats sank some old ships of line but never succeeded in destroying a modern English battleship as now.

Emsmann and von Hennig had tried the same toward the end of World War I. They had not come back. Prien had, and from *Scapa Flow*, the very place the German High Seas Fleet had been scuttled. What a script to inspire the people, champion the great endowments and virtues of Germans. Excite the people's emotions. Captivate their minds. Influence the masses by cheap clichés. That was the psychology of the weapon of Nazi propaganda, the art of capturing public opinion. The deed of Günther Prien could have been told plainly and simply, but for German propaganda purposes it had to be told in a language people could not ignore. It was results that counted. Truth could mix with lies. Misrepresentations could muddle the facts.

One German journalist-propagandist, drawing on as melodramatic style as he could muster, began his story:

> They push through the barriers, the last of the barriers. The blockships are behind them, the damned blockships, and before them is the wide bay of Scapa Flow encircled by desolate barren hills. Kapitänleutnant Prien and the men of 'U– —'. Incredibly they did it; against the current, through swirles and eddies. Scapa Flow! In this very anchorage Admiral Von Reuter sank the interned battlewagons of the Skaggerak fleet. This place.

There is the smell of history here. Kapitänleutnant Prien must have sensed it when he glanced through crosshairs of his periscope and saw the shadows of fighting vessels, the masts and topmasts and mainyards of British warships. But which ships? Kapitänleutnant Prien blinks hard, tries to make them out . . .

On and on goes the story, but now from almost every sentence inaccuracies begin to tumble: the story is too big to be stopped by details. The fact of the deed is enough and the account goes on, so glowing in its treatment of German heroism that the German High Command had it broadcast throughout the Reich.

The ship anchored farthest north bears two funnels. The other ship, lying a little more south, is the *Royal Oak*.

False. The *Royal Oak* she was, but *at the time* Prien knew only that she was a Royal Sovereign class battleship. He identified her as the *Oak* only after the Admiralty's announcement.

The Kapitänleutnant moves in to the attack, lets go his torpedoes and turns to escape from the harbour the way he had entered.

False, or at least not entirely true, for nothing is said of the two misses in the first salvo, the need to try again, possible torpedo failure, the miss from the stern tube.

The U-boat presses ahead to get out. Thunder shoots over the water. Kapitänleutnant Prien casts around. He spies a huge cloud of smoke rise suddenly like a great white flag from the dreadnought farthest north.

False. Prien claimed no smoke from the northernmost ship, saw only spray shoot up, assumed, incorrectly, a hit on the northern ship.

Then fireworks erupted from the smoke.

Completely false and never claimed by Prien.

Then from the battleship closest to the U-boat leaping, beautiful flames, blue, violet, orange, green, yellow, blood red, flicking across the sky like the Northern Lights. The pillars of water are gone and there is only the hungry fire, licking at everything. Parts of the ship, machinery, yard tackle, deck gear, fly through the air, turrets tossed like balloons, pipes and masts and deck planks bent like griddle cakes. It's like the *Queen Mary*, thought the Commander.

False. The *Oak* did not blow up, as this account implies. No major magazines exploded, no flames leapt into the air, and in fact the ship died a dignified death, slipping quietly beneath the sea.

Then again the Commander looks around. He sees the *Repulse*, the ship with two stacks, heavily damaged, her bows now deep in the water.

False of course. Prien saw nothing of the kind.

All over the harbour signals appear, lanterns blinking on all sides, searchlights pointing fingers everywhere, probing for the enemy; then destroyers and motorboats hurl depth charges.

Very misleading. Few signals if any, appeared, the only search beams the ones from *Pegasus,* depth charges dropped only after *U-47* made good her escape.

The account continues, blending propaganda with truth, dealing death to objectivity. The story was taken from Prien, pulled from his hands, embellished for the glory of the *Reich*, glory of the Navy, glory of the U-boat arm. The propagandists censored, cut, or stretched the facts, allowed in print only what would raise morale, add to the aura of the feat, details of the Aurora Borealis, the effort to pass the blockships, 'to sink,' in words attributed to Prien, 'a British ship in a British naval harbour, and to keep my boat and crew for further tasks. It was quite a job to smuggle ourselves into Scapa Flow.'

It made marvellous reading; but the German accounts mixed truths with half-truths, spoke of 'torpedoes,' never 'salvoes,' never mentioning the misses, the torpedo failures, the poor state of the Scapa defences. On the one hand there would be Prien saying he saw shaded anchor lights ('correct and authentic,' said Admiralty experts in analysing German press accounts) but on the other: 'As I left the port I heard two explosions and saw a column of water rising from the ship farthest north' ('obviously untrue,' said the Admiralty. 'The time between the first and second torpedoes was certainly not less than ten minutes').

Prien's personal report to Dönitz, as recounted in the *Grossadmiral*'s memoirs is, though flawed, straightforward, and honest:

> The passage both ways through Holm Sound was accomplished only with the greatest difficulty. I was compelled to pass very close to the blockships, and on the return passage encountered a 10-mile-an-hour current running against us. No watch was being kept on Holm Sound. Off Scapa only *Repulse* and *Royal Oak*. In the first attack one hit scored on *Repulse*'s bows. Having reloaded two tubes, delivered second attack very shortly afterwards. Three hits on *Royal Oak*. The ship blew up within a few seconds. After leaving Holm Sound, observed great anti-U-boat activity (with depth charges) in Scapa Flow. Was greatly bothered by brilliance of northern lights.

Foreign journalists, trying for the truth, would dig deeper, the Berlin correspondent of the Amsterdam *Handelsblad* writing for instance:

> There is a feeling of pride in the exploits of the German Navy, but it is admitted in Berlin that the successes have been greatly helped by 'British negligence.'
>
> As an example of negligence, it is said that a German submarine was able to remain for two days near Scapa Flow and had time to locate the positions of minefields and anti-submarine nets there by observing the course taken by British naval units. The Germans conceded that the precautionary measures taken by the British Naval Authorities in 1914–18 were on a high level. It was expected that this level would have been exceeded now, but this does not seem to be the case.

Percy Knauth, reporting for the *New York Times*, also noted a trace of incredulity among the German populace.

It is flatly denied that Germany lost any submarines in the attack on Scapa Flow [he noted on 17 October] though there are many who are wondering how a submarine could enter the mine-infested harbour, torpedo two large warships and escape unscathed. The deed of Lieutenant Commander Prien is hailed as one of the most daring feats of naval history.

For Prien, glory had come so suddenly. 'It was the only thing in his life he had not had to struggle and strive for,' said Wolfgang Frank. From then on he was applauded or toasted wherever he went. People wrote him adoring letters, he was worshipped, thrown into the limelight wherever he went; the mere sight of him in a restaurant or in a tram or bus was enough to set people talking.

Prien enjoyed the adulation, yet he wasn't swept off his feet by it; he wasn't a braggart. He told his friend Frank, 'I am an officer, not a film star.' And, 'The moment I see somebody at the far end of a tram or in a restaurant nudging his neighbour and gaping like a fish I know that he has just whispered reverently: "Prien!" If this sort of thing goes on much longer I shall learn to lipread. At all events there is one word I can't be mistaken about.'

The Third Reich's first hero yearned to return to the sea.

8

Avenged

For days and weeks after the loss of *Royal Oak*, there were, wherever men gathered, open declarations of concern, much fretting over ways to close the gaps, make Scapa truly impregnable. Almost every officer and ordinary seaman in Orkney thought he knew how it should be done. There was ceaseless reflection on the subject: 'Don't keep the gates in the booms open longer than necessary.' 'Use more loops and controlled minefields.' 'Double the lines of indicator nets.' 'Use more patrol craft, more lookouts, more guns, more searchlights and Aldis lamps.' 'In the relatively narrow gaps, fix small mines or other charges on wires or nets.' 'Don't rely on booms or blockships alone—employ, in conjunction with them, controlled minefields and Asdics, either fixed or in the boom gate vessels or specially allocated patrol craft—use yachts manned by yachtsmen if you have to.' 'Extend the nets at all booms so that the foot of the nets is at the minimum distance above the sea bottom—two or three feet at low water.'

One naval commander, E. H. Hopkinson, suggested (to the Board of Enquiry) that a British submarine come to Scapa, try to do what the German U-boat had done—'with a view to attempting, if possible, entering, and also to demonstrate to the men in the gate vessels the appearance of a submarine passing through the gate submerged.'

The Board didn't take to this suggestion; but it did seem simple, it all seemed so simple now—Scapa Flow could be made impenetrable; and by the time the Board disbanded, action already had been taken to carry out some proposals: men should be able to sleep contented, not be afraid of a devilish U-boat roaming undetected on the surface of 'protected' Scapa Flow. Arrangements already were being made for loops to be put down inside the Hoxa boom; all booms were being extended so as to close the existing gaps, except for a few essential for small craft traffic; and more ships were ordered to block the channels between *Soriano* and *Thames* and south of *Thames* in Kirk Sound and the main channel in Skerry. The Admiralty immediately authorised an expenditure of £30,000 for the required blockships, warning 'In view of the conditions it is considered desirable to use the largest ships which can be obtained and handled and that they should be heavily ballasted.'

'The defences of Scapa should not be stinted,' the Admiralty said.

From now on if there was any sign of attack or internal explosion all deadlights and scuttles immediately would be closed; riding lights would not be shown, sliding armoured hatches on the *Queen Elizabeths* and *Royal Sovereigns* and the *Hood* would be changed to slide fore and aft, not athwartships; individual lifebelts would be provided for every man; immediate visual signals made— a general alarm to indicate the enemy was thought to be attacking, an immediate distress signal to indicate need of assistance.

At month's end, Winnie himself came back to Scapa, the glow of regret in his eyes. The U-boat had spoiled his plans, for the time being at least Scapa could remain as a destroyer refuelling base only; Rosyth would take the Flow's place as the main fleet anchorage. On 31 October Churchill boarded the *Nelson* for a conference on the fleet bases (Scapa, Loch Ewe, and Rosyth) with the First Sea Lord, Admiral of the Fleet Sir Dudley Pound, and Admiral Sir Charles Forbes. In the spring, it was decided, Scapa once more would become home to the big battlewagons— but not until more blockships had been placed, the nets doubled, the gate openings and closings reviewed for security, some eighty guns mounted, the aerodrome at Wick enlarged to take four squadrons.

A feeling of vague relief must have filled the First Lord of the Admiralty. The *Royal Oak* affair wasn't closed, he knew, yet it wasn't politically fatal to him either, as well it might have been, had he not been a newcomer to the government. And when a week later on Wednesday, 8 November, Churchill rose in Commons to explain the loss, the House listened sympathetically, did not press him for reasons why it happened:

'I am unable to enter into details, because a full explanation—

and no explanation is worth giving unless it is full—would reveal to the enemy matters which would throw a light upon our methods of defence.'

Churchill admitted nothing about the complete lack in many places of any sort of defence. By now he knew about the Scott report, which had contained the warning, but he chose not to bring this up. He knew about the perilous height of the nets at Hoxa, as revealed by the evidence disclosed to the Board of Enquiry. This too he ignored: 'It would not be right to discuss in public, in time of war, these intimate matters of naval defence, and I ask the House with confidence to support the Admiralty in their decision.'

So for thirty years and more, no one, other than Churchill and the Board, a few others at the Admiralty, would know the full details surrounding the sinking. Churchill wished the House to forget the past, look to the future. How could one expect to carry on a war without tragedies of this sort? He'd seen it happen before. With reasoning and eloquence, he won over the House:

'The Admiralty upon whom the broad responsibility rests, are resolved to learn this bitter lesson, namely, that in this new war, with its many novel complications, nothing must be taken for granted; and that every joint in our harness must be tested and straightened so far as our resources and ingenuity allow. Having most carefully considered the issues involved in this particular case, I propose to take such steps within the Service as are proper and necessary, but I do not intend to embark upon a judicial inquiry with a view to assigning blame to individuals. Such a course would impose an additional burden upon those who, afloat and ashore, are engaged in an intense and deadly and, as many may well think, not wholly unsuccessful struggle. It is on this struggle that all our thought and strength must be concentrated.'

In Portsmouth this day the *Oak* survivors returned from leave— not a man broke it by a minute—and they all appeared recovered in their self-possession, thought Portsmouth's Commander-in-Chief, who moving among the returnees, sensed, however, that they were shaken in their confidence in the Admiralty. As later he'd note in a letter to the Admiralty:

They dimly felt, being wise after the event and evidently after discussion among themselves, that the Admiralty must have known German submarines could enter Scapa Flow and German bombers reach it. Therefore *Royal Oak* should not have been where she was, nor the *Voltaire* either.

He asked one or two of them point blank if that was what they meant, and they said it was so. They'd follow their officers. They knew who they were. But this 'Admiralty.' What was it? Something housed in a building in London few had ever seen. Most Londoners had never seen it. In the men's minds, said the commander, it was staffed 'by cunning and slippery civilians whose main object in life is to screw down the sailor and to get good marks and promotion for themselves by saving money on necessary works like the defence of Scapa Flow. Distrust of this Admiralty has throughout history been latent in British sailors, very likely because they know so little about it. This distrust shows itself when reasons for events they do not understand are sought. It showed itself in modern times at Invergordon,* and it has shown itself now among the survivors of the *Royal Oak*.'

But that Wednesday, 8 November, the First Lord made his speech in Parliament, and this, said the commander, 'put a different complexion on affairs. In it he accepted on the part of the Admiralty, and without equivocation, all blame for the loss of the *Royal Oak*. No fault was found with the admiral or captain of the ship; the Admiralty had acted with over-confidence and now accepted full responsibility.'

On the morning after Churchill's speech, the commander addressed the survivors: he wanted to try to pull them together, which is what Admiral Drax much earlier had suggested some senior officer try to do, before the men went on leave, lest they become 'centres of depression.' But the commander had bided his time: they were 'a mob and not a crew' when their train pulled into Portsmouth. He didn't dare try to preach words of encouragement then. But now was the time. He knew it. As he walked among the men, he felt it. Churchill's speech had struck the right note, put the Admiralty and the lower deck at one in the war effort. So the commander told the returning men and boys that they were at the bottom of the roster for sea service, but the war

* At the North Sea port of Invergordon, Scotland, in one of the deepest and safest harbours in Britain, there took place in 1931 a mutiny in the British Royal Navy.

would last long enough for them to be at sea again 'in time to give Hitler's Navy a final kick in the pants.'

'A great cheer went up,' he'd remember.

On the morning of the day before Churchill's meeting with Forbes and Pound in *Nelson*, the English had missed suffering—only by the grace of God and German misfortune—their third great disaster in the early days of the war; for around 10 a.m. that morning a Type II coastal U-boat, number 56, commanded by Leutnant Wilhelm Zahn, had found *Nelson* and *Rodney* and *Hood* and a screen of ten destroyers steaming west of Orkney, exactly where Dönitz had thought the British fleet would concentrate after the loss of Scapa as the main anchorage. Zahn got within range, emptied all three tubes on *Nelson**, but received no cause for celebration: in *U-56* the crew had heard the three thumps against the battleship's side but no detonation: all three torpedoes were duds. Zahn turned away in disgust, signaled Dönitz directly: '1000. *Rodney, Nelson, Hood* and ten destroyers, Square 3492, 240°. Three torpedoes fired. None exploded.' So upset was Zahn by his failure to take the prize, so distraught was he when he returned to face Dönitz that the Admiral felt compelled to withdraw him from active service, make him an instructor at U-boat school instead.

And so, so soon after Prien's success, there set in for Dönitz and his U-boat Command a period of agonised frustration, compounded by story upon story of torpedo failure. Almost every U-boat commander reported misfires; sometimes every 'eel' carried was a dud. On the 31st Korvettenkapitän Victor Schütze stopped a steamer off Cape Finisterre, loosed four torpedoes from his *U-25*, only to find every one a dud.

A week later Leutnant Herbert Sohler brought *U-46* home after four weeks without a single strike: once, he lamented, he fired seven torpedoes 'against a mighty wall of overlapping ships'— chance to claim 30–40,000 tons at least—but not a dent did he make in British shipping, his torpedoes running erratically, or too deep, or the magnetic pistols malfunctioning, as perhaps had happened with three of Prien's shots in Scapa Flow.

Some success came with mines. On 21 November the new cruiser HMS *Belfast*, moved from Scapa to the Firth of Forth,

* Churchill was not aboard.

struck a mine, barely limped into her dockyard port. Günther Prien, meanwhile, on 28 November, seeking another fat victim, caught sight of masts on the horizon, smoke streaming from a cruiser of the 'London' class, some 880 yards distant, making about eight knots.

Action stations, Prien ordered: he closed range, fired a single torpedo from his No 3 tube, after a minute and a half heard an explosion, thought the ship's upper deck looked buckled, her starboard torpedo-tube mounting 'twisted backward over the ship-side,' as in his log he'd write.

The cruiser* also appeared to have a 5° list; and when she disappeared in a rain squall, Prien surfaced, set off in pursuit, in haste, as the *over*-water vessel the U-boat really was. He got the cruiser in sight, dived to close her, get head of her, get in her path; but the ship disappeared in the squall.

'Surfaced and searched the area but she could not be found,' was Prien's last comment on the subject.

In December, in the entrance to Loch Ewe, it became *Nelson*'s turn to strike a mine, he put out of action. But Germany's top naval staff was allowing itself no special joy, for latest intelligence had the Allies planning to land troops in neutral Norway and Sweden, in a move to encircle Germany, break off her supply of vital ore from Scandinavia—the beginning of the end perhaps for the *Reich*.

As 1939 yielded to 1940 the Führer ordered a secret plan—Operation *Weserübung*—for the occupation of Norway, a bold counterstroke to forestall invasion, actually contemplated by the British government.

On 4 March, amid the sudden increase of British movements in Norwegian waters, a move to lay mines off the long Norwegian coast, Dönitz was ordered by Raeder to halt all further U-boat sailings, and the next day Vice-Admiral and Grossadmiral met in Berlin, discussed the planned landing of German troops in Norway and Denmark.

Dönitz's U-boats were to keep open the seaways between Norway and Germany, protect German naval forces attacking the Nor-

---

* The cruiser was the *Norfolk*, and although Prien's torpedo had missed, exploding in her wake, German propaganda claimed a sinking, prompting Dönitz to comment, on the propaganda report: 'From the serviceman's point of view, such inaccuracies and exaggerations are undesirable.'

wegian ports, the railhead Narvik the main objective, but also Trondheim, Bergen, Stavanger, Haugesund, Egersund, and Oslo—the whole Norwegian West Coast—and fend off counter landings. Dönitz ordered all his U-boats out, even the small ones used for instruction in the Baltic, even the new and untested IX B's, *U-64* and *U-65*, still running trials.

In 'wolf pack' clusters, Dönitz's boats, forty-two strong, stood at the ready, the commanders holding sealed orders, Günther Prien in Group 5, a pack of six. But then, unpredictably, the same strange problem: after the Germans approached Norway on the decisive Tuesday, 9 April (the sealed envelopes were opened on 6 April), and ten destroyers escorted by *Scharnhorst* and *Gneisenau* in gale-force seas poured two battalions ashore, successfully evading British submarines and ironclads, *U-25* (Victor Schütze), *U-51* (Dietrich Knoor) and *U-48* (Herbert Schultze) sent a total of twelve torpedoes at British destroyers out to intercept and sink the German troopships.

Almost all the torpedoes exploded prematurely. 'Effect after explosion not observed,' complained Schütze on the 11th. Wrote Schultze in his log the same day:

> Cumberland type cruiser salvo of three. Missed, one failed to explode until the end of its run. 2115, salvo of three, cruiser *York*. Salvo exploded prematurely.

The next day Knoor was lamenting: 'Two misses. One exploded at end of safety run, the other after 30 seconds, 300 feet ahead of large destroyer.' And three days later it was Schütze again: 'Westfiord, torpedo failures against *Warspite* and two destroyers.' Other U-boats reported similar experiences. Then on the 15th *U-47* and the 'Bull of Scapa Flow' closed on a patch of water near Harstad in the narrow Bygden Fjord, in the afternoon reported British destroyers steaming erratically, presumably laying mines. In the evening Prien sighted almost as many men-of-war as he had dreamed of finding in Scapa Flow: 'Three large transports (each of 30,000 tons) and three more, slightly smaller, escorted by two cruisers, at anchor in the southern part of Bygden. Troops being disembarked by fishing boat in direction Lavangen–Gratangen. Transports and cruisers in narrow waters of the Bygdenfiord, some lying at double anchor, just clear of each other and in some cases slightly overlapping.'

What a chance! A unique opportunity. In his hands, Prien felt, lay the success or failure of the entire Norwegian campaign. He couldn't fail, he had a 'solid wall' of deep-draught ships before him, stationary, anchored, so overlapping, so close he could guarantee the hits, the nearest vessel only 750 yards distant, the farthest 1,500 yards. He submerged, prepared to empty all four bow tubes, one eel each at a cruiser, a transport, another transport, another cruiser; then he'd reload, send more ships down.

Setting his torpedoes for 12 and 15 foot depths, Prien fired; but the seconds turned into minutes, in astonishment he waited as nothing happened—the same frustration as at first he'd suffered in Scapa Flow: 'Result nil. Enemy not alerted.' Instead of a harvest, a total failure.

But after midnight Prien surfaced, and as coolly as he had at Scapa he ordered the tubes reloaded, went personally with Endrass to check the torpedoes before firing; 'Fire control data precise. Thorough inspection of all adjustments by Captain and First Lieutenant. Four torpedoes. Depth setting as for first attack.'

But again, once again, the misfires: three torpedoes, set to explode on impact—*Aufschlagzündung*—failed to detonate, the fourth a G7a, air-driven, veered off course, exploded at the far end of the fjord; even in retreat, now forced upon him, Prien was suffering frustration and embarrassment, as *U-47* ran aground on the fjord bed.

He prepared to abandon ship, slid off just in time, after ordering the crew on deck, to rock the boat by rushing together from stem to stern. Prien ended his report to Dönitz about this debacle:

> Refloated under extremely difficult conditions and very close to passing patrol vessels. Pursued with depth charges. Compelled to withdraw owing to damaged engines.

A few days later Prien tried again, hurling two torpedoes set this time for magnetic detonation—*Magnetzündung*—at the battleship *Warspite*, a survivor of Jutland. The range was only 900 yards. But again no hits scored. *Warspite*'s two accompanying destroyers chased *47* off.

On return to his berth in Wilhelmshaven, Prien, full of fury, growled, 'How the hell do they expect us to fight with dummy rifles?'

What was wrong with the German torpedoes—at least thirty percent duds? A crisis of 'war-decisive proportions,' charged Raeder, shocked and furious. Dönitz, who had too few submarines, and now ineffective torpedoes, demanded reliable weapons. In his memoirs, he'd moan:

> Final analyses showed that they had delivered four attacks on a battleship (*Warspite*), fourteen attacks on a cruiser, ten on a destroyer and ten on transports.

Later the faults were discovered by a special Torpedo Commission, the problem, it turned out, lying not with the torpedoes themselves but the depth at which they were set to pass beneath their victims' keels, places where the magnetic pull of the vessels was supposed to detonate the non-contact pistols and set off the warhead. Anything might cause the torpedoes to run low, a leak for instance in their compression-air system, putting pressure on the delicate balance chamber mechanism, or demagnification applied by the British to their ships, but if the torpedoes passed too far beneath the keel, the pistols would not go off.

Before the crisis passed, court-martials cut through the ranks of the Torpedo Inspectorate, rocked by a scandal the *Kriegsmarine* would never forget.

In May the 'phoney war' on land ended. The western offensive, so long postponed, began. Over Holland, then Belgium, then all of France moved the German express, non-stop: only ten days to reach the English Channel near Abbeville, pound a wedge between the French and British Armies. Talk of the invasion of England, Operation Sealion, began, and a plan proceeded, tenuously, while Dönitz, watching the German advance closely with an eye to putting U-boat bases on the Biscay coasts—as a way out of his cramped 'backyard' bases in the North Sea—tended to the battering his boats took in the Norwegian campaign.

In the summer of 1940 the dockyards of Kiel, Wilhelmshaven, Hamburg, Bremen, Copenhagen, Glückstadt, and Königsberg bulged with mauled U-boats and dreadnoughts. Chief among the big ships: *Gneisenau* which with *Scharnhorst* on 8 June sank the

British aircraft carrier *Glorious*, only to catch a British torpedo in her bows, be put out of action for months.

Dönitz felt out of touch with the situation in the Atlantic, where once again he was told to concentrate his little fleet of submarines. Were British ships sailing as they were before? Singly? In convoy? What kind of escorts did they have? On the surface? In the air? Most important, Dönitz wondered, what effect would his new torpedoes have? Victor Oehrn was the first to let him know, when as the first to go back to sea, as commander of *U-37*, a new large Type IXA boat, he encountered enemy ships outside the Bay of Biscay—and told the same old story: two prematures and two torpedoes which failed to explode. But on Dönitz's orders Oehrn switched his torpedoes, firing mechanism from magnetic pistols (those 'wretched things,' Dönitz called them) to percussion, and by the time Oehrn returned from patrol on 9 June he could claim more than 41,000 tons of Allied shipping. In the words of Dönitz, 'The spell of bad luck was broken.'

A golden summer, a time of triumph was dawning for the U-boats; the 'happy time,' the German submariners would call this start of the opening campaign of the Battle of the Atlantic, as now there began a putting to sea of U-boat commanders with names soon familiar: Fritz-Julius Lemp, Fritz Frauenheim, Hans-Gerrit von Stockhausen, and many more—Lueth, Schepke, Oehrn, Liebe, Kuhnke, Schultze, Endrass, Jenisch, Rösing, Ambrosius, Rollmann, Kretschmer, Wohlfahrt—and of course Prien, always in the fight, still the best known of all.

Dönitz constantly shifted and re-grouped his forces: not more than two days would he let his boats roam without making a sighting. Thus quickly he found the routes the British were using, and as the tonnage of Allied merchant shipping mounted, there came into being a competition: Who could sink the most?

When Endrass in June, commanding *U-46*, sank the armed merchant cruiser *Carinthia*, 20,000 tons, the former watch officer in *U-47* was propelled to the front of the group—giving Prien, his old boss, who in mid-June did not have the tonnage of his former subordinate, the incentive to improve his own score. 'We mustn't let these junior chaps get too big for their boots,' Prien said.

On 14 June while west of Scotland Prien sighted a convoy: forty-two ships in seven columns of six and destroyer-escorted. The ships outsteamed *47*, were running away, when suddenly a straggler hove in view, the *Balmoral Wood*, about 5,000 tons. A single torpedo leaped from a bow tube, struck the straying vessel amidships, sweeping onto the sea her cargo of fuselages and air-craft wings. Then on the 21st Prien found another convoy, shad-owed it all through the day, finally picked out a victim, a tanker, some 7,000 tons. One torpedo fired, one hit; then another victim selected; another torpedo, another hit, like the first a sinking, then a third ship, another tanker, more than 20,000 tons in all, until the convoy outran Prien.

On 27 June he found still another tanker, watched as his tor-pedo hit and the ship began to sink. 'Despite the gunfire and the torpedo hit,' wrote Prien in his log, 'her radio operator continued to signal, *"Empire Toucan* torpedoed in position 49° 20′ north, 13° 52′ west" and later "Sinking rapidly by stern." Finally he jumped overboard with a flare and was seen swimming away from the ship.' Prien steered for the flare, he'd later say, but found nothing, so left.

Next southwest of Ireland on 30 June he sank the Greek steam-ship *Georgios Kyriakides* 5,000 tons, then more tankers, and on 2 July, in the approaches to the North Channel with only one tor-pedo remaining he came upon and sank the *Arandora Star*, an armed passenger ship.

With the German occupation of France, the U-boats took up more strategically favourable positions, new ports at Lorient, Brest, La Palice, St Nazaire, Bordeaux, La Baule, drastically re-ducing the distance to Britain's main sea arteries, allowing the U-boats, even the small Type II's, to range far west into the waters of the Atlantic, well beyond the range of the anti-sub-marine escorts which rendezvoused with the convoys.

U-30 was the first to put in, at Lorient on 7 July, and more soon followed, meaning that Dönitz's small force was strengthened, not needing to return to Germany for repairs and leave. If only he had a hundred grey wolves, Dönitz kept telling Raeder—Britain could be brought to her knees by U-boat block-ade and mine warfare. What Dönitz did have was about thirty op-erational boats, available continuously, with just enough new boats to take the place of those lost. Even in the successful month of June (fifty-eight ships sunk, more than 500 tons per boat per day, total 284,000 tons), his force had been depleted, first by a

Sunderland flying boat which destroyed *U-26* (Heinz Schringer), then when *U-102* (von Klot-Heydenfeldt) and *U-122* (Hans Loof) failed to return from patrol. The boats were replaced at once, but by the coastal Type II's, not the newer and bigger boats then under construction.

U-boats still carried the offensive: Dönitz was determined not to let a single day go by without at least one Allied ship sunk somewhere, and when in August Hitler proclaimed a total blockade of the British Isles, the grey wolves snapped with increased ferocity, at any ship on sight; any vessel could be attacked and sunk without warning.

Critically short of ships, Great Britain lacked carriers and battleships, needed cruisers and aircraft, but especially destroyers. In the final phases of World War I Britain had 500 destroyers. In September 1939 she had only 185, and dozens of these had been bombed and sunk, or put out of action in the battles of France and Norway. 'Give us destroyers to save ourselves,' cried the British to their friends across the Atlantic. And America did, turning over in September (for the right to establish air and naval bases in British Guiana and British territory in the West Indies) fifty destroyers, old ships, 'tin cans' left over from World War I but still very fast and manoeuvrable. The Royal Navy manned and modernised them, equipped them with Asdic, used them as they had in World War I, to screen convoys, from torpedo attack, hurl depth charges, turn anti-aircraft guns skyward.

But Dönitz pressed forward with the wolf pack tactics he had been wishing to try since the start of the war: find a convoy, signal its position, wait for the arrival of other U-boats operating in the same area, attack simultaneously. A pack that included *U-47* did just this on 10 September, closing on Convoy SC₂ steaming to Britain from the Nova Scotia port of Sydney. Result: five ships attacked, five ships sunk.

A few days later *U-47*, operating with *U-65* and *U-28* (Günther Kuhnke) and *U-99* (Otto Kretschmer), picked at another convoy, then during the night of 21/22 September, the same pack came upon Convoy HX 72, more than fifteen ships steaming from Halifax. Using bearings supplied by Prien, Joachim Schepke joined the pack, sneaked his *U-100* into the convoy lines, plucked off one ship after another, within hours got seven ships, some at almost point-blank range.

Prien and Kretschmer accounted for five more; and once again, it seemed, the U-boat, as in World War I, was threatening to drive Britain, the greatest sea power in the world, right out of the war. In October, the most successful month for U-boats, sinkings rose to a crescendo: sixty-three Allied ships sunk, 352,000 tons—up from the thirty-eight ships downed in July, some 196,000 tons; fifty-six in August, 268,000 tons, fifty-nine in September, 296,000 tons. After a year of fighting, the U-boat Arm had destroyed one battleship (*Royal Oak*), one aircraft carrier (*Courageous*), three destroyers, two submarines, at least five cruisers and about 440 merchant ships grossing approximately 2,330,000 tons.

In one single night in October—the 'Night of the Long Knives'—the wolf packs accounted for thirty-one ships, 173,000 tons of shipping (by British statistics). The next night they added seventeen ships; only thirteen reached Britain safely. It was nothing unusual for a U-boat returning with all its torpedoes expended to report 50,000 tons of shipping sunk on patrol.

See-Löwe—Operation Sealion—was abandoned in late October, Hitler deciding to settle with Russia first (though in fact the plan never had been adopted in earnest by the Führer), and Dönitz, who with Raeder never had had any faith in its success, could forget about U-boat participation in it, turn all his attention to the struggle in the Atlantic, the war against Britain's sea lines of communication.

In preparation for Sealion, he'd been headquartered in Paris, in a house on *Boulevard Suchet,* leaving frequently to personally meet and talk with his commanders and crews returning from patrol to the French ports, seeing them, as in his memoirs he'd say, 'emaciated, strained, their pale faces crowned with beards of many a week at sea and in their leather jackets smeared with oil and flecked with the salt of the ocean.' They seemed 'nearest to my heart. There was a tangible bond between us,' he'd write.

Dönitz left Paris for a villa near Lorient, convinced the war would go on for years. If Germany was to win the Battle of the Atlantic, he felt, the U-boat construction programme must expand. It did. But fortunately for Britain, unfortunately for the entire German war effort, growth came slowly: raw materials were lacking, the dockyards could not handle the increased demand, there was a lack of labour and tools, priority was given to *Panzers*, Junkers bombers, fighters, anti-aircraft guns, engines, ball-bearings, other war needs; while Britain, in the meantime, was taking better bearings on U-boats, using radio direction finders and Sunderland flying boats from Coastal Command equipped with airborne depth charges to force U-boats to submerge, lose contact with convoys they were stalking.

Gradually, convoy sightings became rarer: for every convoy attacked, ten got through unmolested. So the sinkings dropped—to only thirty-two ships, 147,000 tons, in November: up slightly to thirty-seven vessels, and 213,000 tons in December; dropping again in January, to twenty-one ships, 127,000 tons; rising to thirty-nine ships and 197,000 tons in February. In all not bad for Germany, however, more than a hundred ships, more than half a million tons destroyed in the winter of 1939–40.

In January and February 1941, upon Dönitz's urging and Hitler's orders (but against Göring's wishes) the Luftwaffe turned over some of its long-range four-engined Focke-Wulf Kondors to help home the U-boats in on convoys. It worked for a while but communication between planes and boats remained awkward, there were too few Kondors to be effective, and so for the most part the U-boats were left to pick on stragglers, rely on luck, roam the seas alone, often in raging Atlantic storms that made torpedo attack impossible. In the winter of 1941 the battle lay not so much against single ships or whole convoys as against ice and bitter cold. The U-boats often had all they could do just to limp back to port safely.

The fruitful 'happy time' was over.

South of Iceland on 6 March, 1941, *U-47* was riding upon the sea when just before dark a lookout reported smoke curling over the horizon and presently there appeared the ships of a convoy. Prien scented a kill. He had sailed from Lorient in February wearing a freshly starched white cap and a sprig of camellias in his long leather coat, an expression of confidence upon his lips that this was going to be a good trip; he could 'feel it in my bones.' And now ahead the convoy (OB 293) steaming northwest, returning to the United States after a voyage to Britain. Prien radioed the bearings, bringing in Kretschmer in *U-99*, then *U-70* commanded by Korvettenkapitän Matz, who shortly after dark began snapping at the fattest ships he could find.

In short order he fired salvoes at two ships, destroyed both vessels, did damage to two more, then got careless; on submerging *U-70* fell apart from a barrage of depth charges. All hands died. Kretschmer moved in, sank one ship, set another ablaze, was soon driven off by the convoy's destroyer escort. Then Prien gave chase, like Kretschmer was forced off by a Sunderland but he continued to shadow the convoy, reporting STEERING SOUTHWEST, then ENEMY IN SIGHT, and early on the 7th he bore in again. AM RESUMING PURSUIT, he radioed U-boat Command. Shortly after 4 a.m. he brought *U-47* up, began attacking ships on the convoy's starboard flank—until the destroyers, arch-enemy of the U-boat, two of them now, HMS *Verity* and HMS *Wolverine*, gave chase. Twenty-three minutes after midnight *Wolverine*'s skipper, Commander J. M. Rowland, was alerted by a light patch of smoke resembling diesel exhaust, a reading by his Asdic sound locator, and then, suddenly, his watch spotted the wake of a boat moving full ahead.

Wolverine picked up speed to eighteen knots.

'Something ahead of me,' Rowland signalled *Verity*, steaming abaft his port beam.

A U-boat ahead, Rowland felt sure—and it was; it was *U-47* and Prien, who with Schepke and Kretschmer was one of Dönitz's most successful U-boat commanders, could boast twenty-eight ships sunk, the first to personally account for more than 200,000 tons of enemy shipping. In addition to the Knight's Cross he had earned at Scapa he now had the Oak Leaves, the highest decoration possible, held up to then only by four other officers in the Armed Forces.

'Full speed ahead,' Rowland ordered, and *Wolverine* lurched to twenty-two knots.

'The U-boat,' as Rowland would put in his report, 'was zig-zagging wildly at high speed.'

Wolverine tore down on his quarry but Rowland ordered gunfire withheld, 'for fearing of losing sight of the enemy and in hopes of stalking to decisive range before it was scared into diving.'

Thirty minutes past midnight and *Verity* opened up with starshell, the dazzling lights betraying the destroyer, for Prien ducked, crash-dived, *47*'s stern lunging down, in a desperate attempt to get away: he hadn't the gun power or the gun platform of his pursuer;

a single hit in his pressure hull and he might be prevented from diving altogether.

Wolverine hurried over the general area but Asdic contact had been lost, so Rowland sent down a pattern of depth charges; and for the next five hours there followed a remarkable chase, a duel between the instinct, skill, and experience of opposing minds.

Using amazingly sensitive underwater detection devices, hydrophone and Asdic, *Wolverine* swept back and forth upon the rolling, electrolytic sea, exploding patterns about the enemy.

'Phase Two,' Rowland called the long chase that followed.

At thirty-eight minutes past midnight he switched to a new course—one-eight-oh to starboard—began a fresh sweep, beaming his echoes down; seven minutes later the ultrasonic waves were reflected by what sounded like the hull of a submarine off his port bow, course 185°.

'Obtained firm contact,' he put in his report.

Within seconds Rowland began a pattern, ten charges set for 'deep,' released by the 'stop watch' method: 'The A/S recorder, which had been giving trouble for two days was not in action.'

The depth-charges rained down. None struck a fatal blow.

'No visible results,' said Rowland.

A brisk chase ensued and Rowland stayed on the trail of his plodding victim, helplessly slow below water. After twenty minutes of patient manoeuvring, he lost contact. The U-boat had successfully taken evasive action, shaking the destroyer, by twisting and turning, dodging about. A couple of minutes past one, however, and *Wolverine*'s Asdic operator picked up an echo.

The hunt was on again.

The destroyer sped ahead, the echoes stronger, and six minutes later Rowland ordered another pattern: eight more high explosive charges with 'deep' settings.

There was no need for a direct hit: in the incompressible water the pressure waves made by the effect of a single explosion would be enough to collapse the U-boat's hull, force against it the weight of hundreds of tons. If the charge exploded beneath the hull, it could send the boat rocketing up or if it went off near the side it could turn the boat over, break its rivets or buckle its plates, make it leak all over, or send it to the bottom. If just one of the charges came within 50 feet, it could put the boat's tanks and hydroplanes

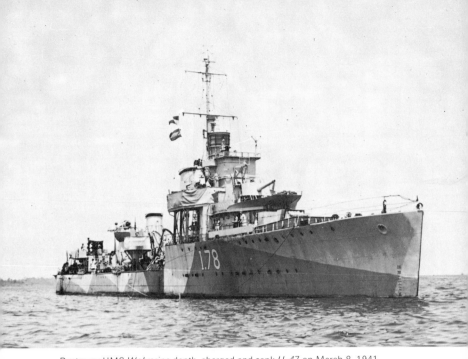

Destroyer HMS *Wolverine* depth-charged and sank *U-47* on March 8, 1941

At Germany's memorial for *U-47:* Wilhelm Spahr, Ernst Dziallas, and Herbert Herrmann

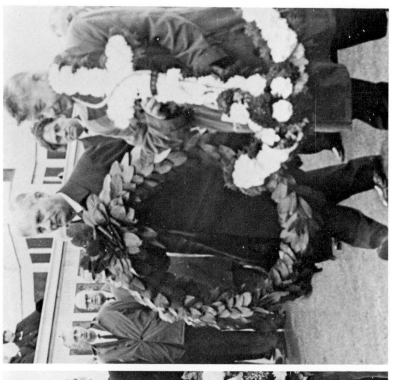

Remembrance and Re-dedication at Portsmouth: *U-47*'s Spahr
and *Royal Oak*'s N. T. Davies

At a 1971 wreath-laying ceremony for the dead of *Royal Oak*: *U-47*'s
Herbert Herrmann and *Royal Oak*'s Philip A. White

(*Above left*) Winner of the Distinguished Service Cross (extreme left) for his rescue of *Royal Oak* survivors, John G. Gatt of Rosehearty, Scotland, holds other medals and watch received in connection with the rescue. King George VI gave Gatt the DSC at a Buckingham Palace ceremony February 6, 1940. (*Above right*) Herbert Herrmann at age 19

U-47 crewman Herbert Herrmann (third from left), now a naturalised Englishman living in Scotland, joins a 1974 reunion toast with *Royal Oak* survivors (from left) Norman Finley, Stanley Thompson and Archie Lawrence

In his villa outside Hamburg, the 84 year old Karl Dönitz poses in 1975 with *U-47's* assistant navigator Ernst Dziallas and Herbert Herrmann and his Scottish wife Ina

out of order, send her completely out of control, produce an almost instant 'kill.'

Wolverine's contacts were taking no effect.

'No visible results,' said Rowland, who had lost sight of *Verity*,
knew that alone he would have to press the hunt, against a tough
and wily opponent: he had no way of knowing it was Günther
Prien.

There'd be no quick kill; but *Wolverine* kept pressing, ploughed
on; she regained contact at nineteen past one, eight and a half
minutes later dropped a single charge.

'Nothing seen,' reported Rowland.

He had had contact for some time, but then he lost it, regained
it, then continued to hold it, while all the time looking for *Verity*
whose signals in the mist and darkness he could not see. Rowland
thought that perhaps the destroyer would pick him up by the
heaving of a pattern; so he dropped four charges, waited, but
failed to guide *Verity* in.

At 0234 he finally sighted *Verity*, quickly passed signals to her;
but in the dim light, as later he'd say, 'attempts to carry out organised attacks were rendered difficult.'

And so it went, into the third hour of the hunt, Rowland keeping track of every detail:

At 0259. Dropped flare to mark position for *Verity*.

At 0320. Engineer Officer reported on bridge that he had unmistakably both seen and smelt shale oil (when he shone a 10-in
light on the water).

At 0337½. Dropped one charge.

At 0343. Marked H.E.* obtained.

At 0350. Contact regained.

At 0354½. Dropped 1 charge. By this time *Verity* had been
lost sight of and R/T communication had broken down. Every attempt was made to guide her back, but without success.

For *Wolverine* the longest chase of her life was on. Built as a
hunter, launched in July 1919, completed a year later, she had as
yet done little hunting, had passed her time escorting Channel and
Atlantic convoys during the first few months of the war. At sea at
the outbreak she had met the first convoy in September, accompa-
nied it round Land's End to the Bristol Channel, then six months

---

* Hydrophone effect.

later sailed with expeditionary forces to France and Norway. In May, she fought off with her guns a flight of German fighters which with a lone bomber had set ablaze a Polish troop transport; in 12 minutes *Wolverine* had taken 690 men of the Irish Guards from the crippled trooper.

Next, during the evacuation of France, she came upon forty Allied merchant ships in Quiberon Bay, helped group them into a convoy, brought them safely home to the Bristol Channel; then again, in July, she was back rescuing survivors, pulling 330 men from the torpedoed French steamship *Meknes*, delivering them safely to Weymouth.

At four minutes past four a.m. *Wolverine* suddenly advanced on an oil slick fifty feet wide, then found a narrow path of thick oil trailing off to starboard. A trail of oil from some leak? The track of a torpedo? Was the clever U-boat commander, forced on the defensive, simply trying to shake his pursuer? For a minute Rowland followed what he believed may have been a torpedo.

'Course two-eight-oh,' he ordered.

He was listening for some sound from the U-boat's revolving propellers and presently his Control Officer, Lieutenant Lacon, reported an HE abaft the port beam.

'Course one-eight-oh degrees.'

It was a game: the old fox below was trying to pull a *ruse de guerre,* trying to steer *Wolverine* away.

Who was this fellow?

Determined not to let the German creep away, or take the offensive, Rowland immediately ordered a new course: 180°.

Pressing his small but highly-manoeuvrable ship on, he charged ahead, picked up the rebound from the ultrasonic sound waves beamed by his Asdic, slowed down on losing contact, then raced ahead on hearing a faint echo, repeating the procedure for almost an hour.

At twenty minutes before five, he slowed to eight knots, fearing he might lose the U-boat altogether: then he heard a very faint HE, shot ahead again, continuing on at twenty knots.

Rowland and Lacon talked over the situation, decided that the U-boat must be about four miles away, five at the most; they'd keep on his tail, narrow the distance slowly, presenting a very small and difficult target for any torpedo from her stern tube.

They couldn't risk giving the skipper a chance with his bow tubes.

'The importance of not over-running the target was fully appreciated', Rowland would later state.

Six minutes passed, *Wolverine* slowed to eight knots, HE was lost, then regained, then lost, heard once more, but not only intermittently.

Trying to break contact, the U-boat was changing course radically. Rowland knew he'd have to close more rapidly; so he ordered four more knots, up to twelve, then switched to a bearing of 200° which allowed him to keep up the Asdic beam.

He boosted speed, only to drop back to eight knots after losing contact.

Creeping forward slowly, the submarine was difficult to hear. But once more HE was heard and this time Lacon thought the sound most unusual, like a 'harsh metallic rattle.' In the bridge it could be heard on the loudspeaker.

Was it a fatal rattle, a sound produced perhaps by a damaged propeller? Maybe the U-boat was not functioning properly.

With the same precision he'd been showing for hours, Rowland changed course, to 200°, and *Wolverine* thundered ahead.

Then, as later Rowland would report, 'At 0518 sighted wake of U-boat fine on the starboard bow.'

Prien had surfaced, trying to speed ahead, outrace—or outbluff —his tormentor: *U-47* was trimming down, moving fast to port.

'Full speed!' Rowland ordered.

'Standby to ram!'

Steeply, almost hurtling down, *47* crash-dived.

'Starboard thirty!' Rowland bellowed.

He wanted the prize, was overhauling the submarine, approaching dead over her, at a course of 208° he put his wheel to midships, looked into the clear water and 'I was able to estimate the U-boat's position with considerable accuracy.'

He saw a rush of bubbles which left a patch of disturbed water and leading out of that a 'V' shaped track, which tapered off and curled to starboard.

An ex-submariner, for six years serving in underwater boats, Rowland felt sure the bubbles were produced by air escaping from the submarine's bow buoyancy vent: 'I could see the bubbles under water near the point of emission. The large patch gave me the impression of air from the main ballast events with possibly some phosphorescence around the conning-tower.'

'Fire one!' Rowland ordered as *Wolverine*'s bridge passed over the centre of the patch of bubbles. Then 'Hard a port!'

'Fire two!' he shouted into the voice-pipe, then four seconds later 'Fire three!' Then more charges, a total of ten in the pattern.

Once more Prien was made aware of the power of his opponent; there must have seemed no end to the ordeal through which he was passing. The steel plates in *47*'s hull and bulkhead might by now have started to crack, the lights probably went out, the dim emergency lighting must have heightened the tension in the claustrophobic small space of the submarine; her inside must have been a mess, paint likely peeling off in blisters, pipes broken, perhaps even the steering gear affected.

Over the starboard side Rowland could see a charge from one of the throwers hit the water on the far side of the 'V'. The U-boat was no deeper than fifty feet, he thought, but he could not estimate the depth with accuracy. If only he had *Verity* with him. The depth settings were wrong, set for 'shallow' instead of 'heavy.' For twenty miles, he'd been pursuing the U-boat and when no wreckage appeared, he knew he had missed again: 'Ship was then turned to starboard and great disappointment felt.'

Daylight broke. Rowland casually radioed news of his attack, then of a sudden at 0543 there was noted from *Wolverine* a faint orange light on the starboard side in approximate position of the last pattern. For about ten seconds the glow continued, then disappeared.

Rowland was worried about losing contact, expending all his depth charges and oil, which he'd been consuming at a prodigious rate. At this critical moment he couldn't afford to run out of fuel. But he kept pressing. He could not give up. He decided to mix his tactics: drop some depth charges quickly, work forward, drop others slowly, send a flare up each time, try to frighten his adversary, weaken his morale, while holding onto a small stock of depth charges until daylight. He didn't want to let the U-boat skipper think he was running out of charges; so he dropped a couple of charges, then made a run or two over the target area. A few minutes later he'd drop another charge, a few more minutes another two, then he hurled more down sparingly, and soon it dawned on Rowland that perhaps he'd already got his prey:

'For the last hour and a half it had gradually been borne in on me, and confirmed by the Control Officer, both during earlier and later attacks, that all contacts obtained, since the 10-charge pattern, had been behaving erratically, although good echoes had been obtained. Besides this, the extent of target had increased, but under the prevailing conditions no one was prepared to believe it was anything other than our "adopted" U-boat.'

The contacts *Wolverine* had been making were probably not with a U-boat at all but a school or schools of fish, porpoises perhaps.

'Perhaps,' Rowland would conclude, 'the amber-coloured light was in fact the key to the whole secret as we never carried out a really thorough search on the actual scene of attack, being led away, I fear, by a school of fish.'

Rowland took *Wolverine* back and forth over the scene, convinced that all that was left were fish.

In fact the U-boat with the Bull of Scapa Flow painted on its conning tower was gone, with all hands, forty-eight men, eight of them members of the Scapa Flow crew, Prien, Biermann, Böhm, Hötzer, Sammann, Steinhagen, Thewes, Werder. Günther Prien was dead, two months past his thirty-third birthday.* HMS *Royal Oak* was avenged, one year and five months since the first anniversary of her sinking.

Over and over for the next few days U-boat command in Wilhelmshaven called in vain. '*U-47*, report your position . . . *U-47*, report your position.' But there was only silence, and against her number at the *Toten Weg* there was put an asterisk, then, as hope dimmed, a second asterisk, to indicate a U-boat lost.

In the open Atlantic there still roamed Schepke in *U-100*, Kretschmer in *U-99*, and on 17 March both began snapping at a convoy from Canada when suddenly Schepke was caught, forced to surface from a barrage of charges; he struggled free of the conning tower, only to find himself staring at a British destroyer (the *Vanoc*) bearing down on him—according to witnesses he was crushed by the destroyer's bows while on the bridge; all hands

---

* Was it Prien? Without a doubt, according to an official British Admiralty statement: 'While escorting a North Atlantic convoy on 8 March 1941 *Wolverine* sighted the *U-47* on the surface and sank her by depth charges in position 60° 47′ N., 19° 13′ W. The submarine was commanded by Günther Prien.'

died with him. Only thirty or so minutes later the destroyer *Walker* rammed Kretschmer's *U-99*, but he lived, was picked up by *Walker*, to spend the rest of the war in a prisoner of war camp.

Incredibly, within a little more than a week Prien, Kretschmer and Schepke, Dönitz's top three aces, had been lost to the U-boat arm, spreading anxiety and uncertainty throughout the U-boat ranks—these were very heavy blows—and to Dönitz deep feeling of a personal loss. In his memoirs he would write:

> Schepke had been a real thruster and had done exceptionally good work from the very beginning; in all he had sunk 39 ships with a total of 159,130 tons. Kretschmer's exploits stood alone; he had sunk no fewer than 44 ships and one destroyer with a total tonnage of 266,629 tons. Prien's great feat had been the destruction of the battleship *Royal Oak* in Scapa Flow; he had also sunk 28 merchant ships totalling 160,935 tons. Prien was all that a man should be, a great personality, full of zest and energy and the joy of life, wholly dedicated to his service and an example to all who served under him. In war, notwithstanding his sudden leap to fame and popularity after the Scapa Flow exploit, he remained a simple, frank and courageous fighting man, intent only on doing his job and adding to his exploits. I held him in great affection and esteem.

Wolfgang Frank recalled how in the days that followed Dönitz

> went about his work with a grim and purposeful dourness which we who knew him recognised as a sign of the depths of his emotion. He never gave expression to his feelings; he kept his grief to himself. But we, the officers of his staff who could not ourselves bear to speak of what we felt, knew without words what this loss meant to him.

April passed and still the news about Prien was not made public, only the news about Kretschmer and Schepke: Hitler worried about public opinion. But in the *Kriegsmarine*, in the dockyards, it was no secret that Prien had not returned from his last patrol. Even Prien's wife was not told: Günther was 'away,' on a 'long voyage.' In confidence she was finally given the news at month's end; but the public knew nothing. Rumours bred: Prien was in a

British prisoner of war camp. The Russians had him. The Americans had him. He was dead. He had fallen from grace; he and the majority of his crew were in a Nazi concentration camp at Torgau. They were in a labour corps on the Russian front.

Only on 23 May, 1941, ten weeks after the Navy knew of the loss of Prien and his entire crew, was the public finally told over the German *Rundfunk*. After his death, Prien had been promoted, from *Kapitänleutnant* to *Korvettenkapitän* (Lieutenant Commander), for 'gallantry in action,' and the High Command of the Wehrmacht stated simply, 'The U-boat commanded by Korvettenkapitän Günther Prien has failed to return from its last war patrol. The vessel must be presumed lost. Korvettenkapitän Günther Prien, the hero of Scapa Flow, was honoured by the Führer with the Oak Leaves to the Knight's Cross of the Iron Cross in recognition of his eminent services. He and his brave crew will live forever in German hearts.'

Dönitz himself composed Prien's obituary notice, issued as an 'Order of the Day.'

Günther Prien, the hero of Scapa Flow, has made his last patrol. We submariners bow our heads with pride and sorrow, in tribute to him and his men. Even though the vast ocean hides him, Prien still stands in our midst. No U-boat will go to sea against the West but he will sail with her, his spirit will bear her company. No blow against England will be struck by us but his aggressive spirit will guide our hand. Ebullient with youthful vigour and reckless courage, he is an eternal pattern for all U-boatmen. We have lost him and recovered him; he has become for us the symbol of our hard and remorseless will to vanquish England. The fight will continue in his spirit.

With Wagnerian grief, the tributes continued. GÜNTHER PRIEN WILL BE WITH US FOREVER, said the mournful headline in the *Volkischer Beobachter*.

The hero of Scapa Flow has made his last cruise. Although the vast ocean covers him, Günther Prien will forever remain among us. We have lost him, but we have won him again. He will for all eternity be the model for submarine fighting.

The war was young then. This kind of grief was a luxury that could be indulged in; but already the tide had begun to swing against the U-boats. After more than a year and a half of war, more than a hundred new submarines had been built, advanced types of the VII and the IX classes were going to sea, would remain in production through almost the entire war, remain Germany's most powerful naval weapons; but generally no more than twenty would make the operational zones at one time; most would be proceeding to or from the hunting grounds or undergoing repairs. For Dönitz's U-boat arm, for Hitler's Third Reich, the 'happy time' would never again be.

Epilogue

On a warm summer afternoon in 1963 two young German women stood amid the heather on the cliffs of Gaitnip and for long minutes, in silence, in sadness, they looked down upon the place, upon the cold, still water where it happened.

On a pilgrimage to Orkney, from Offenbach near Frankfurt, they had crossed from Scrabster on the *St Ola* and come to the spot where lay the wreck of the ship their father had sunk. They were the daughters of Günther Prien, 'Geremy' Dagmar Prien, aged twenty-three, and Birgit, two years older, and they had made the long journey from Germany to Scapa Flow, they said, to see the scene of their father's daring.

'My sister and I are profoundly moved to be here and to re-live the emotions our father must have felt on that dark October night when he accomplished his feat,' Geremy told Gerald Meyer, editor of *The Orcadian*, Orkney's newspaper.

Her father could just as easily have died at Scapa Flow, she said, and 'I have never felt so near to my father as now. We cannot remember him but he is very much alive in our hearts. It is depressing to think that where father performed such a great deed so many people had to die. Scapa Flow looks much bigger than we visualized.'

Over the years Scapa hasn't changed noticeably. It looks much as it did those thirty-eight years ago. The ships are gone of course, the roads are empty of warships. There is not the sight of sailors, or of flags flying or of guns tilted in the air. The sound of bands playing, men drilling on deck, tramping up gang-planks, is gone, no longer do bugles call out the watch, or call men to action stations, for the White Ensign of the Royal Navy was hauled down for the last time at the Flow on 29 March 1957. Yet still it is Scapa Flow, lonely, awesome, majestic, beautiful, bloody Scapa

Flow. Scraggy sheep still make the hillsides home, seabirds still venture over the water, and occasionally, as a reminder of 'that night,' the Merry Dancers dazzle the visitor.

North Sea fishermen come, sometimes a ship seeking shelter, but it is impossible to take the door Prien took, for the eastern approaches are securely sealed. Across the Sound called Kirk through which Günther Prien slipped his boat number *47* in the early hours of 14 October, 1939 there sits today a section of a massive stone, rock, and concrete causeway—the Churchill Barrier—named after the man who ordered it built to prevent an enemy from attempting a deed as insolent as Prien's. Labouring for three years, until the spring of 1945, several hundred Italian prisoners of war captured during the campaign for North Africa put down on the sea-beds between islands more than a quarter million tons of stone and rock—making it possible on the smooth causeways laid over the jagged foundations to motor from island to island and view the peaceful land and seascapes.

Hans Wessels, now 73 and the only surviving officer of *U-47*, did this in 1966, returning to behold Scapa once more, when the BBC was preparing a film on the fifty-year history of the anchorage.

Since the tragedy many of the *Royal Oak* survivors also have returned, singly or in groups; while others, never making the trip back, have kept in touch with one another, still discussing details and incidents of the sinking. But not until 1967, twenty-eight years after the disaster, did the British decide on a formal reunion. Vincent Marchant had organised it, after appealing in the *News of the World* for survivors, and when dozens responded, it was decided as well to invite the Germans, the remaining crewmen of *U-47*, and 'club together' to help meet the expenses of their former enemies.

It was a remarkable display of friendship, as for the first time men from HMS *Royal Oak* and *U-47* met face to face. The former foes gathered first on 13 October at a social evening at Portsmouth's Royal Navy Association club, then, the next day, they met at the Royal Navy War Memorial in Southsea, at a ceremony to mark the anniversary. About eighty British survivors were there, one German-turned British subject, Herbert Herrmann, and three other *U-47* crewmen, Ernst Dziallas, Kurt Römer, and Wilhelm Spahr, the submarine's navigator, who laid a wreath on behalf of the submarine's crew. Spahr also spoke to Mrs Ethel Taylor of Twickenham, who lost a son in the *Oak*, and later he wrote to Dick Kerr, another of the reunion's organisers:

Acceptance of this invitation was a matter of course for us. In all the years which have passed I have never been able to forget the night of 13/14 October. Nor shall I ever be able to. There is a lot that binds us few survivors of both the *Royal Oak* and *U-47*. I have often thought about the bereaved and their sorrow, an outcome of any war. We who have tasted the bitter cup of war and found it distasteful would far sooner be 'heroes of the sea' in peacetime, when there is ample scope for heroics in the rescue of survivors of ships that are the victims of storms or other disasters on the high seas. Before the war sailors of all nations enjoyed life together as a matter of course. We often met British sailors without misunderstanding, and I know from conversations with my fellow sailors that they still cherish this old comradeship. The fuss made by some newspapers shortly before our departure (from Portsmouth) did nothing to deter us from attending the Memorial Service. My comrades and I are grateful for the invitation. We were met like any sailors who have been through a lot. We felt at home, our presence accepted naturally, even though we were the former enemy. We particularly thank you for this and would like to extend our heartfelt greetings to all comrades of the *Royal Oak*, to the bereaved, and to the *Royal Naval Association*.

The 'fuss' Spahr spoke of was set off by the mumbling of sabotage among a small number of survivors but picked up by the press and captured in the headlines. Proclaimed the *Evening News* that Saturday: '*Royal Oak* sunk by sabotage, say survivors.' The newspaper observed that one British group, still doubting the sinking was the work of *U-47*, had admitted they were 'too embarrassed' to confront the Germans with their belief the *Oak* was not sunk by a submarine at all.

It was noted too by the press that a number of British citizens had objected to the meeting and the German government had refused to give its official sanction, claiming the event too sensitive to openly proclaim support of it. Marchant, however, asserted that of the almost 500 letters he had received wishing the reunion well, only a dozen had expressed antagonism toward the visit (he said one came addressed 'Nazi Bastard, Doncaster').

The reunions continued, and Taffy Davies, who after two years took over the organising of them, heard more complaints. They were sparse compared to the expressions of approval but Davies went to his rector, and also to the Navy chaplain in the Portsmouth dockyard. 'Do you think I'm doing wrong?' he asked. 'Or am I doing right in trying to not forget it (the sinking) but at least not to bear a grudge for the end of our days? What is the point of us holding grudges with nations against whom you've been at war? If Britain was to hold a grudge with every nation with which it has warred, we wouldn't be talking to any bugger in this world, even Wales and Scotland, not even the United States.'

The rector and chaplain agreed, said they would support the reunions, and so they continue, to this day.

The *Oak* has produced other controversies: stories of amateur divers with sub-aqua gear ('pirate divers') going down to the wreck, and scavenging, taking brass name plates and portholes, and prompting newspaper stories headlined 'Ghouls dive to rob dead war heroes.' For years there had been no legal ban on unauthorised diving in the vicinity of the wreck, and when in 1958 a suggestion was made that the *Oak* be raised to salvage the precious metals she contained, a cry went up from the Orkney Islanders. Leave this war grave alone, they said. The Admiralty eventually amended its regulations, and placed a notice on the buoy above the upturned battleship: 'This marks the wreck of HMS *Royal Oak* and the grave of her crew. Respect their resting place. Unauthorised diving prohibited.'

In 1974, thirty-five years after the *Oak* went down, a small boat, the RNXS *Loyal Proctor*, heaved-to above the wreck and while eleven of the 424 men who survived the sinking stood with bowed heads a bugler sounded The Last Post, a piper played The Flowers o' the Forest, and as the last sad notes of the lament died away a Navy lieutenant representing the Thurso Sea Cadet Company dropped a wreath overboard to float above the *Oak*'s resting place.

Most missed, not able to make the trip, was 'Skipper Gatt,' as the modest Scottish captain of *Daisy II* is still affectionately called by his friends. Now seventy-five, Gatt in 1960 retired from the sea after forty-five years and today lives surrounded by grandchildren and great-grandchildren in his hometown of Rosehearty, Aberdeenshire.

'I have never looked back,' says Herbert Herrmann, the German-turned-Scotsman who served one year and three months on *U-47* and was taken prisoner in 1944, when his *U-1209* ran into rocks off Land's End. He was interned in prisoner of war camps up and down Great Britain, finally met his Scottish wife Ina while working as a POW farm labourer in Kinmount Estate in Dumfriesshire in the south of Scotland. In Britain he built his life anew, settled with Ina in the Scottish village of Eastriggs, had a son, now twenty-eight, became a mechanical engineer with ICE at Powfoot, Dumfriesshire.

'We are all firm friends, now,' he says of the survivors of battleship and U-boat. 'And I am sure it would have been better to be friends before the incident. I have made friends with everybody and we have exchanged many, many views over the years. We visit each other and have get-togethers apart from the reunions. It isn't bad at all when out of the last world struggle, friendship and lasting friendships develop and long may it continue. Time is running out for all of us who took part in it, as we all get older and older and one or the other sleeps peacefully away and the circle gets smaller and smaller and we will go on meeting and meeting and finally a few will sit down and say "Do you remember?" and by that time more and more will be forgotten of what really happened.'

Appendix A

Extract from the Board of Enquiry report

MOST SECRET

We find that:—

1. *The Cause of the loss of 'Royal Oak'*

We have obtained no evidence that a submarine was seen or heard entering or leaving the Flow. The reports that propellers were heard from the Gate Vessel at Hoxa on the night of 11 October and that the boom was disturbed or moved, are held to have no significance. The latter was due to bad weather while the propeller noises were probably caused by our own ships passing the gate.

2. Contacts were reported by A/S vessels in the Flow after the sinking, and depth charges were dropped. Subsequently Minesweepers located an obstruction in one of the positions in which depth charges were dropped and divers were sent down but have found nothing. There is therefore no further evidence that a submarine was detected or located by these vessels.

3. The evidence of the survivors however definitely suggests that all the explosions were from a source external to the ship on the starboard side, and were such as would be caused by torpedoes fired from a submarine in two salvoes. In addition, there is evidence from one of the survivors that he and another man, who has not been identified, saw the conning tower of a submarine in the direction and at distance that might be expected. We accept this evidence as correct.

4. We consider it is possible for a submarine to have entered the Flow by any of the seven entrances, though entrance by Switha

Sound and Water Sound is thought for various reasons to be less likely.

Conclusion

5.   The evidence available points to the attack having been made by a submarine and there is nothing to suggest that it could have been made by any other means. We are definitely of opinion therefore that HMS *Royal Oak* was sunk by torpedoes fired from a submarine.

The Entry of the Submarine

6.   Though it is possible that the submarine entered the Flow prior to the night of 13/14 October this is not considered likely. In the remarks that follow, those on the organisation of the Patrol Vessels apply to the conditions on that night only; all other statements including those with regard to lookouts apply generally.

7.   The means by which a submarine might have entered Scapa Flow on the night of 13/14 October are:—

(i)   Passing through the gap at the Flotta end of the Hoxa boom on the surface or trimmed down. This gap is wide with at least depth of water of 15 feet at High Water and considerably more over the greater part. There was no lookout on shore at the gap. One drifter was patrolling the whole entrance which is 1½ miles wide. Approaching this gap would take the submarine within 5 cables of the battery on Stanger Head.

(ii)   Passing submerged through the gate in the Hoxa boom while it was opened to allow vessels to pass. No Hydrophone or Asdic watch is maintained at or inside the entrance when the gate is open. Entry here would be a difficult operation but is possible.

(iii) By passing under the Hoxa boom. The foot of the net at this boom is 25 feet above the sea bottom at Low Water and approximately 35 feet above the bottom at High Water Springs. In these circumstances we think it would be quite possible for a small submarine proceeding very close to or scraping the bottom to get through without much disturbing the boom.

(iv) Passing through the gap at the Flotta end of Switha boom on the surface. There was no lookout on shore at this gap and no Patrol Vessel at the boom.

(v) Passing through the gap at the Hoy end of Hoy boom on the surface or trimmed down. This gap is 500 feet wide with a depth of water of 30 feet. There was no lookout stationed on shore at this gap. One Drifter was patrolling this boom, which, with the gap, is 1.7 miles long.

(vi) Passing through the opening in Kirk Sound south of SS *Thames* on the surface: this opening is 400 feet wide with a depth of 4 to 4½ fathoms at Low Water. There is another opening about 200 feet wide with a depth of 15 feet or more at High Water.

Note An additional blockship has been placed in this entrance since 14 October.

(vii) Passing through the opening in Skerry Sound on the surface. This opening is 240 feet wide with a depth of 15 feet or more at High Water.

(viii) Passing through the opening in East Weddell Sound on the surface. This opening is 460 feet wide with a depth of 15 feet or more at High Water. The depth in the centre is 3 to 4 fathoms at Low Water.

(ix) Passing through the openings in Water Sound on the surface. One of these openings is 400 feet wide and the other 200 feet wide; both have a depth of 15 feet or more at High Water.

No lookout is kept at any of the entrances on the East side of the Flow mentioned in (vi), (vii), (viii) and (ix) above.

8. The weather on the night of 13/14 October was fine and clear and the sea calm. The night was fairly light and for periods the sky was lit up by the Aurora and Northern Lights.

High Water at Kirk Sound was at 2338 on 13 October; High Water at Hoxa was at the same time.

9. Any opinion as to which entrance the submarine came in at must be conjecture only but in many respects Kirk Sound would

present the least difficulty. Having found a way in, the submarine would no doubt aim to return by the same route; but if it entered by Kirk Sound at slack water, and left as soon as the torpedoes were fired, the tide would then have been running against it, perhaps as much as 8 knots.

Various statements in the Press attributed to Lieutenant-Commander Prien are considered worth studying as circumstantial evidence.

The Admiral Commanding, Orkneys and Shetlands had to take over a defence scheme that was inadequate and unsatisfactory in many ways. It had however been given much thought, it had Admiralty sanction, and was known to be limited to some extent by the unavoidable absence of certain necessary items such as loops and asdics.

The Admiral Commanding, Orkneys and Shetlands had been there only a few weeks, his Chief Staff Officer arrived on 13 October, he and his staff were constantly harassed by current administrative work, and he had no A/S officer on his staff. Practically all his staff are retired officers, some of whom have been retired for a number of years. The Chief Staff Officer had the additional duty of Maintenance Captain which would certainly occupy the whole of his time.

(Sgd.) G. C. Muirhead-Gould.
CAPTAIN

R. H. T. Raikes
VICE-ADMIRAL

R. E. E. Drax
ADMIRAL (President)

Appendix B

Report of Divers
Message 2010/20 October to Admiralty (R) C-in-C HF from ACOS

Divers have carried out examination of *Royal Oak*. Following is report. Quote ship is lying 40 degs from bottom up. Trim 2 degs aft. Forward damage starboard side starts 80 to 100 ft from stem and extends 40 to 45 ft aft depth of three plates starting one plate below water line. Plating is blown inboard and extreme edges bent in. Damage surveyed aft starts 10 ft abaft after end of bilge keel and extends from water line to bilge keel. Hole about 30 by 50 feet. Plating bent inboard. Bilge keel is blown away and bent outboard. Midship section of ship has not been surveyed. Diver surveyed vicinity of mast and found no trace of Submarine. Nature of bottom soft silt and mud. Unquote. In addition to above divers brought up part of what was almost certainly part of the balance chamber or after body of a torpedo and other small fragments of internal parts. These will be forwarded to the Torpedo Factory, Greenock. TO. 2010/20.

Appendix C

Extract from Log of U-47, 15 September–21 October, 1939*

8/10/39 1100 Heligoland Bight. Wind SE 1. Cloudy.
Left port (Kiel) on special operations, Operational Order North
Sea No. 16, through Kiel Canal, Heligoland Bight, and Channel 1.
[Exact positions cannot be given as under special orders all
secret documents were destroyed before carrying out of order.]

*9/10/39 South of Dogger Bank. Wind SSE 4–5. Overcast,
very dark night.*
Lying submerged. After dark, surfaced and proceeded on our way.
Met rather a lot of fishing vessels.

10/10/39 North of Dogger Bank. Wind ESE 7. Overcast.
During day lay submerged; at night continued on course.

11/10/39 Devil's Hole. Wind ESE 7–8, Overcast.
As on previous day.

12/10/39 Wind SE 7–6, overcast
During day lay submerged off Orkneys. Surfaced in the evening and
came in to the coast in order to fix exact position of ship. From
2200 to 2230 the English are kind enough to switch on all the
coastal lights so that I can obtain the most exact fix. The ship's
position is correct to within 1.8 nautical miles, despite the fact that
since leaving Channel 1 there was no possibility of obtaining an
accurate fix, so that I had to steer by dead reckonings and soundings.

*13/10/39 E. of Orkney Islands. Wind NNE 3–4, light clouds,
very clear night, Northern Lights on entire horizon.*

* British Admiralty translation.

At 0437 lying submerged in 90 metres of water. Rest period for crew. At 1600 general stand-to. After breakfast at 1700, preparations for attack on Scapa Flow. Two torpedoes are placed in rapid loading position before tubes 1 and 2. Explosives brought out in case of necessity of scuttling. Crew's morale splendid. Surfaced at 1915. After warm supper for entire crew, set course for Holm Sound. Everything goes according to plan until 2307, when it is necessary to submerge on sighting a merchant ship just before Rose Ness. I cannot make out the ship in either of the periscopes, in spite of the very clear night and the bright lights. At 2331, surfaced again and entered Holm Sound. Following tide. On nearer approach, the sunken blockship in Skerry Sound is clearly visible, so that at first I believe myself to be already in Kirk Sound, and prepare for work. But the navigator, by means of dead-reckoning, states that the preparations are premature, while I at the same time realize the mistake, for there is only one sunken ship in the straits. By altering course hard to starboard, the imminent danger is averted. A few minutes later, Kirk Sound is clearly visible.

> *It is a very eerie sight. On land everything is dark, high in the sky are the flickering Northern Lights, so that the bay, surrounded by highish mountains, is directly lit up from above. The blockships lie in the sound, ghostly as the wings of a theatre.*

I am now repaid for having learnt the chart beforehand, for the penetration proceeds with unbelievable speed. In the meantime I had decided to pass the blockships on the Northern side. On a course of 270 I pass the two-masted schooner, which is lying on a bearing of 315 in front of the real boom, with 15 metres to spare. In the next minute the boat is turned by the current to starboard. At the same time I recognise the cable of the northern blockship at an angle of 45 degrees ahead. Port engine stopped, starboard engine slow ahead, and rudder hard to port, the boat slowly touches bottom. The stern still touches the cable, the boat becomes free, it is pulled round to port and brought on to course again with difficult rapid manoeuvring, but we are in Scapa Flow.

14/10/39 0027

It is disgustingly light. The whole bay is lit up. To the south of Cava there is nothing. I go farther in. To port, I recognize the Hoxa

Sound coastguard, to which in the next few minutes the boat must present itself as a target. In that event all would be lost; at present south of Cava no ships are to be seen, [*0055*] although visibility is extremely good. Hence decisions: South of Cava there is no shipping; so before staking everything on success, all possible precautions must be taken. Therefore, turn to port is made. We proceed north by the coast. Two battleships are lying there at anchor, and further inshore, destroyers. Cruisers not visible, therefore attack on the big battleships. Distance apart, 3,000 metres.

0116 (time queried in pencil, 0058 suggested)
Estimated depth, 7.5 metres. Impact firing. One torpedo fixed on the northern ship, two on southern. After a good 3½ minutes, a torpedo detonates on the northern ship; of the other two nothing is to be seen.

0121 (queried to 0102) (suggested time 0123, in pencil)
About! Torpedo fired from stern; in the bow two tubes are loaded; *three torpedoes from the bow*. After three tense minutes comes the detonation on the nearer ship. There is a loud explosion, roar, and rumbling. Then come columns of water, followed by columns of fire, and splinters fly through the air. The harbour springs to life. Destroyers are lit up, signalling starts on every side, and on land 200 metres away from me cars roar along the roads. A battleship has been sunk, a second damaged, and the other three torpedoes have gone to blazes. All the tubes are empty. I decide to withdraw, because: (1) With my periscopes I cannot conduct night attacks while submerged. (See experience on entering.) (2) On a bright night I cannot manoeuvre unobserved in a calm sea. (3) I must assume that I was observed by a driver of a car which stopped opposite us, turned around, and drove off towards Scapa at top speed. (4) Nor can I go further north, for there, well hidden from my sight, lie the destroyers which were previously dimly distinguishable.

0128
At high speed both engines we withdraw. Everything is simple until we reach Skildaenoy Point. Then we have more trouble. It is now low tide, the current is against us. Engines at slow and dead slow, I attempt to get away. I must leave by the south through the narrows, because of the depth of the water. Things are again difficult. Course,

058, slow—10 knots. I make no progress. At high speed I pass the southern blockship with nothing to spare. The helmsman does magnificently. High speed ahead both, finally 3/4 speed and full ahead all out. Free of the blockships—ahead a mole! Hard over and again about, and at 0215 we are once more outside. A pity that only one was destroyed. The torpedo misses I explain as due to faults of course, speed, and drift. In tube 4, a misfire. The crew behaved splendidly throughout the operation. On the morning of 13/10, the lubricating oil was found to have 7–8% water in it. All hands worked feverishly to change the oil, i.e. to get rid of the water and to isolate the leaking point. The torpedo-crews loaded their tubes with remarkable speed. The boat was in such good form that I was able to switch on to charge in the harbour and pump up air.

0215
Set SE course for base. I still have 5 torpedoes for possible attacks on merchantmen.

0630 57° 58′ N 01° 03′ W
Lay submerged. The glow from Scapa is still visible for a long time. Apparently they are still dropping depth charges.

1935 ENE 3–4, light clouds, occasional rain, visibility bad towards land, otherwise good.
Off again, course 180°. This course was chosen in the hope that we might perhaps catch a ship inshore, and to avoid *U-20*.

15/10/39 0600 56° 20′ N 0° 04′ W
Submerged and lay at 72 metres. From 1000 onwards, depth charges were dropped from time to time in the distance. 32 depth charges were definitely counted. So I lie low, submerged, until dusk.

1823 Wind NE 5, sea 4, swell from E, cloudy, visibility good.
Surfaced. On surfacing, Norwegian steamer "METEOR" lies ahead. W/T traffic from the steamer is reported in error from the W/T office; I therefore fire a salvo far ahead of the steamer which is already stopped. The steamer is destined for Newcastle on Tyne, with 238 passengers. Steamer immediately allowed to proceed. It is reported later by the W/T office that the steamer did not make any signals.

16/10/39 0702 54° 57' N 2° 58' E Wind NNW 2–3, visibility good.

General course 180°. Submerged on the Dogger Bank. 3 drifting mines sighted, 54° 58' N 2° 56' E. No measures taken, owing to the proximity of fishing vessels. Proceeded submerged throughout the day.

1856 54° 51' N 3° 21' E Wind NW 2, light clouds, visibility good.

Surfaced. Course 128°. Steered course of 128° into Channel 1.

17/10/39 0404

Channel 1 passed. From 0404 to 0447 chased fishing vessel escort ship no. 808; gave recognition signal eight times—no reply received. This fool did not react until V/S was used at a distance of 500–600 metres. With such guardships, an incident such as my operation could occur in our waters also.

1100

Entered port—Wilhelmshaven III.

1144

Tied up.

1530

Crew flown to Kiel and Berlin.

20/10/39 1600

Crew returned.

1830

Sailed for Kiel.

2330

Met an armed fishing trawler at anchor with riding lights in the stretch between Elbe I and Elbe II. I pass him with darkened ship at a distance of 40 metres. Apparently he sees nothing, because no call for recognition signal is made.

21/10/39 0120
Tied up at Brunsbüttel Lock.

1300
Tied up at Holtenau Lock. Operation completed.

Appendix D

Scapa Flow Crew of U-47

* Died in *U-47*, sunk March 8, 1941 by HMS *Wolverine*

*Biermann, Heinrich, *Maschinist Obergefreiter* (Leading Stoker)
Blank, Hans, *Oberfunkmaat* (Petty Officer Telegraphist)
Bleeck, Kurt, *Obermechaniksermaat* (PO Mechanic)
*Böhm, Gustav, *Stabsmaschinist* (Engine Room Artificer)
Brehme, Kurt, *Masch. Obergfr.*
Dittmer, Ernst, *Matrose Gefreiter* (Able Seaman)
Dziallas, Ernst, *Bootsmaat* (PO)
Endrass, Englebert, *Oberleutnant zur See* (Lieutenant-Junior)
Hänsel, Gerhard, *Mt. Obergfr.* (Leading Seaman)
Hebestreit, Herbert, *Ob. Funk. Gfr.* (Leading Telegraphist)
Herrmann, Herbert, *Ob. Mech. Gfr.* (Leading Seaman)
Holstein, Kurt, *Masch. Maat* (PO Electrician)
Hölzer, Erwin, *Masch. Hauptgefreiter* (Leading Stoker)
*Hotzer, Gerhard, *Masch. Obergfr.* (Leading Electrician's Mate)
Loh, Willi, *Ob. Mech. Gfr.* (Leading Seaman)
Lüddecke, Werner, *Masch. Obergfr.*
Mantyk, Heini, *Mt. Obergfr.* (Leading Seaman)
Marquard, Herbert, *Mt. Obergfr.*
Meyer, Willy, *Bootsmaat*
*Prien, Günther, *Korvettenkapitän* (Lieutenant-Commander)
Radloff, Walter, *Masch. Obergfr.*
Römer, Kurt, *Obermaschinist* (Chief PO Electrician)
Roth, Ronni, *Masch. Obergfr.*
*Sammann, Hans, *Bootsmann* (Chief PO)
Schmalenbach, Werner *Masch. Maat* (Stoker PO)
Schmidt, Ernst, *Mt. Obergfr.*
Schmidt, Friedrich, *Masch. Obergfr.*
Scholz, Werner, *Masch. Maat*

Smyczek, Rudolf, *Mt. Obergfr.*

Sollig, Werner, *Masch. Gfr.* (Able Stoker)

Spahr, Wilhelm, *Obersteuermann* (Chief Quartermaster)

Sporer, Karl, *Masch. Obergfr.*

*Steinhagen, Karl, *Funkgefreiter* (Telegraphist)

Strunk, Otto, *Stabsobermaschinist* (Chief ERA)

*Thewes, Peter, *Ober. Mech. Gfr.*

von Varendorff, Amelung, *Oberleutnant zur See* (Lieutenant-Junior)

Walz, Friedrich, *Mt. Obergfr.* (Cook)

*Werder, Gustav, *Masch. Maat*

Wessels, Hans, *Oberleutnant* (Lieutenant)

Winzer, Ernst, *Masch. Obergfr.*

Appendix E

Survivors, HMS Royal Oak

Adams, Robert L., Chief Mechanic
Affleck-Graves, Gerald, Lieutenant
Alford, Edward C., Able Seaman
Allridge, Arthur, Boy
Amer, Aubrey S., Royal Marine
Anderson, R., Able Seaman
Andrews, George R., Acting Corporal, RM
Anslow, Benjamin J., Comd. Gunner
Aplin, William H., Chief Stoker
Archer, Lawrence, Marine
Arnell, George R., Able Seaman
Ashley, Roger, AG
Askham, Reuben W., Boy
Atmeare, George W. C., Engine Room Artificer
Atter, John, Leading Seaman
Ayles, Victor L. T., Able Seaman
Babb, Allen J., Lead. Seaman
Baker, George R., Able Seaman
Baker, Rufas, Leading Cook
Balch, Henry C., Lead. Cook
Ball, C. W., PO
Bardsdell, William J., Act/PO
Barrett, Walter, Stoker PO
Bateman, Robert H., Stoker 2nd Class
Batterbury, William G., LSA
Belben, David, Boy

Bell, Ian. O Sig.
Bendell, Reginald, SBA
Benn, W. G., Capt.
Benton, Michael H., Lieut., RM
Bevis, Alfred H., Able Seaman
Bignell, Charles S., Musician
Billingham, John P., Boy
Birch, Reginald George, Ord. Seaman
Bish, H., CPO Mech.
Bishop, Thomas G., Ord. Seaman
Blake, Maurice, Able Seaman
Blackmor, D., ERA, 5th Class
Blowers, Arthur F., Pay. Lieut-Cdr.
Blundell, Thomas W. A., Act/PO
Bond, Albert, Stoker 1st Class
Booth, George H., Sgt. RM
Borchwick, Samuel, Able Seaman
Bowes, Matthew, Cadet Seaman
Boxall, Edward A., Lead. Seaman
Breen, John, RM
Brierley, Arthur, Able Seaman
Brigden, William S., SBPO
Britt, Edward R., Boy
Brocker, E. R. A., 5th Class
Bromyard, Jack, Boy
Brooke, Frank, RM
Brown, Allen D., Ord. Seaman
Brown, John, Stoker 1st Class
Bryan, Leonard, Lead. Cook
Bryant, Jack E., RM

The Royal Oak Disaster

Bryant, Henry, Able Seaman
Bulley, Frank J., Wt. Engineer
Burnside, James, Stoker
Burton, Ronald D., Ord. Seaman
Butcher, Norman, Stoker
Caldwell, Dick, Surgeon-Lieut.
Camenzuli, Anthony, OS 1st
  Class
Campbell, William M., Stoker 1st
  Class
Cartwright, Charles P., CERA
Casey, William P., Lead. Seaman
Chalder, James, PO
Chalker, Arthur, Steward
Chatfield, Alex. G., RM
Childs, George J., PO
Childs, Leonard, WL Wtr.
Chown, Williams, E., OCI
Clarke, Ellis, Able Seaman
Clarke, W. H., Tel.
Clayton, John W. J., Lead. Stoker
Clayton, Kenneth B., S. Lieut.
Clements, Frederick S., Lead.
  Cook
Cleverley, H. P., Stoker
Coade, James A., ERA
Coady, John, Lead. Stoker
Cole, Stanley, Ord. Seaman
Collier, Jim, Able Seaman
Combes, Frederick, S. Lieut.
Combes, Philip C. W., Musc.
Connelly, Michael, St. 1st Class
Connor, Ronald, ERA
Conway, Kenneth G., Sig.
Cook, Dennis S., S. Musc.
Cook, Frederick N., Lieut. Cdr.
Cook, Gordon F., Boy
Cook, Sydney Henry, Stoker PO
Coombes, John J., Cpl. RM
Coote, Arthur G., RM
Coulson, Tom S., Able Seaman
Cowen, William, Stoker
Cox, Henry P. T., Boy
Crichton, Ord. Seaman

Cripps, William A., Stoker PO
Cross, Fred., Lead. Seaman
Crowther, W. H., ERA
Cruse, Victor, A/PO
Cundall, John R., Pay. Cdr.
Cutler, Frank, Able Seaman,
  RFR
Dall, Frank O'N., Boy 1st Class
Davey, Michael F., RM
Davidson, Kenneth E., Ord. Sea-
  man
Davies, Norman T., Cpl. RM
Davis, Ernest E., Able Seaman
Dawson, Sidney R., Able Seaman
Densham, Eric D., Ord. Seaman
Devlyn, James Charles, Ord. Tel.
Dewey, Kenneth G., CPO
Dommett, Edward, Ord. Artificer
Dove, Gordon E., Boy
Dowling, Harry V., Stoker
Drew, Thomas R., RM
Duncan, Henry, Lieut.
Dunne, William A., ERA 5th
  Class
Dunstone, G., Wt. Engineer
Edmunds, Robert, ERA 4th Class
Edwards, William A., Lead. Sea-
  man
Ellis, Gerald, RM
Elmes, Alfred, Able Seaman
Evans, Edward A., Gunner
Evans, Sydney, Able Seaman
Fairney, Edwin H., ERA
Farley, Alfred J., Able Seaman
Farmer, Harry, Lead. Seaman
Farquhar, John, Able Seaman
Ferrugi, John, PO Steward
Fiddler, Edwin J., RM
Figg, Joseph, Able Seaman
Finlayson, Reginald H., Lead.
  Seaman
Finley, Norman, Supply PO
Fisher, George William, Able
  Seaman

Fleming, Edward, Stoker
Fletcher, Oswald L., Stoker
Forder, Kenneth B., Able Seaman
Fordham, Alfred L., Musc.
Fossey, William J., Lead. Sig.
Foster, Thomas J., Able Seaman
Fox, W. T. J., Mid.
Freer, Thomas F., Ch. Mech.
Frost, Albert V., Boy 1st Class
Gardiner, Richard H., Ord. Seaman
Gattrell, Frederick M., Able Seaman
Gearing, Arthur, Able Seaman
Gibbs, Arthur R. F., Blacksmith
Gibson, Wilfred, Chief ERA
Gilmore, Ernest J., PO
Goodlad, John R., Lead. Seaman RNR
Goodson, Henry J., RM
Grant, Norman W., RM
Green, Reginald C., Lead. Seaman
Green, Ronald C., Boy 1st Class
Gregory, Richard, A. V., Lieut. Cdr.
Grove, Robert C., Tel.
Haig, James D., A/Lead. Seaman
Haigh, Stanley W., Boy
Halford, Jack L., RM
Hall, Clarence J., Boy 1st Class
Hall, John, Boy
Hall, Ronald E. A., 4th Class
Hancox, William, Able Seaman
Hanharan, Frederick, RM
Harbord, Ronald V., Boy
Harding, W. E., Wt. Shipwright
Harland, Thomas, Stoker
Harmer, A., Leading Seaman
Harrington, Kenneth, Boy Tel.
Harris, Donald T., Ord. Seaman
Harris, Edward, ERA 5th Class
Harris, Edward J., Lead. Seaman

Harrison, Gilbert S., Pay. S. Lieut:
Hart, Donald J., Boy L/C
Hartley, James A., Marine
Harty, John, Lead. Seaman
Hasler, John E., Able Seaman
Hastings, A., ERA 5th Class
Hawes, Barry, Marine SE
Harks, Frederick L., Tel.
Hayhow, Robert, ERA 5th Class
Head, Samuel P., Able Seaman
Hearn, James V., Ord. Seaman
Hickman, Kenneth, Lead. Stoker
Hickmore, Alfred, Ord. Seaman
Higgins, P., PO
Hilkin, Bertram H., RM
Hinde, Norman L., Ord. Seaman
Hine, C., Chief Stoker
Hine, Norman J., Marine
Hobbs, Frederick J. C., Ch. Stoker
Holligan, M., Pay. Cadet
Hollis, James E., Able Seaman
Hoskin, Alfred J., Lead. Seaman
Howard, Alexander R., RM
Howe, H., Stoker
Howell, Ronald S., Yeo. Sig.
Hughlock, William, Marine
Humby, William E., CPO
Hutchings, William K., Sig.
Hutchison, Wm., S. Lieut. (E)
Ingpen, James P., Lieut-Cdr.
Ings, Alfred G., PC Std.
Instance, H. J., Leading Seaman
Jackson, Robert E., Ord. Tel.
Jacobs, E., ERA 3rd Class
Johnston, Herbert R., Stoker
Jones, Raymond S., Lead. Tel.
Jones, Thomas H., Lead. Stoker
Jordan, A. R., RM
Judge, Fernleigh G., Musc.
Keen, Bernard B., Lieut.
Kelly, Horace A. G., Musc. RMB

Kenny, Ronald J., Able Seaman
Kerr, J. R., PO
Kersley, Sub-Lieut. RNR
Ketcher, Arthur D., Cpl., RM
Kichener, Ronald, Ord. Seaman
Knott, Arthur H., Able Seaman
Lakin, Thomas H., PO Tel.
Langlands, George A., Lead. Stoker
Lawrence, Alfred, Ch. Stoker
Lawrence, William A., Ord. Seaman
Lazell, Norman, Ord. Seaman
Leadley, K. R. S., Lieut. RN
Lee, J. H., Sig.
Lees, Robert, Stoker
Lettin, John T., Ord. Seaman
Lidget, Eric E., Stoker
Lipscombe, Cyril G., Boy 1st Class
Lloyd, David J., Lead. Seaman
Lockyer, George L. J., Ord. Seaman
Lucking, Cecil J., Stoker
Lutman, Henry J., Lead. Stoker
Maggs, George J., Lead. Seaman
Main, Henry W., SBC, PO
Makin, John Henry, Stoker
Mallis, Laurence, Steward
Marchant, V., Ord. Seaman
Martin, Frederick A., RM
Martin, R., Ord. Seaman
Marsh, William A., ERA
Masters, Dennis W., Ord. Seaman
Mawson, Michael G. H., Pay. Cadet
McCabe, C. B., Able Seaman
McCarthy, Frank, Boy
MacLean, Queardley G. S., Pay Lieut-Cdr.
McLaverty, James, Cpl. RM
Mead, John N., Boy, 1st Class
Melrose, James R., Lead. Tel.
Merrick, Thomas, Seaman RNR

Miles, Ronald S., RM
Milligan, Lawrence W., Ord. Seaman
Mitchell, William C., Yeo. Sigs.
Moore, Edward A., RM
Moppeti, Arthur J., RM
Morley, Reginald, Stoker
Morris, Peter J., Able Seaman
Murray, John, Able Seaman
Murrin, Charles W. T., Lead. Stoker
Neville, Percy, Able Seaman
Newton, Douglas, Boy, 1st Class
Nichols, R. F., Cdr.
Nichols, Wilfred, Able Seaman, RFR
Noble, Thomas A., PO Tel.
O'Byrne, Desmond P., RM
O'Leary, James D. F., Lead. Cook
Orges, Richard H., RM
Owen, Peter H., Cadet
Owens, William, RM
Pagett, Ivor H., Ord. Seaman
Palmer, Walter G.
Patterson, Andrew, Stoker
Pattison, Herbert, Cpl. RM
Parham, George E. T., Sgt. RM
Payton, John A., Cplr. RM
Pead, Norman V., GH ERA
Pearce, J. T., Comd. Gunner
Pearman, Anthony H., S. Lieut.
Peay, Joseph F., CPO Cook
Phillips, Walter G., RPO
Pipes, Henry, Able Seaman
Pirie, Roger P., Mid.
Pitcher, Alfred T., Lead. Seaman
Pither, Henry W., Able Seaman
Pocock, Herbert E., Boy
Poling, George R., Lead. Seaman
Pope, Reginald A., Stoker 1st Class
Potter, Thomas W., RM
Potts, Herbert H., Ord. Seaman

Pouttner, Cyril S., Musc.
Pritchard, Brinley W., RM
Prowse, George, Senior Master
Protheroe, Gwyn, Act. WSO
Radford, James A., Lead. Seaman
Randall, Edward, Joiner
Randell, Hector, Ordnance Artificer
Ransome, Frederick J., Lead. Cook
Redman, Alfred, Able Seaman RNR
Renshaw, J. W., Engineer Cdr.
Richard, Peter, Sub. Lieut.
Riley, Charles H., Ord. Seaman
Ritchie, George L., Surgeon-Cdr.
Roberts, G. O., Lieut.
Roberts, L. H., Able Seaman
Robertson, Norman Claude, Tel.
Rockingham, Norman W., Mid.
Rose, P., Stoker
Ross, James, Able Seaman, RNR
Ross, John, Able Seaman
Rowland, E. A., PO
Rowlands, Stanley, RM
Sammit, Edward, Off. CK
Saltmarsh, Stanley R., RM
Sandifer, William E., Pay. Lieut.
Scarff, Arthur W., PO
Sclater, Claude E. L., Lieut.
Scott, Edgar L., Painter
Scovell, E. W., Boy
Seaburn-May, Ronald M., Mid.
Seal, Leonard, Cadet Seaman
Seymour, A. M., Lieut.
Seymour, Albert E., PO
Sheldrick, Douglas W. V., Stoker 2nd Class
Sherwood, Jesse, Lead. Seaman
Shuter, James W. D., RM
Sidley, William F., Ord. Seaman
Sims, Frank G., LSA
Skilling, Matthew, Boy 1st Class

Smart, William H., Able Seaman
Smith, Arthur W., Boy 1st Class
Smith, Arthur, Boy
Smith, E., Ord. Seaman
Smith, George A., Able Seaman
Smith, George, Cadet Seaman
Smith, John H., RPO
Smith, William, Marine
Smithalls, John K., Mid.
Spitary, Paolo, Off. CK1
Spurling, William G., Stoker PO
Stares, G. R., Cook
Stephen, George P., Ord. Seaman
Stevens, Thomas B., PO
Stewart, Edwards S., Seaman RNR
Stimson, Ronald Frank, Stoker 1st Class
Storar, T. R., ERA
Sturdee, P. D., Mid.
Symes-Thompson, M. F. J., Mid.
Symonds, Henry G., Lead. Seaman
Sylvester, Reginald G., PO
Tate, William, Stoker
Taylor, Thomas W. R., Asst. Cook
Terry, Anthony H., Lieut.
Terry, Philip, Chief Stoker
Thackeray, Norman E., RM
Thompson, John F. P., Musc. RM
Thompson, Stanley W. H., CPO Writer
Thompson, Victor R., Boy
Throssell, William H., Mech.
Tily, R., Lead. Seaman
Timms, Jack, Ch. Mech.
Took, Kenneth H., Boy
Trewinnard, George, SV Boy
Tunnicliff, Leslie H., RM
Turner, Reginald A., RM
Turney, Albert R., Boy
Tutton, Albert E., RM

Upham, Ernest F., Boy Tel.
Vincent, Jeffrey T. E., S. Lieut.
Vennel, George F., CPO
Wadham, H. F., Stoker
Wallace, Richard S., Lieut.
Ward, David H., Able Seaman
Ward, Michael R. F., Lieut-Cdr.
Ward, Robert M., Ord. Seaman
Warren, James G., Sig-Bsn.
Watten, Reginald P., Boy
Weare, Walter Thomas, Able
    Seaman
Weir, William, Boy
Welch, John Wm., Stoker PO
Wernham, Harold J., Musc.
Westcott, Clifford, SBCPO
Wheatland, Alfred J., RM
Wheeler, Douglas R., 2nd Lieut.
Whincup, Reginald W. G., Ch.
    Shpt.
White, Frank, RM
White, George R., Boy 1st Class
White, Philip A., Ord. Seaman
Whitebread, Edward, Wt. Engi-
    neer
Whitehouse, Gordon, Stoker PO

Whitlock, James T., ERA
Wilkinson, Anthony P., Pay.
    Lieut.
Williams, Frank, Bosn.
Williams, George B., Musc.
Williams, Mac., Able Seaman
Willoughby, Kenneth H., Leading
    Wtr.
Wilson, Cyril J., CERA
Wilson, Ronald E., Boy
Wiltshire, Frederick W., Joiner
Winterbottom, George E., Lead-
    ing Stoker
Wisden, Thomas F., Lieut-Cdr.
Wood, Kenneth J. J., RM
Wood, Richard H., RM
Wood, Stanley R., Boy 1st Class
Woolnough, George H., Cpl. RM
Woodnutt, William E., Able Sea-
    man
Woods, Harold J. C., Pay. Lieut.
Woods, H. J., Able Seaman
Woods, J. W., RM
Wright, Herbert, Able Seaman
Zarb, Paulo, Off. Std.

Sources

BOOKS

Bekker, Cajus. *Hitler's Naval War,* Oldenburg and Hamburg: Gerhard Stalling Verlag, 1971.

Brown, Malcolm and Meehan, Patricia. *Scapa Flow,* London: Allen Lane, 1968.

Busch, Harald. *U-boats at War.* New York: Ballantine, 1955.

Churchill, Winston S. *The Second World War, Vol. I. The Gathering Storm.* London: Cassells, 1948.

Dönitz, Karl. *Memoirs: Ten Years and Twenty Days.* London: Weidenfeld and Nicolson, 1958.

Dönitz, Karl. *Der Krieg sur See, Vol. 5.* Frankfurt: Mittler & Sohn, 1966.

Frank, Wolfgang. *The Sea Wolves.* New York: Holt, Rinehart and Winston, 1955.

Frank, Wolfgang. *Enemy Submarine.* London: William Kimber, 1954.

Korganoff, Alexandre. *The Phantom of Scapa Flow.* London: Ian Allan, 1974.

Lenton, H. T. *German Submarines I.* London: Macdonald, 1965.

McKee, Alexander. *Black Saturday.* New York: Holt, Rinehart and Winston, 1959.

Poolman, Kenneth. *Ark Royal.* London: William Kimber, 1956.

Raeder, Erich. *My Life.* Annapolis: United States Naval Institute, 1960.

Roskill, S. W. *The War at Sea, Vol. I.* London: Collins, 1960.

Shirer, William. *Berlin Diary.* New York: Knopf, 1941.

Showell, J. P. Mallmann. *U-Boats Under the Swastika.* New York: Arco, 1973.

Trevor-Roper, H. R. (ed.) *Blitzkrieg to Defeat: Hitler's War Directives 1939–1945.* New York: Holt, Rinehart and Winston, 1965.

Von der Porten, Edward P. *The German Navy in World War Two*. London: Arthur Barker, 1969.

Werner, Herbert. *Iron Coffins*. New York: Holt, Rinehart and Winston, 1969.

DOCUMENTS, MAGAZINES, NEWSPAPERS
PUBLIC RECORD OFFICE
Admiralty: War of 1939–1945.

ADM 199/158 X/J 5845	Loss of HMS *Royal Oak*—Board of Enquiry Sub-Committee of the Board, Survivors' Statements.
ADM 199/158 X/K 1651	Narrative of Events in *Royal Oak*, Conclusions and Recommendations of the Board.
ADM 1/1840 XJ 5823	Report of Admiral L. M. Forbes and Board of Enquiry.
ADM 1/9840 X/J 5823	Report on Rescue Work and Assistance to Officers and Men, Remarks on Carley Rafts and Life-Saving Arrangements.
ADM 138/417–19	*Royal Oak* 'covers,' or construction plans, in the Draught Room, Natural Maritime Museum, Greenwich.

FREIBURG

PG/61871/NID *Kriegsarchiv der Marine* file on UB 116.

PG/61526/NID *Kriegsarchiv der Marine* file on U 18.

Fuarbringer, Wagner, Report of 3 April, 1941 ('The U-47's Scapa Flow Undertaking').

Führer Naval Conferences, 1939.

Imperial Club Magazine, Spring, 1940.

Isle of Man Times, October 9, 1964.

Log of U-47, 15th September–21st October 1939 (British Admiralty Translation).

Microfilms of the German Naval Archives and Related Records, 1922–1945. Washington, DC: US Naval History Division, Operational Archives, July 1973.

Naval and Military Record, November, 1914.

Orcadian, The, September–October 1939, July 25, 1963.

Orkney Herald, September–October 1939.

Portsmouth Evening News, October 1939.

Profile HMS Wolverine, Imperial War Museum, August 1948.
Scottish Sunday Express, Glasgow, February 3, 1974.
United States Naval Institute Proceedings, Vol 81, No 4 April 1955 (German U-Boat Construction).
United States Naval Institute Proceedings, Vol 85, No 12 Scapa Flow article by Vice Admiral Friedrich Ruge.
United States Technical Mission in Europe (technical reports)
War Diary of the German Naval Staff Operations Division, September–October 1939.

INTERVIEWS AND/OR CORRESPONDENCE WITH:
John Atter, Victor L. T. Ayles, Rear Admiral Peter N. Buckley, George H. Booth, Edward R. Britt, Charles P. Cartwright, William Casey, H. P. Cleverley, Robert Crawford, Norman T. Davies, Grand Admiral Karl Dönitz, Ernst Dziallas, J. G. Faulkner, DSM, Norman Finley, George W. Fisher, Captain Dr Friedrich Fortsmeir, John G. Gatt, DSC, Admiral Eberhard Godt, Gerhard Hänsel, Herbert Herrmann, F. J. C. Hobbs, M. L. Hulbert, A. R. Jordan, Richard Kerr, Willi Loh, Werner Lüddecke, Vincent M. Marchant, David D. Merriman, Douglas Newton, Dieter Oehrn, James T. Pearce, Professor Dr Jürgen Rohwer, Captain S. W. Roskill, CBE, DSC, Commander William E. Sandifer, Frank G. Gordon Sims, Wilhelm Spahr, Ernst Schmidt, Friedrich Schmidt, Stanley W. H. Thompson, Fred L. Tunnicliff, Harold J. Wernham, Hans Wessels, Alfred J. Wheatland, Commander Philip A. White, MBE, Frank Williams, Herbert Pattison, Gerald Meyer.

Index